The Boy Who Lived With
GHOSTS

The Boy Who Lived With GHOSTS

A TRUE STORY OF CHILDHOOD HAUNTING

JOHN MITCHELL

This memoir is based on my experiences over a ten-year period. The events occurred over forty years ago and, as is the case with works of creative non-fiction, many details have had to be imaginatively re-created. This is a story of childhood, as observed, interpreted or imagined by the child, and as recalled by the adult who experienced them. Some names and other identifying details have been changed. Some characters are not based on any one person but are composite characters.

ISBN-10: 0615793207
ISBN-13: 9780615793207

For Margueretta
and Emily

and all children who
sleep without
a nightlight

Acknowledgements

My wife, the beautiful Michelle, dug me up after I had been buried alive. She encouraged me and cajoled me to write. She found a way to keep our daughter quiet.

Sophia, you can be noisy again.

My editor, Laura Burns, inspired me. She helped me realize that the best stories are the ones that make people care.

The Cellar

Portsmouth, England
December 1962

1

live in a haunted family, in a haunted house, on a haunted street. One day I will live in a place where there are no ghosts but right now they're everywhere. Some people don't believe in ghosts but that's alright. Those people have orange nightlights glowing in their bedrooms after dark, reflecting little moons and stars on the ceiling, and cups of hot chocolate to make them sleepy before their blankets are tucked in cozily around them by their mums. I don't think my mum believes in ghosts. If she did, she would not turn out all the lights when she puts me to bed at night.

I am almost five years old and I was born in our front bedroom with my twin sister Emily. It was on the Twelfth Night. That's the night when the Three Wise Men visited the baby Jesus with their gifts. It was also my sister Margueretta's fourth birthday. So we are three gifts for the baby Jesus. If I am a gift, I would like to be a lamb. Animals don't go to Heaven but I am sure there is a lamb up there. I think there is also a donkey.

Margueretta hates me because I was born on her birthday and now she has to share it with me and Emily, so she locks me in the cellar in the dark. And there's something scary down there in the corner that goes drip, drip, drip. If I die down there I will go to sit at God's feet because Dad says God suffers all the little children to come unto him. And Jesus loves dead children the most because they will never grow up to become sinners.

God wears brown sandals and no socks but Jesus doesn't wear anything on his feet and he washes God's feet for him because there is a lot of sand in Heaven and it gets between God's toes. Dad says Heaven is a warm place and you are never hungry in Heaven because you can have as much bread and jam as you want to eat. So you shouldn't cry if a little boy dies, having been killed by his big sister who locks him in the cellar in the dark.

Nana says we will all go back to God one day so long as we are not sinners. Because if we are sinners, we will go to live with the Devil and we will scream and burn as we catch fire in a lake for all Eternity, which is a very long time. And Nana knows what a long time means because she is very old, which is also why she has hair that comes down to her knees. She ties it in braids on top of her head but I mustn't see my Nana's hair when it is down or that will mean I have been in her bedroom and a little boy should never go into his Nana's bedroom or she will hit him on the back of his head with her hairbrush.

2

can hear those people inside my bedroom walls, whispering and knocking in the night. Nana says they are waiting for someone to die and when that person dies they will stop their knocking and it will be quiet until someone else is going to die and then they will start knocking again. Nana knows all about dying.

Mum says it is very silly to think that there are people living inside the walls of my bedroom and they are actually deathwatch beetles. I don't know anything about deathwatch beetles but it's true that they are waiting for someone to die. And then the house will be very quiet because we will all be dead.

This afternoon, we were in the hospital waiting for Great-Auntie Maisie to die. She's Nana's sister and it took all afternoon for her to go. Boots is already dead. Mum said it was her time but Dad said it was a bus. They found her last week in front of the library where Mum gets her books. Dad brought her home and Emily cried even though Boots was very flat. She didn't even look like a cat. And Dad buried her under the wall in our backyard next to Judy. Judy started having fits and running around in circles and we all knew that soon enough she would bite me or Emily in the face and that would be the bloody end of it. I think Dad killed her with the coal shovel but we weren't allowed to watch.

Pop will be dead soon. This is because he thinks he is a train. He looks right at me and shouts, "Choo-choo goes the train! Stand back! Stand back!" I always run under the kitchen table with Emily and the cat. But now it's just me and Emily because the cat is dead.

Pop also wets himself and his tongue no longer fits in his mouth. And he hides in the corner of the kitchen and screams if you come near him. The only one who knows what he is screaming about is Nana and so far she has only told me that it has something to do with my Auntie Beryl and a pack of playing cards with pictures of naked ladies. Also from spending a lot of time on his own in our garden shed, doing God knows what.

They always make me stand by the hospital bed because there are never enough chairs and if I stand on one leg Mum cuffs me round the ear, even though I'm just trying to rest my other foot. And I have to keep my hands in my pockets at all times or Emily will try to hold my hand and I am not holding hands with a girl. Mum says I should take my hands out of my pockets and show some respect. And Mum will be even more angry if I keep my hands in my pockets and try to stand on one leg at the same time, because then I will fall over.

I also try to hold my breath in hospitals because they smell of boiled meat and disinfectant. And old ladies who are dying smell of perfume and onions and pee. But Great-Auntie Maisie smelled of sick. There's only so long that you can hold your breath. And her lips were all gray and sagging and covered in brown spots with little bits of slimy spit in the corners, making tiny creamy bubbles that didn't pop. So there was no way she was getting a kiss from me, even if she was going to sleep for all Eternity.

And because everyone else kissed her goodbye and I wouldn't kiss her, they made me say the beginning of the Lord's Prayer out loud. I have almost learned the Lord's Prayer by heart. It's God's prayer but no one has told me what it means.

Our Father, which art in Heaven. Hello be thy name. Thy king done come.

And then we said the rest of the prayer together and held hands because Great-Auntie Maisie was dead, and they put her teeth back in her mouth because Nana says you want to look your best when you're dead and about to meet your Maker. They were in a jar beside the Bible. Old ladies can take their teeth out just like that. Nana can push her teeth up over her nose and she does it to scare me but I just laugh, even though it is quite frightening. Emily screams the way girls always do.

"Och, it's the end, right enough," Nana said. "I'll be all alone soon. One by one, they're leaving me. I thought Maisie would be with me long after her time. But her time has come before her end. That's right enough. Her time has come before her end, and she has left me."

"She's in a happy place now," Mum said.

"Aye. A happy land. I'll be next. There is a happy land. Far, far away. Where they eat bread and jam three times a day. She'll dance again, barefoot in the heather. We danced, you know. Maisie could dance! And skipped with the golden-tailed dragonflies just out of her reach."

Nana touched the air in front of Maisie's face like there was something there.

"I know," Mum replied and started to cry.

"Just wee lassies. Wee lassies playing," Nana said. "We're all wee bairns, inside. She wore a pink dress. Pink with yellow flowers. Dancing with the dragonflies. Maisie could dance, you know! Aye, she could dance."

And Nana cried too and Mum cried even more and that made Emily cry but I did not want to cry so I stood on one foot and stared at the floor and it was plastic and shiny with gray swirls and tiny red flecks. But I did not put my hands in my pockets.

Great-Auntie Maisie is in Heaven now. Just as soon as they are sure that she wasn't a sinner, it will be St. Peter who meets her when she arrives in Heaven. God has quite enough to do keeping locusts away from crops and fighting the evil that's inside all of us. But there isn't any evil inside of me because I am just a little boy.

I'd better behave on the bus going home because it is very selfish of me not to kiss my Great-Auntie Maisie right before she died, with Nana holding her hand and whispering to her about when they were girls dancing together

7

in their bare feet and chasing dragonflies in the heather. And now it's too late and there's no point in harping on about it but I should be ashamed of myself.

So I will not make my usual fuss even though Margueretta has just flicked the back of my ear.

3

All the houses on our street are falling down. Our house is very dark because it's in the middle of a long row of houses and there aren't many windows and the electricity keeps going off. There's a narrow black passageway that goes all through our house and at the end are some broken stairs that go up to our bedrooms. I must not play on the stairs because the railing is mostly missing and I will fall off and break my bloody neck and die. And I can only blame myself if I get my foot caught in that hole at the top of the stairs because I've been told enough times to watch out for it. If my foot gets caught in that hole, I will never get it out and I will be forced to live at the top of the stairs for the rest of my life without my foot.

The best thing about our house is that there is no bathroom so we don't have to wash until our feet are really black. But when I need to go to the toilet, it is out through the scullery door and halfway down our backyard and there is no light in there and I keep telling my mum that it's not my fault if I pee all over the floor. And only someone really brave would go there in the middle of the night—or if you had very bad diarrhea. I had diarrhea once but I never made it to the toilet.

Pop's son hanged himself in the toilet. Nana said he was just going for a wee but he took his shoes off and hanged himself with his tie from the pipes. I don't know why he took his shoes off but Nana found him dead swinging from his tie. She said his eyes were popping out of his head like my marbles—the big green ones. She mostly stayed away from toilets after that. But she says you have to go eventually.

Mum said I shouldn't listen to Nana's tales and not to worry that Pop's son was also called John, the same as me. And Mum says a rhyme when I am scared to go into the toilet in case his terrible ghost is in there, hanging with his eyes popping out like my green marbles. The rhyme is supposed to make me feel better.

Diddle, diddle, dumpling, my son John,
Went to bed with his trousers on,
One shoe off, and the other shoe on,
Diddle, diddle, dumpling, my son John.

I'm not going to tell my mum again but that rhyme does not make me feel at all better. If she wants me to feel better she should not make me go in the toilet on my own in the dark.

Nana says it will be a blessing when Pop goes to join her first husband on the other side, although she doesn't know whether Pop deserves to go to Heaven because of something he did with those playing cards and my Auntie Beryl. And then after he dies, some men in black suits will bring Pop back home and they will put his coffin in the front room so we can give him a night-night kiss for all Eternity. I will be hiding under my bed.

Dad keeps his bellows organ and his piano in the front room, so he will also be able to play some sad music for Pop. Nana likes "Abide With Me." I like "Twinkle, Twinkle, Little Star."

Dad also plays funeral music in the middle of the night and it's a very loud organ and it makes Mum scream but he's only doing it to annoy the woman next door because she is spying on us. Dad says it's bloody obvious that she's spying on us because no one goes out to hang up washing after dark. She's just trying to look through our scullery window to see what we are up to.

I used to have a bath in the sink in the scullery but now I'm too big and I have to go to the public baths, which are quite a long walk away. I tried to hide my feet this morning but I had to agree with Nana that they were extremely black and neither of us could remember when I last had a bath. I should also know that cleanliness is next to godliness and even though Emily's feet are not as black as mine and there are no little parcels of dirt between her toes, we will both be having a bath today because it is cheaper at the public baths to share, even though I complained that I do not want to have a bath with a girl. But Nana said it is also my birthday tomorrow and I need to look my best because I am going to be wearing a kilt.

On top of that, Nana has noticed that I have been scratching my head a lot lately which she says is nothing that a good wash with a bar of carbolic soap won't cure. But I have stopped picking my nose because Nana said I will get very fat nostrils like an Eskimo and then I will have to go to live in the North Pole.

There's no point in arguing with Nana because she is stronger than my dad, and she can arm wrestle with grown-up men, even though she is quite short and never eats except for an occasional pickled egg. I saw her hit a man once outside a pub and he never got back up. He didn't see it coming because you don't expect a very short grandmother to punch you on the chin so hard you fall over. She distracts them by swinging her left arm around so they think she is going to hit them with her left fist but then she catches them on the chin with her right.

Nana comes from the Highlands, which is a place in Scotland where the soldiers wear kilts and play bagpipes to frighten the English who always run away, screaming like little girls. I am Nana's Scottish soldier.

"Dunnee ever admit that you're English, wee Johnny! You should have been born in Dunfermline."

The English are Sassenachs and are never to be trusted. I must not under any circumstances tell anyone that I was born in England.

4

I t's our birthday today. Emily got some lavender bath salts wrapped in Christmas paper. And Nana gave me a set of six whisky glasses. They have pictures of Scottish soldiers on them. Mum said it makes no sense for a five-year-old boy to have a set of whisky glasses so I will keep them under my bed.

"Aye. That's right enough," Nana said. "I have no use for them now. I'm giving away all ma worldly possessions before I meet ma Maker. Possessions imprison you! It will be easier for a needle to go through the eye of a camel than for me to enter the gates of Heaven wi' ma possessions. That's right enough. You mark ma words, laddie! All this talk has made me thirsty. A wee dram is what I'll have. Och, aye."

"For God's sake, Mother. You're not going anywhere!" Mum replied.

"You'll all be fighting over ma things before I'm even cold. I'll be lying there in ma bed, waiting for one of the archangels, hopefully Gabriel, while someone is measuring my tallboy to see if it will fit in their recess."

And even if it is my birthday, I am still very upset that Nana has made me wear a kilt because it is obviously not a Scottish soldier's kilt and is in fact a girl's tartan skirt. She said you can't find kilts in Portsmouth and it is a soldier's choice whether or not to wear any underpants. Obviously I am wearing my underpants or Margueretta will lift up my kilt to show everyone my willy.

And so that I will look extra handsome in my kilt, Mum took me to get my hair cut really short like a movie star even though I only had it washed yesterday.

"You shall have a crew cut for your birthday. You will look just like Tony Curtis."

I do not ever want to look like Tony Curtis, whoever the bloody hell he is, because now there is a white patch on my forehead where my fringe used to be and my ears stick out like they aren't part of my head. I do not look like a movie star. All my hair is gone.

So Nana gave me a sherbet lemon to cheer me up. And I was only halfway through sucking it when I swallowed it by mistake and it stuck in my throat. It was a good thing that Nana was there because she could see I was about to faint because you always faint if you can't breathe. So she thumped me really hard on my back and the sherbet lemon shot across the room and landed in some dirt by the fireplace so I left it there, even though I was only halfway through it. Nana said she saved my life. But she was the one who gave me that sherbet lemon in the first place.

Margueretta thinks it's very funny that I have no hair and I'm wearing a girl's tartan skirt and she said I had fleas and that's why they cut off all my hair. My mum lied. I am not going to forget that she lied to me about looking like a movie star. I know what a lie is. A lie is saying I have a tummy ache so that I don't have to go to Sunday School and can stay at home to watch *Bill and Ben the Flower Pot Men*. But *Bill and Ben* only comes on during the week. And Mum said that was God's punishment for lying.

Mum says that all boys tell lies.

"Oh, yes, m'laddo! You can't believe a word your father says. Your father told me he was a pilot in the air force during the war. But you know what? He was nothing more than a NAFFI cook in the army kitchen. A pilot, indeed! The only action he saw was peeling potatoes. And brussels sprouts."

I do not like brussels sprouts. And I'm sure Mum is wrong because Dad showed me a picture of himself in his uniform with a cap and everything. I'm sure it was his air force uniform but when I told Mum she said that he got his first job working on the buses in London and when I asked Dad for another look at that picture, I saw there was a bus in the background and not a bomber plane. So it is possible that Dad is lying.

But I don't think Margueretta was lying about the fleas because I have been scratching my head like a dog for weeks. Now you can see the scratches because all my hair is gone.

There are nine candles on the birthday cake but Emily and me are only five. We are sharing the cake with Margueretta, who is nine. And anyone can see it's not a birthday cake. It's bread pudding.

"I will mend that bicycle for your birthday!"

Well, Dad's not going to mend it right now because he has to go and see a man about a dog. He was going to mend it for me for Christmas but he had to see a man about a dog. He always has to see a man about a dog. I think it's in a brown room. I don't know that for sure because when I go with him to see a man about a dog, he makes me wait by the door outside the pub. And when he comes out to go home, I have to hold his hand to make sure he doesn't fall over. It's easy to fall over after you've been to see a man about a dog. Especially in the dark.

I don't like the dark. And Margueretta knows that I don't like the dark and it's completely dark in the cellar with the door closed. That's why she has locked me in the cellar. She waited until the grown-ups went out to the pub for a birthday drink and left us with Pop. And Pop is useless because he just makes noises like a train and then stands in the corner and wets himself and screams. So he doesn't care if she's locking me in the cellar.

I'm curling up into a ball. I'm biting my lip. Now I'm counting to a thousand. It's so dark down here that I don't even know if my eyes are open or closed. But I've screwed them up tight because I don't want to see the thing that lives in the corner. I'm sure it has eyes that bulge like my big green marbles. It makes a sound that goes drip, drip, drip.

Drip, drip, drip.

I'm holding my hands over my ears so I can't hear it. And I'm curling tighter and tighter into a ball. One day, that thing in the corner is going to come out of the cellar in the night and come into my bedroom. And it will hide under my bed and reach its arms up under the blanket and strangle me until I am dead.

Now I'm whispering the Lord's Prayer.

Our Father, which art in Heaven. Hello be thy name. Thy king done come.

Now I'm crying. But no one can hear me.

5

She let me out when she heard them coming. Dad was the first one to come into the kitchen so I held onto his leg with both arms, which I do quite a lot, and it made him fall over and Mum shouted at him even though he only fell over because I was holding onto his leg.

Nana always cooks them supper when they come back from seeing a man about a dog. She makes bubble-and-squeak from cabbage and potatoes. It lasts forever and she heats it up the next day and the day after that. You can even have bubble-and-squeak for your birthday supper.

"Cabbage and potatoes? That's not much of a birthday treat," Dad said.

"Aye, that's right. And you didn't put your hand in your pocket for a single thing for their birthdays!" Nana replied.

"It needs something to spice it up!" Dad said.

So he put sugar and mustard and treacle and brown sauce and pepper and strawberry jam and vanilla essence on it and I helped him. He said I was a good boy to help him like that. And Pop even came out of the corner, which he never does, to watch Dad putting all those things on his bubble-and-squeak.

"Choo-choo! Stand back! Stand back!" Pop shouted and he put his hands over his face when Dad put the syrup on top of it all.

"A meal fit for my children's birthday!" Dad shouted.

And Dad added a little salt for extra flavor. Emily thinks that you put salt on your dinner to cool it down but it is actually the draft that comes from the gap at the top of the window. You just have to wait, and it will cool down. I keep telling her that but she still thinks it's the salt, which is why she always burns her tongue on her food.

Dad ate the birthday dinner in two bites but you mustn't gobble your food down or people will think you are a glutton. And that's a deadly sin. But he doesn't care because most of the time he doesn't eat.

"Tomorrow I will mend that bike!" Dad said and told me to come and sit on his knee.

And Emily sat on his other knee and Margueretta looked at me with that smile, which means she is going to lock me in the cellar again as soon as she can.

Here we go loopy loo, here we go loopy light,
Here we go droopy-doo, all on a Saturday night!
My droopy-doo! My droopy-doo!

Daddy swung Emily around and lifted her little feet off the ground and she squealed.

"Do it again, Daddy. Do it again!"

"Do you love your daddy?"

"We do! We do!" we cried.

"Choo-choo! Choo-choo!" shouted Pop and wet himself, which was the second time today.

Happy Birthday to you! Happy Birthday to you!
Happy Birthday dear Emily, John, and Margueretta!
Happy Birthday to you!

And Emily danced, holding hands with Dad, singing.

"And tomorrow, my wee Johnny, you will go for a ride in a police car!"

"Can I go too?" Emily asked and jumped up and down.

"No. It's man's work. Little Johnny is a man."

And Emily cried because she wasn't a man.

And I cried too because it wasn't a police car. It was a milk float.

6

That's why we had to get up so early this morning. It was freezing and dark when we loaded the milk onto the back of the float and Dad said I could help but the crates were too heavy and we pretended I was lifting them but everyone could see it was just my dad. And the man at the depot said I was a good boy to help my dad like that and then he asked what happened to my hair.

Dad never said anything about the fleas or Tony Curtis. He said I wanted it cut that way, which was not true at all. Why would anyone want to have all their hair cut off so you can see scratches all over their head from where they had fleas?

The milk rattled as we went up the street and Dad made siren sounds and said we were chasing baddies in our police car. And even though it was only a milk float, I made my fingers into the shape of a gun and blasted at the baddies through the open door.

"Faster, faster!" I shouted.

"We will be able to go faster once we have delivered all this milk," Dad said.

"Bang, bang! Bang, bang!"

"They'll never get away!" Dad shouted.

But they did get away because we were not in a real police car and we kept having to stop to deliver the milk.

"Did you know that your dad had tea with the Queen of England?" Dad asked.

I have heard this story before and I have checked with Mum if it is true. And even though he sometimes tells lies, it is true that my dad went to tea with the queen.

"The king died suddenly. That's how it all started, and she was a princess when the king died. She was beautiful, it goes without saying, and I was a very young man. She was going to be the Queen of England. And I had tea with her!"

"Did you cry?"

"Why would I cry? Och, you say the funniest things."

"The pussycat went to London to visit the queen."

"That's right! And what did the pussycat do?"

"She frightened a mouse from under a chair."

"She did. Very good! Well, let me tell you the story. The princess was sad, and she wanted someone to play the organ at the king's funeral. The king was her daddy."

"Her daddy died? Did she cry?"

"I'm sure she did. She loved him very much. Anyway, the Royal College of Music told her about me. Daddy has a gift. A gift from God. That's how I can play the organ. I found out one day when the choirmaster gave me a lesson in the church. I was a wee laddie like you. And that's how a poor grocer's son got to go to the Royal College of Music and have tea with a princess who was about to become the Queen of England."

"Can I play the organ?"

"Perhaps. But perhaps God gave you a different gift. We all have a gift from God."

"Mum said I am a gift from God."

"Well, that's right enough, Johnny."

"She said my name means 'Gift From God.'"

"It does."

"But there are a lot of people called John so are they all gifts from God?"

"You ask too many questions."

"Your name is John too. So are you a gift from God?"

"We're all gifts from God."

"If I am a gift from God, I would like to be a lamb. Can I be a lamb, Daddy?"

"You are a blessed lamb, wee Johnny. A blessed lamb."

"What happened to the princess?"

"She chose someone else. There was another princess called Margaret. I forgot to call her a princess. I just said, 'Hello, Margaret.' So they never asked me to come back."

"Then did you cry, Daddy?"

"I did, Johnny. I did. I cried for all that could have been but never was. I could have played at the king's funeral in Westminster Abbey. I could have played but for my own stupidity. Don't make the same mistakes, wee Johnny. Don't make the same mistakes as your old dad. Well, all this talking has made me thirsty!"

"Have a pint of milk, Daddy!"

"No, Johnny, your daddy needs pints of a different kind. You guard the milk like a Scottish soldier!" Dad said and stopped the milk float to go inside the Fitzroy.

I think he must have been really thirsty because he was gone for a very long time. That's why I climbed over into the driver's seat and pulled at the steering wheel. When I am a grown-up I will go to see a man about a dog. Or I might be a policeman and kill baddies.

"Bang, bang, you're dead!"

But it's really tiring shooting baddies and anyway Dad was gone so long that I ran out of baddies to shoot so I lay down on the seat and fell asleep.

He was still gone when I woke up. And I thought he would never come back from being so thirsty and seeing a man about a dog in the brown room. And I would have to stay there forever with the milk and the baddies. If he was so thirsty, I don't know why he didn't have some milk. There was lots of milk.

I don't know who that woman was who asked me why I was crying. She looked very worried about something.

"What are you doing here?" she asked.

"Waiting for my dad," I answered but I'm not supposed to talk to strangers.

"Where is he?"

"He's in there."

"Dry your tears. And wait here. It's a disgrace. A disgrace, I say."

She came back out of the pub with Dad and wagged her finger at him and he blew a raspberry at her and she shook her head the way that people do when you have done something very bad but he was only getting a drink because he was thirsty. Dad laughed and made his voice sound like hers but I didn't laugh, even though it was funny, because that lady looked even more angry. I don't like it when people get angry.

Dad drove much faster in the afternoon. We weaved in and out of the white lines and a crate of milk fell off the back and two men shouted at us but we kept going because we were in a speeding police chase.

And when we slowed down, Dad started singing. I like it when he sings.

She was lovely and fair as the rose of the summer,
Yet 'twas not her beauty alone that won me.

I could see him looking down at me, snuggled under his arm.

"Och. Dear wee Johnny. My dear, wee boy," he said and he started to cry and I watched the tears trickle down his rosy cheeks.

"What is it, Daddy?"

Oh no, 'twas the truth in her eyes ever dawning,
That made me love Mary, the Rose of Tralee.

"Who's Mary, Daddy?"

"Och, it's just a song, Johnny. Just a sad song."

"Why are you crying?"

"It's a sad song."

"Are we going home soon?"

"Just as soon as we deliver all the milk."

"I'm tired, Daddy. And I'm hungry."

"Well, just close your eyes, wee Johnny. Close your eyes and pretend you are in a police car."

So I closed my eyes and fell asleep again on his arm while the bottles went chink, chink, chink behind us.

Chink, chink, chink.

Dad was fired when we got back to the depot. And when we got home, Dad kept falling over. Usually he falls over because I hold onto his leg but I wasn't holding onto his leg this time and Mum was shouting at him but I don't think you should shout at someone just because they fell over. You should help them get back up. I tried to help him up but he's too heavy.

"You are an irresponsible good-for-nothing! A useless piece of...and how are you going to get another job when you keep getting fired?" Mum shouted.

She lit a cigarette, but she still didn't help him get back up so he got back up on his own, which he can do sometimes.

And Dad laughed and said, "There's no demand for pipe organ players, except in churches. And horror films."

And he laughed so much he fell over again. And still no one helped him get back up.

"You are drunk!"

"Och. Don't be like that, my sweet rose. Come here and give me a wee kiss."

He sat up on the kitchen floor and held out his arms.

"A kiss? A kiss? That won't put food on the table. How could you do that? You're drunk..." She lowered her voice so that me and Emily couldn't hear her. "And, with Johnny there too. How could you? A five-year-old boy. Seeing his father like this."

23

"Help me up, Johnny."

"If your dear father was here now, he'd turn in his grave!" Nana said.

"The front of my trousers. Someone has sewn up the front of my trousers!" Pop screamed. "My trousers! Sewn up my trousers!"

I could see Pop had his trousers on back to front but I never said anything and then he wet himself and hid in the corner. And everyone slammed the door when they left, Dad first and then Mum and Nana chasing after him.

I pulled Emily by the hand and we sat under the kitchen table and picked at the piece of Dundee cake that Nana made at Christmas. It's stuck to the floor behind one of the table legs. I managed to pull a sultana out of it. It looked like a dead fly. But I didn't eat it. Then I made tracks with my fingers in the cigarette ash on the floor.

Margueretta came over and grabbed me by the neck and dragged me to the cellar door and pushed me in. Normally she would pull me by the hair but I don't have any. She strangled me a little bit before she pushed me in. Strangling is when you put your hands around someone's neck and squeeze so hard that they can't breathe and then their eyes nearly pop out like marbles.

I don't always curl into a ball. So I'm pulling my knees up to my face and rocking back and forwards on the stone floor. Backwards and forwards. Backwards and forwards. Backwards and forwards in the dark.

And the thing in the corner goes drip, drip, drip. I don't know why it makes that sound.

Drip, drip, drip.

I'm shivering now. But I'm keeping my teeth shut tight so they don't make a noise. Tight like my eyes. I don't want that thing to know I'm here. But it knows I'm here. And it's not very nice.

7

Today did not start well. Just after I arrived at school, my best friend Tommy dared me to climb over the wall of the knackers yard which is right across the road from our school. Everyone knows that the knackers yard is haunted, and they take dead horses and their headless riders in there and boil them down into glue. It's a terrible place.

Then the others joined in with Tommy and dared me, so I had no choice but to climb up the wall. There's a bomb site beside the knackers yard so we piled up some old bricks against the wall, and I climbed on the bricks and pulled my head over the top to look.

That's when I saw it. It was the skeleton of a horse's head with no body. So that proves it.

"There are skeletons and dead horses and dead men with no heads! Aieeee! Aieeee!" I screamed.

And Emily screamed and then the other girls screamed. Everyone turned and screamed and ran so I had to let go of the wall and the pile of bricks gave way and I slid down on the front of my shoes and now they are ripped and I know for sure my mum does not have money for new shoes, so my toes will be sticking out the bloody ends for God knows how long because there is no way I am going to show her what I have done to my shoes.

And then things got worse when we ran across the road to the school gate. All the other children were gathered around the front window of the assembly hall because someone had set fire to it. It wasn't still on fire but the big window was smashed and the wall was black.

Daisy was lying there on the ground all broken with one of her eyes hanging out and her hair was matted down on her head like a swimming cap. And her lips were on the wrong side of her face. It made her look like she was trying not to kiss someone. She was beautiful before she was burned like that and the girls took turns to brush her hair. There were lots of toys and books lying beside her, black and burned. But Daisy made the girls cry.

"That's what happens when you play with fire! Do not ever play with fire!" Miss Jones said.

Miss Jones is our schoolteacher. We love Miss Jones. She said it was Teddy Boys who set fire to the front of the school by throwing a petrol bomb through the small open window that Mr. Clegg the caretaker only left open to let some fresh air in.

"Yes, indeed. That's what happens when you play with fire. So let that be a lesson to you all!" she shouted.

We have an open fire in our classroom and we don't even need a fire-guard. Mr. Clegg makes the fire for us in the morning and Miss Jones has taught us a rhyme to help us remember that unguarded fires are extremely dangerous around small children.

> *Wee Willy, all bows and sashes,*
> *Fell into the fire and was burned to ashes.*
> *Now the room grows cold and chilly,*
> *For no one wants to poke poor Willy.*

I have asked around but no one knows who Willy was or when he fell into the fire. I also do not know why he didn't just climb back out because it's not a very big fire. There is no way that I will stay in that classroom on my own because the ghost of Willy will climb out of the fireplace, all black and crispy, and pull me back into that bloody fire with him. I just know it.

"So, children. Today we will continue with our sewing. I am sure that will make us all feel better about Daisy," Miss Jones continued.

The girls clapped their hands. I am sure they felt better about Daisy now that they could get back to their embroidery, but I was not at all happy. Miss Jones just doesn't understand that sewing is for girls, and I do not want to embroider my name with a sunburst above it. Tommy agrees. We have been working on this project for weeks and most of the girls have already finished and started on some quilting. I have only done a *J* and an *o* and haven't even started on the sunburst. Tommy has only done part of a *T* because he says it's a big letter but that's just an excuse because it's no bigger than a *J*.

So we started the sewing class, but I stopped in the middle of my *h* and started to chew on the end of my needle because I was worried about my shoes. That's when I saw Gloria McIntosh secretly picking a giant green bogey out of her nose and eating it. A line of snot was dangling all the way from her nose to her mouth, probably still connected to the bogey. It was therefore no surprise that I bit into the needle and the point broke off.

"Miss Jones!"

"Get to the end of the line, Johnny."

"But Miss Jones!"

"Johnny! Get to the end of the line. You are not the only one with problems with your cross-over stitches, you know!"

"I-bit-the-needle-and-it-broke-and-I-think-I-swallowed-it!"

That was the first time any of us had heard Miss Jones scream. Even that time when a small mouse ran in front of her desk she didn't scream because anyone should know that a small mouse is actually more afraid of us.

"Everyone take their seats! Johnny has swallowed a needle! And stay away from the fire!"

We ran down the corridor to Mr. Clegg but he said there was no way he could get a needle out of my mouth with a pair of pliers or any of his other tools for that matter so we all went to see Miss Nugent because she's the headmistress and she would know what to do.

"Have you swallowed it?" Miss Nugent screamed.

"I don't know."

"Come here by the window and open your mouth!"

"Can you see it?" asked Mr. Clegg.

"There it is!"

It was stuck in my gum just above my back tooth. Miss Nugent pulled it out with her eyebrow tweezers.

"Did you do this deliberately?" Miss Jones demanded.

"No! I saw Gloria McIntosh pick her nose and eat it!"

You always have to tell Miss Jones the truth because she can read your mind and she knows if you are lying. That's why Jimmy Grundle confessed last week that the puddle on the floor was not in fact where he had knocked over his jam jar of water for his paintbrushes but was actually where he had peed himself. It wasn't really his fault because he had his hand up and was hopping from leg to leg trying to get Miss Jones' attention, but she was very busy showing us how to make orange paint by mixing red and yellow together. You can also make green by mixing yellow and blue.

And last month, she made Gary Gordon admit that he was the one who had taken a shit in the boy's toilet and not in the sit-down place. He said there was only one sit-down toilet working and someone was in it and he couldn't hold it in any longer. We all rushed to take a look at it during play-time. Mr. Clegg was not very happy. He had to get it out with his mop.

Miss Jones said it's been a very difficult day and we could all go home early, so I walked back home from school with Emily. It's only a mile and we have to hold hands but only to cross the street because I am not holding hands with a girl. You absolutely must look both ways and listen before you cross but a few weeks ago I forgot and was run down by a man on a bicycle. He picked me up and told me to watch where I was going. Luckily, he missed Emily. Nana said it was also lucky that he was on a bike and not driving a bus.

Anyway, I'm home now and Mum has seen my shoes, which I had completely forgotten about and for some reason she started crying, which made me very sad. So I have decided to grow her some daffodils.

They will make her think of the sun and then she will be happy again. As soon as he gets home, I will ask my dad where I can buy some daffodil seeds.

8

Two men came to live in our house today. Nana calls them "The Irish," and they dig roads in all weathers, which is something only Irish people will do because they had a famine. That's what happens when you completely run out of food because locusts ate the crops. If there is no food at all then you end up eating anything including rats and worms and dirt. I would not want to eat rats but I did eat a worm once and Mum made me spit it back out. I also ate some dirt.

The Irish are going to be our lodgers, which means they are going to live with us and pay us money. So now, Margueretta will have to sleep in the tiny room that's at the back of the bedroom that I share with Emily. Margueretta said it should be me who has to sleep in there because she's the oldest one and I'm much smaller and it's only big enough for a small bed and it doesn't even have a window.

We have a window in our bedroom but no curtains and Dad says that's so we can watch the moon and the stars at night and dream of Heaven. I like to dream of Heaven but mostly I dream about that thing in the corner of the cellar with the bulging green eyes. It makes me scream and sometimes when I scream, nothing comes out but I keep screaming all night long. Screaming and screaming. But no one comes.

Emily always dreams about the baby Jesus because she held him when she was Mary in the Nativity play. They put a blue scarf around her head and she looked so much like Mary that we all wanted to touch her. Some of the girls cried to be so close to the Holy Mother. But I didn't cry because she was really my sister.

I wanted to be Joseph or a lamb but I had to be Wee Willy Winky with a candle to light you to bed. Miss Jones put me in a man's shirt for a nightshirt and it was obviously a very stupid thing to do because it was far too long and I tripped on it and fell off the stage into the audience. And it was a real candle with a real flame. Luckily, I fell on top of the flame and the shirt put out the fire.

And that is why you must never ever play with matches or candles.

Dad told us that if we lay in bed and stare long enough at the night sky, we might see an angel.

"And that angel might come down and bless you and that would be the most wondrous thing you will ever know because an angel is a messenger of God."

I have been staring and staring at that dark night sky. I'm sure I've seen an angel. I know it had to be an angel because Daddy said they shine with the most beautiful heavenly light and you will feel warm inside, warm like a cup of hot chocolate in your tummy. It was a light like I had never seen before and I felt the warmth inside me, the way Daddy said I would.

In the morning, when I told my mum that I had seen an angel she laughed.

"Next time you should make a wish and maybe you should wish for your dad to come home and get the stove working!"

So I wished.

Margueretta flicked my ear and said it wasn't a real angel—it was just a star. And she said wishes never come true anyway. But I still wished.

And she was wrong because Dad did come home and he finished knocking out the fireplace in the kitchen and put the stove in there and it was working again.

But Nana is still angry at my dad because of what happened. You are supposed to have the chimney swept if you are going to knock out the bloody fireplace in the kitchen and put the stove in there so all the cooking smells can go up the chimney. And if you don't have the chimney swept it should not be a surprise if the steam from the bubble-and-squeak loosens the soot and it all comes tumbling down over the frying pan and your nana. Dad said she looked like a Black and White Minstrel.

She didn't think that was funny. But she couldn't catch him to hit him over the head with the frying pan because her legs are too short and my dad can run really fast. And she had soot in her eyes.

We still haven't had the chimney swept, so that's why The Irish have to have fish and chips from the shop for dinner tonight. But they shouldn't get used to it because you can't have fish and chips from the shop for dinner all your life. We are not made of money, you know. And Nana says they can have a drink of whisky and a wee song on her gramophone.

Oh, stop yer tickling, Jock!
Dinna mak me laugh so hearty or you'll mak me choke!

Nana likes to sing along to her records and she holds her apron up when she dances. She dances the Highland Fling with me because I am her Scottish soldier. Round and around and around we go. And when the record stops, she puts her hand down my pants and grabs my willy.

"Stop yer tickling! What have I got hold of here? Ha! Ha! Stop yer tickling, Jock! What have I got hold of here?"

That made The Irish laugh. It makes people laugh if someone puts their hand down your pants and grabs your willy. So Nana played another record and put her hand down my pants again to make The Irish laugh some more. I like it when The Irish laugh. The old one mostly smiles and smokes his cigarettes but the young one laughs and slaps his leg and asks for more whisky. His name is Sam and Margueretta danced with him because I was getting far too much attention with Nana singing the tickling song and grabbing my willy.

Sam twirled Margueretta around so that her short dress flew out and we all could see her knickers and her skinny white legs. And he stroked his big hands through her long blonde hair and held her up close to him like he was her boyfriend even though she's only nine. Then he rubbed his hands on her legs all the way up near her knickers.

Mum says Margueretta always wants to be the center of attention. Anyway, my sister has never seen an angel and she's wrong because wishes do come true.

9

The electricity is off tonight. Margueretta loves it when the electricity goes off because it's so dark in our house that no one can see what she's doing to me. And she's angry tonight because she had to look after me and Emily outside the pub while the grown-ups were inside singing and laughing. I've never been inside the pub but I like the inside. I look at it through the door when it opens. It smells of smoke and sweet things. It's warm and bright on the inside.

But we were on the outside. And Margueretta ran off and left us there and a big man came out of the pub and was sick all over the pavement, which wasn't very nice because some of it splashed onto Emily and me. His sick was all brown and frothy and it ran down into the gutter and floated away under the street lamp. And then he wiped all of the snot and sick onto his coat sleeve, which you are not supposed to do because that is what hankies are made for. But I never said anything.

And now we're home in the cold and dark and I don't know where any of the grown-ups are. I just know I'm going to be in the cellar soon.

Margueretta knows all about the thing in the corner of the cellar. She was the one who told me about it in the first place. She said they had to cut him down after he hanged himself because they couldn't undo his tie. And then they dragged him into the house and dumped him in the corner of the cellar with his eyes bulging out like marbles. And he's still there. Waiting for a chance to come out in the dark. His name is John and now he wants to get inside me because my name is John too and I'm still alive and he is dead. Margueretta says I will never escape from him because he always knows where I am.

I'm sure I've seen him behind me. There's a dark shadow following me sometimes and it's much bigger than me so I know it's not my shadow.

There's another reason Margueretta likes the dark. She says she can see things that no one else can see. And our house is full of bad things—like the thing in the cellar and the people who are inside the walls of my bedroom knocking to get out. One day they will kill us all in our beds. One day. And then everyone will be dead.

She wants to twist my hair tonight but there's still not enough of it for her to get hold of. So she's twisting my ears instead. She says she will make me pray to Jesus to save me from the thing in the cellar. I'm not telling her that I already do that. And because I wouldn't beg her to stop she's locked me down here again.

She says death is waiting for us. And so is the Devil. He wants to come inside our heads and make us do bad things. Then we will be sinners and burn in a lake of fire. We can't stop the bad things from coming inside our heads. No matter how hard we try to think of good things and even Jesus will not be able to save us.

Margueretta's head is full of bad things. And those things talk to her. That's what she says.

10

I t's a good thing that I have learned my address, in case a policeman wants to know where I live. This afternoon I was in a very dark boiler room with Emily, and Margueretta turned out all the lights and locked the door when she left us there. She also said that the boilers were going to blow up in five seconds, which is not very long. So we both took turns screaming.

The caretaker from that block of flats was really unhappy when he found us screaming in his boiler room and he asked me where we live and I told him our address, even though strictly speaking he was a stranger and I should not be speaking to him. But this is how we were able to get back to our house with the caretaker before the boiler room blew up.

And even though it's Dad's birthday today, he still took down Margueretta's knickers and spanked her because the caretaker wanted someone punished. That's only right because it was very annoying having to drag us home with Emily and me crying the whole way.

But being locked in a boiler room that was about to explode is not why I am so upset. I am upset because nobody told me about my dad's birthday until now and I am very sad because I cannot buy him a birthday card. Birthday cards cost money and so do flower seeds. I only get one penny of pocket money per week and I saved for six weeks to buy the daffodil seeds, which cost sixpence a packet. Mum is sad a lot of the time, so I have to grow the daffodils as soon as possible to make Mum think of the sun so that she will not be sad again. And now I don't have any spare pocket money to buy Dad a card. That's why I am upset and that's why I am going to make him a card.

I'm not going to have much time to make a birthday card because it's getting late and I've only just got back from the garden shop. The man in the shop was not very nice and he said there's no such thing as daffodil seeds. I don't know how you can grow daffodils without seeds but he said it doesn't matter anyway because you can only grow daffodils in the spring. And it's the end of spring now.

And when I started to cry, he asked me why I was so sure I wanted daffodils and I told him I needed yellow flowers like the sun for my mum and then she won't be sad. And he said that's a very good thing to do for my mum but I should grow sunflowers, not daffodils, and sunflowers grow in the summer. I have not heard of sunflowers before but there is a picture on the packet and the man looked at me and told me to wipe away my tears because any idiot could grow sunflowers. But you must not forget to water them.

I have not told anyone about the sunflowers. I have especially not told Emily because girls cannot keep secrets. That's why I have also not told Emily that I have a box of matches in my pocket that I found on the sideboard.

I will plant the sunflower seeds soon, in the backyard near the wall, being careful not to dig up Boots or Judy. Also I will not forget to water them.

Nana said not to worry that I can't buy a card for my dad.

"He didnee buy you ones so much as a card for yer birthday! And he still hasnee mended that rusty old bicycle."

But she gave me an old paper bag and we folded it in half like a card and I drew a picture of Daddy and me on the front, riding in a police car. And she showed me how to write inside, "Happy Birthday, Daddy!" And she wrote out "With all my love from Johnny," and I copied it in my best handwriting. And I added four kisses. I think four is the right number. We don't have any envelopes so I've put it on the sideboard for him and he will see it at soon as he comes home and it will make him happy and I hope he doesn't notice that it is an old paper bag from Timothy White's. I also drew a blue flashing light on the police car with my crayon.

"Let's have some wee tunes," Nana said. "Some wee tunes while we wait for your father to come home."

"Why bother?" Mum replied.

But Nana put a record on the gramophone.

> *Oh, roamin' in the gloamin' on the bonnie banks o' Clyde,*
> *Roamin' in the gloamin' wi' ma lassie by ma side.*
> *When the sun has gone to rest; that's the time that I like best...*

And Nana told me to dance with her but she never put her hand down my pants to grab my willy because The Irish weren't there and it wasn't the tickling song.

"When will Daddy be home?" Emily asked.

"Only he knows," Mum replied.

"When will we sing 'Happy Birthday'?" I asked.

"Soon. Soon enough," Mum replied.

"Och, I'll put this one on. It's your father's favorite. Enrico Caruso. 'The Lost Chord.'"

"Oh, he's lost the chord alright!" Mum added. "Lost everything more like it!"

> *Seated one day at the organ,*
> *I was weary and ill at ease,*
> *And my fingers wandered idly,*
> *Over the noisy keys.*

"It's such a waste," Mum continued. "Wasting his gift from God. What a bloody waste."

> *I know not what I was playing,*
> *Or what I was dreaming then,*
> *But I struck one chord of music,*
> *Like the sound of a great Amen.*

"Caruso sung that wee song for the victims of the *Titanic*, you know," Nana said.

"What?" Mum replied and lit a cigarette while handing one to Nana.

"After the *Titanic* sunk. He's Italian. That's why you cannee understand the words. It's his accent. And I think you'll find that he's dead now. He said he wasnee feeling well and no one listened to him. Then he died, poor wee beggar. Ha! Ha! Yer a lang time dead. Right enough, lassie."

"Right enough, Mother."

"Do you think he will like my card?" I asked.

"He will, Johnny. That he will," Nana replied.

"Can we play party games when he comes home?"

"Yes, Johnny."

"And will we dance with him?"

"You will, little lad," Nana replied.

We don't have any real swords because you could cut your foot off with a real sword. So we put the broom and mop on the floor and danced the Highland Fling and Nana made whooping sounds like a Red Indian. I danced with her but I didn't make any whooping sounds.

And Mum kept looking at the clock and I kept looking at my card on the sideboard, ready for my daddy's birthday party. Four kisses. Maybe I should have put five.

"It's time you were all in bed," Mum said.

So I left my card on the sideboard and Daddy will see it when he comes home. He will have a Happy Birthday with four kisses.

11

tried to stay awake and I don't know when I fell asleep. When I woke up, I couldn't remember if I had said my prayers or not. I always say my prayers, down on my knees on the bare boards by the bed. Mum makes me ask God to bless Margueretta even though she beats me every day and locks me in the cellar. You are supposed to love your enemies. But that doesn't make sense because there's no point in having an enemy if you love them because then they won't be your enemy and they might even be your friend.

And when I say my prayers, I bless Mum and Dad and Emily and Nana and Pop and Uncle Bertie in Arundel and Great-Auntie Wilma in Peckham, who's been burgled three times. Mum even made me bless Boots and Judy when they were alive but I don't think you should ask God to waste his time blessing a cat and a dog. A lamb would be different. And I don't have to bless Great-Auntie Maisie now because she is dead and you don't need to bless a dead person.

But I can't remember if I said my prayers last night.

It was the screaming that woke me up. The screaming and the funeral music that makes the walls shake. And even if Dad is only trying to annoy that woman next door who is spying on us, I don't think he should play funeral music in the middle of the night.

I wanted to stay in bed and hide under the blanket but all I could think about was the thing in the corner of the cellar and I know that one day it will come out of there and crawl up into my bedroom. I'm sure it's behind me all the time but when I turn around there's nothing there.

In the end, I just had to creep downstairs while the funeral music sounded like thunder in the night. I moved really slowly on the wooden boards in the passageway, so slowly anyone would think I was standing still. No one heard me coming down the stairs with all that noise. I could hear the blood in my ears like the ocean as I got closer and closer to the door to the front room— the front room where all the screaming was coming from.

I was all alone in the dark in the long passageway, tiptoeing on the balls of my black feet.

But a huge hand landed hard on my shoulder and another hand pressed against my mouth. It had to be him. He was out of the cellar in the darkness.

"That room is no place for little boys. You shouldn't see your father like that. No one should. Get back to your bed. Get back to your bed while you still have a bed."

But it wasn't the thing from the cellar. It was The Irish, just the old one and he didn't mean to frighten me. I still ran like a dog. Up the stairs, two at a time, through the bedroom door. Jumped into bed and I tried really hard to hold it in but it was too late and it felt warm, the piss running through my legs onto the mattress.

12

I didn't say anything this morning. All the piss in my bed had dried up. Mum says I can go into her bedroom and try to wake Dad up if I want because no one should spend all day in bed asleep.

It smells of piss and vinegar in here. There are gray blankets lying on the floor around the bed and Dad is lying on the bed in his underpants. I've been shaking him for ages but he isn't moving.

I'm going to sit by the bed and wait for him to wake up and then he will mend the bicycle and take me for a ride. There's not much light in this bedroom because there's a big brown blanket hanging on a string over the window. I can see the dark mold growing up the corner of the wall and across the ceiling and just above the corner I can see the sky through the small hole by the chimney breast.

He's groaning now so I think he is waking up.

"Daddy! Daddy!"

But he's turned over and he's snoring.

I want to help my dad but I don't want to empty his piss pot. It's full with dark orange piss right to the top and it's spilled over the edge. I think that's why it smells of piss in here. Mum won't empty his piss pot because she says that my dad can do his own slopping out. Sometimes Dad just throws it out the bedroom window but that's not very nice if you happen to be walking by on the street below.

I can hear them again, inside the walls. Whispering and knocking. They're waiting for Pop because he will be next. Then I hope they will be quiet or someone else will die.

I've got the card with me to show him when he wakes up. You shouldn't be asleep this late and I've been waiting all day for him to wake up and see my card.

"Johnny! Johnny!"

That's Nana. She's calling me for supper. But Dad still won't wake up so I'm going to leave the card on the bed beside him and he will see it when he wakes up. And that will make him very happy even if his birthday was yesterday and not today.

We're having cabbage and potatoes again tonight. The Irish are having eggs and potatoes because Nana says they are workingmen and they are paying to be here so they expect more than cabbage for dinner.

"Och! Let's have a wee tune," says Nana. "I think we'll have some Harry Lauder."

Sam is smiling and there's egg yolk running down his chin but I don't think he knows. He's mopping up the egg with a thick slice of bread and butter. I can see the bread and egg yolk mashing around in his mouth because he talks with his mouth full, which you should never do.

The old one never says anything but I can see he thinks a lot. Mostly he rolls cigarettes and smokes slowly like he's in a far-off place. He never said anything this morning about last night. I don't know what it was that I shouldn't see and why there was so much screaming and why Dad was playing the organ in the middle of the night if it wasn't to annoy the woman next door. She's spying on us, you know. Always spying.

"Oh, Danny Boy, the pipes, the pipes are calling," Nana sings.

"Come and dance, Margueretta," says Sam.

And he's twirling her around again and I know her dress is too small for her because it's really short and we can all see her knickers again.

"'The summer's gone and all the roses falling.' Come and dance with me, Johnny!"

So I'm dancing with Nana and she's putting her hand down my pants and grabbing my willy for The Irish and Sam is laughing even though it's not the tickling song.

"Choo-choo! Stand back! Stand back!" shouts Pop.

He hasn't pissed himself yet today. But he will.

> *But come ye back when summer's in the meadow,*
> *And I shall hear though soft you tread above me.*
> *And then my grave shall warmer, sweeter be,*
> *For you will bend and tell me that you love me,*
> *And I shall sleep in peace until you come to me.*

Now Sam has sat down and Margueretta is sitting on his lap. And he's sliding his hand up her leg, right up to her little white knickers and she's smiling at him and he's keeping his hand there, by her little white knickers. And she's turning to look at me and it's a look that means she is special and Sam has chosen her and not me and I can be Daddy's favorite because now she has got Sam.

And Sam's whispering something in her ear while he's looking at me and smiling. I think he's telling her a secret.

"Choo-choo goes the train! Stand back! Stand back!" screams Pop.

Pop's rolling his eyes around and spit is dripping down off his long tongue and wetting the crusted porridge that's still on his chin from breakfast. And we all know that his tongue doesn't fit in his mouth. So he just leaves it hanging out.

"There is a happy land far, far away; where they eat bread and jam three times a day," sings Nana.

She's grabbing my willy again.

We have bread and jam sometimes for dinner but Nana says you must never have bread and butter and jam together. You need a lot of money to have butter and jam together.

I hope Daddy will like my birthday card when he wakes up. I think I should have written more kisses.

13

I saw it tonight. I knew it would come into my bedroom. Climb out of the cellar and come up here. I knew it would.

Drip, drip, drip.

When we came to bed, Nana read us the story of "The Little Match Girl" and that made Emily cry because the little girl died and went to Heaven to be with her grandmother. Nana says it's a happy story because the little girl is now safe and warm, sitting at the feet of God with her grandmother instead of starving and freezing to death on the street trying to sell matches to rich people who don't even care if she dies. And the little match girl made that wonderful warmth when she set fire to all the matches she had left and the glow was like the first time you see Heaven when you die. Like seeing an angel.

So you shouldn't cry because now the little girl is in Heaven. But Emily cried herself to sleep because the little match girl died and no one cared.

It was very dark when I woke up and saw that huge hand coming round our bedroom door. It was the creaking of the door that woke me up. Then it floated into the room. I thought I would scream but I didn't want it to find me so I stayed very quiet and still. I was scared that it would hear me breathing so I held my breath.

But it came nearer and nearer to me. Nearer and nearer. I could hear it make the sound.

Drip, drip, drip.

It floated over to Emily's bed and put its huge face up close to hers. Then it turned and floated over to Margueretta's door and went inside.

Perhaps it would kill her. I hoped it would kill her. Don't kill me. I heard some sounds. Surely it would kill her.

Drip, drip, drip.

Kill her.

And then it floated back into our bedroom and out the door. I know where it went. It went back into the cellar. Back with its bulging green eyes into the darkness. And the next time I am locked in there, it will kill me.

14

I will not get anything by whining. It's about time I realized that I will miss out on a whole lot of things in life because of my constant whining. But when I start a whine it's hard to make it stop and then Emily starts whining and she can whine even better than me and then none of us can stop.

And that is why we never go to the seaside. Mum does not want to hear me whining about toffee apples and candyfloss and doughnuts and going to Billy Manning's Funfair. But two days ago she said that we could go to the seaside soon but only if she does not hear one more bloody whine coming out of us or we will stay behind and everyone else will go without us, and that will be that.

I have only whined once in two days and I can't even remember what it was about, which just goes to prove that whining does not get you anything. And Mum was prepared to overlook this as it was only the once.

So that is why we are here on the beach with the smell of fish and chips and the beautiful bright colored lights going around and around on the big wheel at the front of Billy Manning's Funfair. And there are other wonderful things but I am trying to ignore them or they will start me whining.

The man who has stripped down to his string vest with the black hairs poking out is my Uncle Jack. He's got a thick black belt holding up his trousers. And he doesn't thread it through the belt loops—that's so he can whip it off quickly if he needs to.

He's drinking Whitbread's Mackeson Milk Stout because he says it looks good, it tastes good, and by golly it does you good. Dad is having one too but Auntie Ethel is drinking sherry with Mum and Nana. They like to drink sherry because it comes in smaller glasses and no woman should be seen drinking a pint of beer, especially not from a bottle.

We would have had pickled eggs for lunch but someone left the jar on the sideboard, even though my mum reminded my dad three times to bring them. He never bloody listens. Someone also forgot the towels and we don't have any swimming costumes so we will just have to swim in our underwear. That is fine for me but it means that I can see Margueretta's nipples and she has blue veins around them and she can't keep her hands over them if she wants to swim. Nana says we can dry ourselves on her skirt when we come out of the water.

Emily won't be going in the water. It's not her fault that some thoughtless idiots left broken glass on the beach and she didn't see it because it was lying amongst the stones when she trod on it. It's green glass and Dad says it's probably from a cider bottle. Or it could be from a wine bottle but Uncle Jack doesn't think anyone would drink wine on the beach in Portsmouth. And when Dad pulled the glass out of her foot, there was blood everywhere and it dripped onto the stones and looked like little purple beads. You can make purple by mixing red and blue together.

"Do not step in that tar!"

Mum was talking to me, not Emily, because Emily can't walk anywhere. I was just on my way down to the water and there was a big lump of tar on the stones in front of me and Mum said that if I get that on me it will never come off. And even if we carried her, which I suggested, Emily cannot go into the water because it's got sewage in it and then her foot will get infected and it would have to be amputated, which means they would cut it off and she would be a cripple because you can't just grow another foot. I do not want my sister to be a cripple, even if Nana says that Jesus can make the lame walk again.

Dad will come into the water later and teach me how to swim, which he says is really easy because you just have to put your arms out in front of you and kick your legs. But he needs to drink his beer for now because he is very thirsty and I can play in the water with Margueretta but she does not want to teach me how to swim. She just waited for a big wave and held my head under the water. And that's how I found out that you can open your eyes under water and then I could see bubbles and black seaweed, like a cloak all around my head.

It is impossible to breathe under water. We have lungs and fish have gills and they are totally different. That's why fish can't breathe out of water. Which is why it is a good thing that Margueretta let me back up to take a breath before I died but then she pushed my head back under again and held it down with her knees.

Complaining about your older sister trying to drown you is not the same thing as whining. But it didn't matter because absolutely no one was listening to me when I was trying to tell them about nearly drowning because they were all singing and it's hard to hear a little boy complaining about nearly drowning when you are singing very loudly on the beach about a brass band playing tiddley-on-pom-pom.

> *Oh, I do like to be beside the seaside!*
> *I do like to be beside the sea.*
> *And I do like to stroll along the prom, prom, prom,*
> *Where the brass bands play, tiddley-on-pom-pom!*

You shouldn't try to dance on stones, which is why Auntie Ethel fell over and broke her sherry glass. Luckily, they brought spare glasses with them and Mum got her a refill. I didn't tell Auntie Ethel that she put her arm in some of the black tar when she fell over. She will have that tar on her arm for the rest of her life, and she will have to tell people that she was being stupid trying to dance on stones on the beach.

It is also not whining if you are really very thirsty and you ask for a drink just once. I only asked once and Mum said there was nothing for me to drink and she offered me an Opal Fruit pastel because they are made to make your mouth water, which is the same thing as a drink. So I ate the fruit pastel and it did not make my mouth water. It is not the same thing as a drink. It made me even more thirsty.

If you ask for something twice then that is possibly the start of a whine. And when I asked for a drink a third time, while running around in circles, it was definitely a whine. Mum said there was a really good chance that she would take me home and leave me there if I didn't stop and Uncle Jack agreed that he did not come all the way here from London just to listen to my whining so I should bloody well shut up.

And I thought I was going to pee myself when he told me to come over and stand in front of him. All the time, his fingers twitching around that belt buckle.

Twitch, twitch, twitch.

I stared at that belt and he stared into my eyes.

Then he poured me a big glass of sherry and handed it to me and that made him and Dad laugh and they laughed even more when I gulped down the whole glass because I was so thirsty.

"Just like your dad! You're a real man now, sonny," Uncle Jack shouted.

"That's my boy!" said Dad.

Dad was really proud of me and I am a real man now. But Auntie Ethel looked angry.

"What the bloody hell did you just give him?" demanded Auntie Ethel.

"It was Harvey's Bristol Cream Sherry! The boy said he was thirsty," Uncle Jack replied.

"You can't do that!" Auntie Ethel replied.

"Why not? He said he was thirsty!"

"Well, that's our sherry. The sherry is for the women. You should have given him one of your beers! Bloody cheek of it!" said Auntie Ethel.

And everyone started laughing and singing again and Uncle Jack said I could have another drink if I wanted one but I said no because I was feeling very dizzy.

"Och, come on, wee ones. Let's get you out of here."

Nana said I would feel much better once we get to Billy Manning's. I was only sick once on the beach and Uncle Jack said I needed a lot more practice and he said that would be no problem with my dad around and next time I should just have a beer instead of drinking a whole glass of sherry so quickly.

And I knew it was a mistake when Nana said we should go into the House of Mirrors. The mirrors make you fat with a tiny head or like a dwarf with massive eyes and I was looking in the mirror with Nana and noticed there were three Nanas. No, four. Five. Six Nanas. And they were going around and around.

Those people in there did not like it when I was sick all over the mirror. It's also hard to get out of the House of Mirrors in a hurry because some of the doors look like mirrors and you don't know which ones are real.

"Och, those mirrors even made yer old Nana feel unwell! How about the carousel?"

Sometimes Nana doesn't listen to me and I was not whining when I said over and over again that I did not want to go on any rides and they were not making me feel better. And she lied when she told those people on the carousel that it wasn't me when the ride stopped and I slid off my horse. Everyone could see it was me who had sprayed sick everywhere. There was sick all down my shirt and the horse.

And then she put me on the Helter-Skelter and they will have to close that ride for the day. And the Laughing Sailor was funny with all those people watching until I was sick in the middle of the crowd.

"Get your bloody brats out of this place!"

That man doesn't know that Nana could thump him and he wouldn't get back up.

"Och, you big bag o' wind. It's just a wee bit o' excitement. Can't you see the wee laddie is just a bit dizzy from all the rides?"

"Dizzy? Dizzy you call it? He's been bloody well sick in the House of Mirrors, the carousel, the Helter-Skelter, and the Laughing Sailor. What in God's name is next? The bloody Ghost Train?"

"Och, we're not staying where we aren't welcome. Come on kids. We're leaving."

We're going home. And no one wants to sit next to me on the bus.

15

Tommy is not my best friend anymore. It is bad enough that he almost killed me. Offering your best friend a sweet, which he said was definitely a mint imperial, and then sucking them together was very nice. But when I got home, Nana wanted to know what that dreadful smell was, and it turned out to be me. It is incredibly dangerous to eat mothballs because they are made from poison, which is why they were in his grandmother's coat pockets where Tommy found them. They are definitely not mint imperials and I could easily have died if Nana had not stuck her fingers down the back of my throat three times to make me sick.

And making mud pies together and patting them around and turning them into shapes with your fingers is fine if you are making them with mud. It is not fine if you are making them with dog shit. It was a lot of fun until we took our mud pies to show my Nana.

And then while Nana was washing my hands with carbolic soap, Tommy ate our cabbage just like that without even asking. We were in our scullery and there wasn't much cabbage left, mostly leaves, and he ate it all. Well, that made Nana even angrier and I'm not surprised. And it wasn't because Tommy hadn't washed the dog shit off his hands before he ate the cabbage. Tommy said he was starving and that's why he ate it but Nana said we will be starving too if we have no cabbage and we will be like those people in Ireland who had the famine and ate worms. So he can't come round again or the next thing you know he will be eating our potatoes and then all we will be left with is worms and dirt.

We obviously need more food so I have decided to take the eggs from the kitchen cupboard and hatch them into chickens. I think eggs need to be warm to help them hatch so I have put them in my cowboy hat and wrapped them in Nana's scarf, the tartan one with the tassels. When they hatch, I will make them a small pen in the backyard and then they will grow into chickens and lay lots of eggs and everyone will be able to eat eggs—not just The Irish.

I have checked the eggs all day and there is no sign of them hatching yet. I am not sure how long it takes for an egg to hatch into a chicken. I hope it will be today, although it is nearly suppertime already and Nana is looking in the kitchen cupboard.

"What in God's name has happened to ma eggs?"

Nana is looking at me and I know she thinks that Tommy has been round here again and eaten the eggs, which is really stupid because one of us would have to cook them first because you can't eat raw eggs. And we don't know how to cook eggs.

Nana will be very pleased when she hears what I have done and how we will have all the eggs we can eat just as soon as those chicks hatch out.

I will go and check on them again.

"It's a mystery to me," says Dad.

Dad has no idea what happened to the eggs but he will also be very proud when he knows that we have chickens in a pen in the backyard laying eggs all day. He could even have eggs for breakfast. Yes, he is going to be really proud of me. I know he is. Even more proud than seeing me drink a glass of sherry on the beach.

But The Irish don't seem very happy because there are no eggs for their supper and that only leaves potatoes. I will check on the eggs one more time.

"Och, I know I had a half a dozen eggs in that cupboard! Someone has stolen ma eggs! Who would do such a thing? Johnny? You've got that guilty look on your face, laddie!"

It was when I told Nana my chicken plan that she slapped me round the face, right there in front of The Irish. Eggs are dead and I am a very stupid boy for thinking that I could hatch them into chickens.

"There will be no supper for you! You need to learn your lesson, stealing ma eggs!" she said.

"He was just trying to help," said Dad.

"And what would you know about that?"

"Well, I know enough to know that a five-year-old boy was just trying to put food on the table!"

"Aye! And that's something that his forty-year-old father cannee do!"

"And now you're going to make him go to bed hungry? That's heartless."

"He needs to learn his lesson."

And Dad turned away and grabbed his coat from the chair. I ran after him as he walked up the black passageway to the front door.

"Stay and play with me, Daddy!"

"I can't."

"Please stay! Stay and play with me, Daddy!"

"I can't."

He opened the front door and pushed me back but I sprang forward and held onto his leg. He peeled my fingers off his leg and pushed me back again.

"Your daddy has to go. You'll understand one day. One day you will be a man. Then you will understand."

"But I want you to stay with me!"

"I have to go, wee Johnny. Be a good boy and go back to your nana. Go back now."

He's gone.

And I'm going too. I'm leaving home. And I am taking my cowboy hat with me. But not Nana's tartan scarf.

I am going to live in the backyard but I only have two planks of wood and five nails. I cannot build a shelter. I also do not have a hammer out here with me. There is only one answer because it's cold and dark and I am hungry. I will have to sleep in the garden shed and eat worms for the rest of my life.

I have never been inside our shed because Nana said that Pop spent a lot of time in there when he first came to this house and that is why he now thinks he is a train. I need to stop asking questions because the shed is full of things a little boy should not know. I think that's where Pop keeps his playing cards with the pictures of naked women. But I don't know what that has to do with my Auntie Beryl or if she has ever been inside our shed. Anyway Pop does not go into our shed anymore because he is not allowed out on his own now that his tongue hangs out all the time.

I almost jumped out of my bedroom window onto the shed roof once. I was trying to escape from Tommy who was a screaming, bloodthirsty Comanche Indian. I was a cowboy but I don't like heights so I just ducked when he tried to scalp me with our coal shovel.

It's very dark inside our shed. That is why I keep my secret box of matches in my pocket at all times. I've never lit a match before and I've never lit a candle. It glows and makes lots of shadows in the dark. Bad things and shadows in the dark.

I don't like those shadows. I don't like those bad things.

16

I am never going in that bloody shed again. It is full of terrible things. Pop probably killed someone in there. God knows it was much better being back in the warm with Nana, singing along to Freddie and the Dreamers on *Ready, Steady, Go!*

> *You were made for me,*
> *Everybody tells me so.*
> *You were made for me,*
> *Don't pretend that you don't know. . .*

And Margueretta was dancing with Sam and he was twirling her around and we could all see her knickers again. And they were smiling at each other like they knew a secret.

The telly was really loud and that is why we never heard those people banging on our front door. And we never lock our front door, which is why those people didn't wait for us to hear them and they came bursting in and ran down our passageway. That was the end of Freddie and the Dreamers singing "You Were Made For Me."

"What in God's name is going on?" Nana shouted.

"Did you know your shed is on fire?" they shouted back.

Now that is a stupid question, if you ask me, because if we knew our shed was on fire we would not be dancing and singing along with Freddie and the Dreamers. No, we would be outside throwing a bucket of water on it.

THE BOY WHO LIVED WITH GHOSTS

But no one seemed to care because everyone was running down the passageway to the kitchen and out through the scullery and the backdoor and into the backyard.

"How in God's name did our shed catch on fire?" Nana yelled.

The fire engine was bright red and shiny and made a fantastic clanging sound when it came down the street. And they ran their hoses all the way through our house to the backyard. I really wanted Tommy to see it but he's still not my best friend anymore.

"Quick! For God's sake, it will burn down the whole bloomin' street!" shouted the woman from next door.

Nana ignored her because she is spying on us. But the fire was quite big and the flames were reaching up to my bedroom window and that's the problem with a shed that's on fire when the shed is built against the back of your house. And our house is in a row with all the other houses so the woman from next door was right because it could burn down the whole bloody street. And that's why they had to get another fire engine.

"Stand back! Stand back!" shouted the Fire Chief because all the windows were exploding.

"Stand back! Stand back! Choo-choo! Choo-choo goes the train!" shouted Pop.

Then all the other neighbors came into our backyard because they heard the fire engines and that's how the whole street knew our shed was on fire and they would rather watch our shed burning down than watch Freddie and the Dreamers. And the women and children screamed each time one of the windows exploded but I didn't scream. I just stayed quiet and watched the sparks floating up into the dark sky over the roof of our house.

Everyone cheered when the firemen put out the last of the flames and Nana made them all cups of tea.

"How in the world did our shed catch on fire?" asked Nana.

"Sheds don't just burst into flame on their own," said the Fire Chief.

"Och, that's right enough!"

"I think it's reasonably certain that someone left a candle burning in there."

"A candle? But no one was in the shed."

"Well, someone was in there and that person left a candle burning on the shelf."

"It was me!" I shouted.

So I deserved to be locked in the cellar. And they took away my matches. The Fire Chief said that he should really call the police and have me arrested and I would go to jail. I don't want to go to jail and never see my mum and dad again so it is better that I am locked in the cellar in the dark.

And it's here with me. It's whispering.

Drip, drip, drip.

But I don't want to hear it. I don't want to hear it whisper. I want it to kill my sister. Not me. Go into her bedroom again and kill her. Go inside her head like all those other voices.

Sometimes I think I can feel it. It feels like something is touching my arm in the dark. I can't scream because then it will hear me and know where I am. Even though it has eyes bulging out of its head, I don't think it can see. Nana says we would all go blind if we lived in the dark. That thing has been living in the dark for a long time. Blind in the dark.

Dear Jesus, save me. Please, Jesus.

17

must apologize to everyone for burning down the shed—and I must pay for it. Nana has given me a pair of her bloomers and one of Pop's shirts. It's the one he spilt his tomato soup on last week and the stain won't come out. He can only eat soup now because Nana has taken away his teeth because his tongue no longer fits in his mouth and he kept biting it.

She has also given me a Woolworth's paper bag, six pairs of my dad's socks, and all of last week's copies of the *Daily Mirror*. I have to screw up all the newspaper and stuff it down her bloomers. And Nana has taken her lipstick out and she has drawn a face on the paper bag, which makes it look a little bit like a clown.

Emily is helping me and Nana says we have to make a gruesome tortured Guy, which we will then take out and ask for a, "Penny for the Guy!" A long time ago, a man called Guy Fawkes tried to blow up the Houses of Parliament but they caught him and tortured him and hanged him. Nana said they were supposed to cut out his guts while he was still alive but he jumped off the scaffold and broke his neck. I would not want someone to cut out my guts while I was still alive but I would also not like to be hanged. Nor do I know why someone would want to take off his shoes and hang himself in the toilet with his tie until his eyes bulged out like marbles when he was just supposed to be going for a wee. And then stay in the corner of our cellar waiting for a chance to kill us all in our beds.

Nana said we have to make our Guy look very realistic if we want to get a lot of pennies for the Guy but this is hard to do when he is wearing her knickers

THE BOY WHO LIVED WITH GHOSTS

and has a face that looks like a clown. However, Pop has started talking to the Guy so it must be quite realistic. Mind you, Pop also talks to the kettle.

I would like Mum and Dad to see our Guy but they are both in bed asleep. Mum is working the night shift and Dad spends most of the day in bed because he is up half the night playing funeral music on his organ to annoy that woman next door who is spying on us.

But I really want Mum and Dad to see our Guy.

"Och, that's nae bother," Nana said. "Go and wake them up! They'll not mind. Show them your Guy!"

The Guy is actually bigger than me but I dragged it up the stairs with Emily and I was careful not to step in the hole because that would mean I would have to stay there with my foot caught for the rest of my life. Emily pushed the bedroom door open and it was not quite dark inside.

We crept across the bare floorboards and I said to Emily that she should wake Mum first and I will hold up the Guy for her to see. But Emily didn't need to wake Mum because the floorboard creaked really loudly and Mum opened her eyes just as I was standing there behind the Guy.

"Aieeee! Aieeee! Aieeee!"

That's when I knew that our Guy was very realistic. It's one thing for Pop to talk to it but it must look very realistic to make my mum scream like that.

And although Dad never wakes up when you want him to, the screaming was so loud that he turned over to see what was going on and when he opened his eyes he started shouting.

"My God! Your bloody mother is in the room!"

By which he meant that he thought our Guy looked like Nana. He actually thought it *was* Nana, which is not very nice because it has a face made from a Woolworth's paper bag and it looks like a clown. I will not tell Nana that Dad thought our Guy looked like her.

And then Dad tried to get out of bed really quickly but his leg was caught on the blanket and that made him fall halfway out of the bed and knock his piss pot flying and Mum turned over and hit him.

"How dare you say that thing looks like my mother!"

"Och, come out of there, wee ones. I told you not to wake them up," Nana said from the bedroom door.

Nana said it was for the best to leave Mum and Dad to their fighting. So we dragged our Guy back down the stairs.

"I want you to stand on the steps outside the Conservative Club," Nana said. "There's a better class of people there. It's dark now, but Pop will go with you. I told him to wave his arms when he sees someone coming."

Margueretta flicked the back of my ear when Nana told her that she had to go too. And Nana gave me an empty cocoa tin and put two pennies in it and told me to rattle the can when people come by. She also said she wanted the two pennies back when we get home.

Pop is waving his arms already and we haven't even left the kitchen. He looks like a windmill. With a tongue.

"Choo-choo goes the train! Stand back! Stand back!"

So here we are now on the steps of the Conservative Club and it's dark and windy tonight. Pop is waving his arms like a lunatic and his tongue is lashing from side to side in the moonlight. But just as we got here, a gust of wind took our Guy's head off and it sailed up into the air and over a wall into someone's backyard. They will be really scared when they find that head, all gruesome and tortured. They will probably think it's a real head and call the police. It will be a relief for them when they find out that it is just a Woolworth's paper bag stuffed with my dad's socks.

Margueretta has given Pop the Guy to hold. She never wanted to come here in the first place and she doesn't want to hold the Guy. Besides, it means Pop can't wave his arms around anymore, which is a blessing. So he's holding the Guy up in front of him, without its head.

Someone is coming. It's an old lady with glasses and a fur coat. She looks like she's got a lot of money.

"Penny for the Guy, Missus!"

"My, what a realistic Guy."

I knew it!

Rattle, rattle, rattle.

"Penny for the Guy, Missus!"

She's moving up close to our Guy now and looking at Pop's face, which looks a bit like he is the Guy because our Guy has no head.

"It is realistic! Yes, a very realistic Guy."

She's reaching into her purse for money. Nana's plan is working very well. I will be able to pay for the shed and still have money left over, maybe for a bike.

"Stand back! Stand back! Choo-choo goes the train!"

It wasn't Pop's fault that the old lady thought he was the Guy. Still, she did give us a whole sixpence just before she screamed and ran into the Conservative Club.

A man is coming.

"Penny for the..."

"Fuck off!"

Margueretta thought that was funny but I thought it was very rude. I am absolutely not allowed to use that word and Nana washed my mouth out with carbolic soap the last time I said that word so I don't even say that word inside my head now because God can even hear what you are thinking and He doesn't want to hear someone saying that terrible word.

Margueretta has grabbed me by the hair because it's all grown back now. And she's swinging me around and my feet are off the ground.

"Choo-choo! Choo-choo goes the train!"

"Leave him alone! Leave him alone!" Emily is shouting.

"Stand back! Stand back!"

"Let him go!"

Around and around with my feet off the ground. Around and around we go. Spinning faster and faster by my hair.

"Wee! Wee!" Margueretta is shrieking with delight. "Wee! Wee!"

"What the hell are you doing on these steps?"

It's a man in a suit, coming out of the Conservative Club.

"Choo-choo!"

"What in God's name is that?"

"It's our Pop," says Emily.

"No, that thing there. Shouldn't it have a head?"

He's pointing at our Guy.

"Blew off!" shouts Emily.

"Blew off!" shouts Pop. "Choo-choo!"

"Why is his tongue hanging out like that?"

"Nana took his teeth away!"

"What was she doing with that boy there?"

"Dancing," says Margueretta.

"Well, you can't dance here. We don't have a license. Now clear off the lot of you!"

We have to take our headless Guy home. Nana wants her bloomers back. But first I need to be sick because my head is dizzy and my hair is falling out. Dad will be upset that all his socks are gone. But I won't tell Nana that my dad thought our Guy looked like her.

18

Pop is dead. Nana said it's for the best and he's with Saint Peter and the bright lights of Heaven. But I will miss him. We were watching the telly when Pop rolled up his bed blanket and said he wanted to go home because the war is over now. Then he died near the front door and some men came to take him away.

But he's back in the front room now. Nana said I have to say goodbye to him but there's no way I'm going to give him a kiss for all Eternity. I will not kiss someone who is dead. It was bad enough that time with Great-Auntie Maisie smelling like sick. And anyone should know that a dead person would have no idea that someone is giving them a kiss. Nana still says I have to give him a kiss.

Well, I'm not doing it.

But I did look at him.

He's in his suit and he has his medals from the war on his chest. And someone has put his teeth back in and his tongue isn't hanging out. I don't know how they did that because it was a really big tongue. He's also wearing lipstick and makeup. I think Nana must have done that but he does not look like a clown. He looks like a ghost.

"I'm glad he's gone!" Mum said.

I don't think you should say you are glad that someone is dead. But Pop was my mum's stepfather and she says he wasn't a very nice man. I think this may have something to do with Auntie Beryl and the playing cards with the naked women. Anyway, Mum's glad he's dead.

"I'm going to bury him with Grandpa," Mum said. "It was a two-for-one burial plot. They never agreed in life so now they can fight in the grave!"

"Well, there's no money to bury him any other way. Will they be buried, side-by-side? Dead beside each other?" Nana asked.

"No. We'll bury them one on top of the other. When Grandpa died, the man at the Co-op said it would be cheaper in the long run to get a double burial plot. But only if I knew someone else who was going to die soon. Quite a bargain, I thought. But it's not side-by-side."

"Aye, sounds like a bargain, hen. Who did you tell him the second dead person would be?"

"I didn't have to tell him a name. It's just that there's no point in buying a double burial plot if you only have one person to bury and no one else is going to die anytime soon."

"Och, that would nae be a bargain, lassie!"

"Anyway. It's worked out well with Pop being dead. So Pop can fight with Grandpa for all Eternity. Serves him right. And I got two whole books of Co-op dividend stamps. If I had two million of those books of stamps, I'd be a millionaire!"

"Aye. And if we had bacon we could have bacon and eggs. If we had eggs," said Nana.

Nana glanced at me. You cannot hatch eggs into chickens. Anyone should know that.

"Well, things are looking a lot better. Now that he's finally got another job."

Dad's been working for a removal company called Humphries. He says it's the best job he's ever had and sometimes he brings the big brown removal truck home and let's me sit at the driver's wheel. But we don't pretend it's a police car because it's too big.

But Dad's not working today because we're having a wake, which is what they call a party for a dead person. And Dad's in the front room now playing the "Twenty-third Psalm," which is the one about the Lord being my shepherd I shall not want. Dad says he misses Pop too and he cried when they told him Pop was dead. He's been playing funeral music on his organ all day.

"Have you thought about something?" Nana asked.

"What's that?" Mum replied.

"When you go up to Heaven, will you be the person you used to be?"

"Used to be?"

"Well, there'd be no use in being Pop as he was when he died, sitting with the Archangel and not knowing who he is. Or hiding in a corner with his tongue hanging out."

"True enough. I never thought of it that way."

"Well, which *me* will it be who meets ma Maker? Will I be a young lassie? Or will I be old?"

"Well, it will be you, of course. Whatever you want."

"Aye, but when I go to meet ma Maker will ma first husband be there too? That could be very awkward, you know! I canny live for all Eternity wi' two husbands. One at a time was bad enough!"

"Ha! Right enough. Well, there was no love lost with the second one!"

"Careful! He's nae in his grave yet, lassie!"

"Aye. But he's dead. And I'm not."

"And what if I was to marry again? Then I'd have three husbands. And all of them lazing around in Heaven wanting cups o' tea. That doesnee sound like Heaven to me!"

"I think you probably have whatever you want in Heaven, Mother."

"Well, what I want is some peace and quiet."

"I've always said you get your reward in Heaven."

"Well, I need a reward now. Let's have a wee dram to say goodbye to the old beggar. And a tune. I canny listen to that awful organ music a minute longer."

"Don't worry. He'll be off down the Fitzroy soon enough," said Mum.

"Not when he finds out I've got a bottle of Teacher's Whisky! Here, Johnny, take this glass of whisky to your father and tell him to come into the kitchen."

I'm walking up the black passageway to the front room. One sip. I'll just take one sip. God, it's burning my mouth! One more sip. One more. Not the same as the sherry. One last sip.

"Daddy! This is for you! And Nana said you are to come into the kitchen."

"Come over here and sit with me, wee Johnny."

"Have you been crying, Daddy?"

"I have, son. I have. It's a sad time. Do you love your old dad?"

"Yes! I love you!"

"Ah, and I love you too. And your sisters."

"And Mum!"

"Of course I love your mum."

"I don't like being in here with Pop. He scares me."

"Dead people canny hurt you. It's the living ones you need to worry about. Aye, the living ones will do you harm."

"Will you die one day, Daddy?"

"Och, you say the funniest things. We will all die one day, but you shouldn't worry your wee head about these things."

"I don't want you to die, Daddy."

"Don't worry. Your daddy is not going to die. I'm not going anywhere. I'm staying right here with my wee laddie. Hold my hand, Johnny. Hold my hand tight. Hold on tight."

"I want to stay with you forever."

"Of course, wee Johnny. Of course. You are my boy. My bonny, bonny boy. Forever and ever. My boy."

"Can I go with you to see a man about a dog?"

"Och, there you go again, saying the funniest things!"

"I want to go with you. I want to be with you, Daddy. I want to be with you forever and ever and ever!"

"You will, wee Johnny. You will, my dear, wee boy. Forever and ever."

19

We will never be cold and hungry again. Miss Jones said there are really hot places in other parts of the world where it never snows and you can walk around in nothing but your underwear all day if you want. She said they have bananas and coconuts growing on trees and you can just reach up and take one—and no one even cares. And they have flying fish that jump right out of the ocean onto your plate for you to eat. One of those places is called Australia and it's right under our feet. If we could dig all the way through the earth we would be there and we would never be cold and we would have as much food as we want to eat.

I have therefore started digging to Australia.

I told Emily she has to help me. She was not very happy about that because it's so cold outside but I can't dig all the way to Australia on my own—any fool would know that. So I said she could use the hammer and I would use the coal shovel. But the ground in our back garden is very hard and Mum said that's because it's the middle of bloody winter and it's frozen solid. And I said that's why we need to dig our way to Australia and then we will never be cold again. Mum said that's a very good idea because we've run out of coal for the fire and she hasn't seen my dad for three days.

We had only been digging for about an hour in the dark when those men started banging on our front door. Mum was in the backyard with us when all that noise started. She told us to wait in the backyard but we didn't and even though our shoes were covered in mud, we ran through the house after her. We took the hammer and coal shovel with us.

Those men were not very nice and they shouted at my mum because they said my dad has got their money and it's in a biscuit tin under my mum's bed.

"There's no biscuit tin under my bloomin' bed!" Mum shouted back at them.

But they never listened. They said Dad told them all their money was in a safe place and a biscuit tin under your bed is a very safe place. So they pushed past my mum and ran down the dark passageway to the stairs. Mum grabbed the coal shovel from me and ran after them. I grabbed the hammer from Emily and ran after my mum. Emily screamed—the way girls do.

We chased them all the way up the stairs and the fat one got his foot caught in that hole at the top of the stairs and serves him right. And I thought he would have to stay there for the rest of his life with his foot caught in that hole. But he pulled it out just like that so it isn't true that your foot will be stuck forever.

Well, Mum was just as surprised as me when one of them shouted out that he had found the biscuit tin under her bed. Of course, it was really dark in the bedroom and anyone could make the mistake of thinking it was a biscuit tin when it was, in fact, my dad's piss pot. And it made the man very angry when he found out it wasn't a biscuit tin full of money but was a piss pot full of piss and all the piss splashed on him and the other man.

My dad hates emptying that piss pot.

"We'll be back! Mark my words! We'll be back, and this time we will have the police with us. Do you understand? We want our money! That thief will not get away with this!" they shouted and drove away in their big brown Humphries van.

Mum said it was bloody obvious that my dad had not hidden a biscuit tin full of money under her bed. No one listens. And anyway, if there was any money in the house, she would use it to buy coal for our fire and then we wouldn't be freezing to death. Yes, and we would not have to dig all the way to Australia. Although we are also hungry and it would be quite nice to have some bananas and coconuts.

We do have a biscuit tin. It's in the pantry and that's where Nana keeps her Dundee cake but I didn't tell the men about that biscuit tin because the cake's all gone so you will only find a few crumbs in there and certainly no money.

If I was going to hide some money, I wouldn't put it under my bed. I would dig a hole in the backyard and bury it. That's what pirates do. They bury their treasure and make a map with a cross on it. I would make a treasure map in invisible ink and keep it in my pocket and if anyone found it they would just see a blank piece of paper and I would laugh because only I would know that it was a secret treasure map. Nana told me you can make invisible ink with lemon juice but I've never tried it because we don't have money for lemons. But I saw a real lemon once in the grocery shop.

If we were in Australia right now, I would go outside and pick a banana off a tree. A banana and a coconut. And I would give them to my mum because she is crying. She cries a lot and I think it's because we don't have any coal for the fire and my dad is away seeing a man about a dog. But I think he will come home soon and bring some coal with him and we will be warm again.

Yes, he will come home soon and we will sit around the fire and he will tell us stories about where he has been and all the adventures he has seen. Maybe he will have a treasure map with him because he's hidden some money somewhere and he's not stupid enough to hide it in a biscuit tin under his bed.

Mum has wrapped some blankets around us and told us to sit close together. Now Emily is crying too and the tears are making little tracks on her cheeks through all the mud on her face. I gave her back the hammer and told her to keep hold of it.

I don't want to dig to Australia now. It's cold and dark tonight.

20

Those men came back again with a policeman and they searched our whole house. They even looked under my bed but they only found my empty piss pot and my set of six whisky glasses with the Scottish soldiers on them. And the policeman was really excited when he found the biscuit tin in the kitchen cupboard but it only had some crumbs in it from the Dundee cake. I already knew that.

The policeman said my dad is in a lot of trouble and that made my mum cry and the two men said there would be more tears before this is over. They're going to get their money back one way or another. Then they all left.

"What did they say?" Nana asked.

"They said he's a thief. He's got the money from all those house moves and he should have handed it in at the end of the week. It's not his money," Mum replied.

"So where is it, lassie? Where is all the money?"

"Where do you think?"

"Spent."

"Aye, spent. Spent on all his pals down the Fitzroy. Down his bloody throat, that's where."

"My God. A sinner under our own roof. I've never heard the like of it. I will say an extra prayer tonight, that's right enough. A sinner under our very own roof."

It's not very nice to say those things about my dad. My dad is not a sinner because a sinner is a very bad person who will go to live with the Devil.

I don't want my dad to live with the Devil. He might be lost and that's why he has been gone so long.

So it's good that Mum has now gone looking for him. I think she wants to find him before the policeman does but Nana said it's a waste of time and we'll never see him again. But she is wrong because he said he would never leave me. And if he has to run away from that policeman, he will come back for me and we will go far away to a place where no one can find us.

And even though she said it was a waste of time, Nana has gone looking for Dad too.

I don't know why it's so hard to find my dad because he always goes to the Fitzroy to see a man about a dog. But he might be hiding from those men and if I was hiding I would hide in one of the houses on the bomb site. You could also hide in a tree but there aren't any trees around here. I would not hide in the old knackers yard because there's a dead horse in there and I would not want to wake up in the middle of the night with a dead horse.

But it doesn't matter about hiding because I should not have been born. If I had not been born then my dad would still be here. That's what Margueretta says. She says it over and over again. And she says she wishes I was dead and that's why I have to be locked in the cellar with the Devil until the grown-ups come home. She says that thing in the corner is actually the Devil.

The Devil isn't dead. He's alive and he wants to live inside all of us when we grow up and it's up to us if we listen to him and become sinners. I don't listen to the Devil because I love Jesus. But the Devil is always there in every-thing we see and everything we do because the Devil can never die.

There are seven steps down into the cellar. It's very cold down here. I'm shivering and hungry but I don't care about being hungry. You also shake when you are frightened. So I'm shivering and shaking at the same time but I don't know which is which.

Jesus died but if you pray to him, you can feel the hand of Jesus no mat-ter where you are. They put a crown of thorns on his head and it cut into his skin and made it bleed and they spat at him. And when he died they took him down from the cross and put him in a cave. But he came back to life and rolled away the stone in front of the cave. And after three days he went to Heaven to live with God for all Eternity so even though he is dead he is still alive and I think he is the only person who can be dead and alive at the same time.

If I die, I want to live with Jesus. Most of all I want to hold his hand because it is very warm and he will look down and smile at me and keep me by his side and that will make me feel very good.

Yes, I want to live with Jesus if I die down here in the cellar.

21

want to swing on a star. And carry moonbeams home in a jar. You can be better off than you are or would you rather be a pig? I don't want to be a pig because a pig is an animal with dirt on his face and his shoes are a terrible disgrace. But I am a pig because I've got mud on my face and my toes are sticking out of my shoes.

My daddy sings that song. I want to swing on a star. He taught me the words and he says we can carry moonbeams home in a jar together. They will make me think of angels.

If Dad was here, he would take her knickers down and spank her and I could watch. He would spank her for twisting my hair around in her fist until I screamed and for spitting in my face and locking me in the cellar.

She only let me out because Mum and Nana came back. And she says I'm a pig. She says oink, oink like a pig, little boy. But I won't oink, oink like a pig. So she slapped my face.

But Dad wasn't with Mum and Nana when they came back so it's best if I hide under the kitchen table for now with Emily. The grown-ups are angry and crying, and I don't want to be with them. They know I'm here so I'm not really hiding but it feels like I'm hiding. I hope Dad will be here soon. If Dad was here, we would swing on a star. Dad will swing me around on a star, and he will sing for me. We will carry moonbeams home in a jar. And I won't be a pig.

"Och, I couldnee find him anywhere!" Nana said.

"The police aren't the only ones who want to find him. Mick at The Connaught wants to find him. He's an angry man," said Mum.

"The Landlord at The Connaught? What's he got to do wi' it?"

"That liar of a husband of mine convinced Mick that the way to bring in the crowds was to get an organ. He said he would play it for a share in the business, all the beer he could drink, and an occasional pork pie!"

"That sounds like him. He's always thirsty, but he's nae much of an eater."

"So, Mick cashed in his entire Navy pension and bought a Hammond M-3 organ."

"A Hammond M-3 organ?"

"Yes, like in the picture houses. It's blooming huge. It's in the saloon bar, blocking the ladies toilet."

"What will they do?"

"They're using the gents toilet. But it can't last, Mum."

"I wouldn't think so. The gents toilet is outside."

"Be Serious! And there's a cabinet of sheet music," Mum continued.

"Sheet music?"

"Yes, Cilla Black. And the Bachelors. And all sorts of pub favorites."

"The Bachelors?"

"Yes."

"Which one?"

"'Diane, I'm in Heaven, When I See You Smile.'"

"I like that one. And pub favorites?"

"Yes. 'My Old Man's a Dustman.'"

"You could sing along to that song..."

"That's not the point, Mother! Mick was in the Merchant Navy for thirty years. He survived two attacks by German U-boats in the war you know. He nearly drowned. He was never the same after that."

"Which Cilla Black song?" Nana asked.

"'Anyone Who Had a Heart,' I think."

"She's a good singer for such a young girl."

"Mick says he will have to be calling *last orders* until his *last breath*," said Mum, "and that's not all. Two men in the pub said they lent him money and they're looking for him."

"Och, no!"

"Aye. And they said they would not give up. They're not nice men."

"This is bad, lassie."

"There's more."

"More? What more could there be?" Nana asked.

"This letter came today. It's from the mortgage company."

"Mortgage company? What mortgage? He bought this hoose with the money his father left him. That poor man worked hard all his life building his grocery shop just to give it to that waster."

"We don't own this house."

"It's nae much of a hoose to own."

"Yes, well even if it isn't much of a house, we don't own it. He mortgaged it and never paid a penny back."

"What does that mean, hen?"

"I don't know, Mum. I don't know. But it's a lot of money."

"And where's that money?"

"Same place. Pissed away. Into the piss pot with all the rest."

"Och. No wonder it was always needing emptying!"

And Mum started crying and Nana sent us to bed with a slice of bread pudding but I didn't eat mine.

Mum's not here in the bedroom so I can say whatever I like. But God is listening. God is always listening. But I'm not going to ask him to bless Margueretta.

God bless Mummy. God bless Nana. God bless Emily. And God bless my daddy, and please find him and ask him to come back.

Amen.

22

I don't like that man who's making my mum cry. He's in a suit, sitting at our kitchen table. I thought he was a nice man when he smiled at me, when Mum let him in. He rubbed my hair with his hand the way grown-ups always do. But he's not a nice man. He's making my mum cry. I wish my dad was here.

"I don't enjoy this, Mrs. Mitchell. But the fact is, you do not own this house. It is owned by the Building Society, and they want it back. We can let you stay for another month, but that is it."

"A month? Then what?"

"Have you talked to the Welfare people?"

"I've had no choice. We would starve on the money I get working at the Metal Box Factory."

"Well, let's not have the amateur dramatics. No one is going to let you starve. We live in a Welfare State you know."

"Don't patronize me."

"Look. You have three children. The authorities have to provide a roof over your heads."

"Oh yes, if I go with my begging bowl, and they give me a handout."

"Why would you want to stay here? It's a bloody slum for God's sake!"

"We're waiting for my dad," I shouted.

"Where is your father?"

"He's gone to see a man about a dog," I replied.

"Mrs. Mitchell, these children look like they need a square meal. They look very pale. And thin. You have to face the facts. I have to go now. You have a month. That's more than generous."

"Och, don't do us any favors!" Nana added.

"Leave it, Mother. He can find his own way out."

"Good-bye, Mrs. Mitchell. I have to leave now. Good-bye."

"I've a good mind to thump him. Heartless beggar," said Nana.

"That would just make things worse, Mum."

"Aye. But I could have flattened him. Blithering piece of English shite! Useless excuse for a man!"

"What's that?" Mum asked, looking down at a suitcase by Nana's side.

"Ma suitcase," Nana replied.

"Oh, God. Is it today?"

"I told you, hen."

"I've had a lot on my mind."

"Have you told the wee ones?"

"No."

"No?"

"No."

"What is it, Mum?" Emily asked.

"Come here, you twins. And Margueretta, come here."

"What is it?"

"It's Nana. Nana has to go home."

"Home?"

"Her real home is in London. She stayed here to help me with you and to nurse Pop. But that's all changed now, and Pop has gone to his Maker. We have to move to another place. So Nana needs to go back home."

"When?"

"Today. She's leaving today. I forgot to tell you. She has to leave today."

23

I want to be a mudlark. They live in the mud in the harbor under the train station, and they never have to wash. I would dive for a penny in the mud and find it, and I would make lots of money and save it to give to my dad and sometimes someone would throw me a shilling and one day we would be rich.

But Mum says those mudlarks are just common beggars. Nana shouldn't encourage them by throwing them pennies. Nana says they're just wee boys playing in the mud that's left when the tide goes out. I don't care what Mum says about them being beggars. I would live down there under the pier until I was rich.

The Queen is rich. The Queen only has to ring a bell and her servants come and she can ask for a cheese sandwich or a roast chicken or even lemonade when all she really wanted was a glass of water. And if the Queen asked for water, they would still bring her lemonade. Toast with butter is the best. If I was the King, I would eat toast with butter all the time. But never with butter and jam together.

Nana threw a penny to the mudlarks when we said goodbye at the train station. And she said that Scottish soldiers shouldn't cry, and she gave me her lucky silver thrupence and the mudlarks screamed for more money.

And I screamed for my Nana. And she screamed for me.

"Och! Give me a hug! Hold on to your nana. Hold on. Hold on, for the love of God, wee laddie! My wee Scottish soldier!"

And I held on.

But she had to get on the train and trains don't go choo-choo because that's just a sound that Pop made because he thought he was a train. Trains screech and squeal and screech and squeal. And a Scottish soldier must be brave and hold his sister's hand and it's no shame to cry in front of all those people on the platform beside the train when your nana is leaving.

"Och, dear boy. Dear, wee boy. Don't cry. Your nana loves you. Oh, Johnny Boy, the pipes, the pipes are playing. I'll come back when summer's in the meadow...oh Johnny Boy, my Johnny Boy. Och, how I love you so."

When people go away, you will still see them again, one day. Going away is not the same as dying because the only way to see your nana if she dies is when you die and go to Heaven to be with her again and then you can be with her forever and ever and you will never be alone. She will hold your hand as you walk down the street, singing together. And when you get home she will cuddle you on her lap by the fire and she will sing you one of her songs and whisper in your ear that she loves you and she will always love you.

She will always love you.

And you will be a man, one day, and always love her.

You will always, always love her.

24

cannot be the milk monitor anymore. It shouldn't come as a surprise because you have to drink milk if you want to be the milk monitor and I can't drink milk now after I was sick all over Geoffrey Wilson who was sitting in front of me and was not expecting to be covered in sick. He doesn't like it, but we now call him Sicky Back. It was Miss Jones who made me drink sour milk and I don't know why she made me drink it and now I am completely refusing to drink milk and I will get rickets. That means my legs will be bandy and I will have stunted growth and that's my own problem. The only thing that could be worse is if I start smoking because then I will grow up to be a midget.

None of this matters because I am never going back to that school. Miss Jones told the class that I am going with Emily to a happy place where there are trees and grass. And Gloria McIntosh asked if there are flying fish and coconuts growing on trees and Miss Jones said not to be so silly because it is only a council estate up the road.

Mum says we will have an indoor toilet but we should not expect to have anything fancy like toilet paper. Apparently, the *Daily Mirror* has been perfectly good enough for generations and we are not changing now. But I am very unhappy that we will have our very own bath as this means that I will be having a bath every Sunday because we will also have hot and cold running water. Mum said that I will be having a bath every single week, even if my feet are not black. She is making no sense at all these days.

I am going to have my own bedroom because I am the man of the house now that my dad has gone missing and is unlikely to ever be seen

THE BOY WHO LIVED WITH GHOSTS

again—especially while the police have him on a wanted list and those two nasty men who lent him money in the pub want to find him and break his arms. Mum is giving away all of Dad's possessions and she has already given his bellows organ to the church because she is never going to listen to funeral music in the middle of the night again as long as she lives. She is, however, going to keep the piano because it was in fact not his but was given to Nana by a black man who owed her money. Mum will also keep Dad's underpants.

I told Tommy that I am moving to another house and he hit me on the head with a brush pole. Fortunately I saw it coming and it only caught the side of my head and my left ear. Mum said he could have cut my whole ear off and then it would have to be sewn back on again or I would never be able to wear glasses. I did not think that was funny and I lost a lot of blood but it always looks worse than it really is when you cut your ear because your ear is full of blood and not much else. The only time I lost more blood was when I went head first off my plastic trolley bus because Margueretta was pushing me too fast. I told her to slow down—she didn't slow down and it hit a bump and I flew off and landed on my mouth on the pavement. There was enough blood to cover a whole towel and two of my teeth came out and Margueretta said it was an accident, which it was not, but it was her word against mine.

The Irish are going to move our furniture for us. They've brought an enormous great dump truck round and Mum said it's a blessing that it isn't raining or our furniture would get wet as well as having cement dust all over it and the cement would set and then we wouldn't be able to open the bloody dressing table drawers.

And the policeman came round one more time when we were packing, just to make sure we didn't find the biscuit tin with the money. But all he found was some cat turds under the sofa from when Boots was alive. Mum said she thought that cat was blooming well house-trained and someone must have kicked those turds under the sofa because no cat could squat down in that tiny space.

"The past is the past, and we are starting a new life now," Mum said.

"But how will Dad know where we are?" Emily asked.

"Don't worry. He'll know, right enough. He's like a dog, your father. He'll come home when he's hungry."

"My father is not like a dog!" shouted Margueretta.

"You'll understand one of these days," Mum replied. "Your father is your father, and that's all I will say on the subject. It's entirely his fault that we are in this God-awful mess."

"I'm going to search for hidden treasure when we get to the new house!" I announced.

"Well, don't get your hopes up," Mum replied. "It's a council prefab from just after the war."

"Does it have a cellar?" Margueretta asked and looked over at me and smiled.

"Actually, no. It's got a coal bunker by the back door. But no cellar. Why do you ask?" Mum replied.

"Oh, no reason."

I will never be locked in the cellar again. Now I am really excited about our new house. I'm not sure what a coal bunker is, but it can't be as bad as a dark cellar with that thing in the corner that goes drip, drip, drip. And I'm sure that the thing can't follow us to our new house. It will stay behind in the old cellar and maybe kill someone who goes down there to take a look. They won't find anything. But the thing will be in the corner, waiting.

Drip, drip, drip.

But even though I am glad the thing will not follow us to our new house, I have been crying a lot lately because I miss my dad. And because I kept crying for my dad, Mum gave me a robot. She got it from the Methodist Church jumble sale. It has scenes of alien planets on its chest, and they move from left to right while the lights flash. Its legs don't work anymore but its arms swing up and down. I will keep my robot with me at all times, especially in the dark. At night, I will turn it on and frighten away anyone who comes near me. Ghosts are frightened of robots because you can't scare a robot.

I expect Dad will be angry that Mum gave all of his clothes to The Irish, but at least he will still have his underpants. He needs to come home soon because it is very scary being the man of the house.

I have not told Tommy our new address. He has a box of matches, and he says he will burn down our new house with us still in it. He's still jealous about the shed. And that bright red fire engine that went clang, clang, clang.

And I'm glad I never showed him my robot.

The Attic

The Garden City of the South, England
July 1965

25

My robot has run out of batteries. I have also taken it apart and I should have known that I could not get it back together again. I cannot expect to get another robot. So I am therefore hiding under the blanket because there is always something to hide from in the night.

I am not in my new bedroom because Mum found some small creatures making their way across my bed when I was down on my knees, trying to say my prayers. She caught them in a matchbox and I will have to sleep here on the sofa in the front room until the man comes round with the special poison to kill the other creatures that are still running loose.

I don't like this new house. The toilet is just as scary as our old one but now it's right next door to my bedroom and I have to run past it when the door is open otherwise I will see that green rubber handle that's swinging and twitching on the end of a rusty chain. And then I will see a dead man hanging there with his eyes bulging out like my big green marbles. I know it's just my imagination because that thing is still back in our old cellar where it will stay forever, I'm sure.

But the worst thing is that door on the ceiling above my bed. I don't know how my mum can say there's nothing in the attic when she hasn't even been up there to have a look. And it's easy for her to say I should ignore any stories my big sister is telling me about an evil murderer who has left a child up in the attic. It starved to death and now it's trying to get out through that door. Mum told me not to stare at the attic door or it will give me nightmares.

Then there's that madwoman next door called Joan. She came round with a pot of tea this afternoon because Mum has lost the kettle.

"Ooo-er! Don't mind me. There are some things you should know about this place. I'm not sure where to start really. Let's see if there's another cup in the pot," Joan said.

"What is it? What should I know?" Mum replied.

"There were twelve of them. And they were filthy. They left in the night. At least that's what we think because we didn't see them go, and we haven't seen them since."

"Twelve? All in this house?"

"Gypsies. Should never have been given a real house. They don't know how to treat it unless it's got wheels and a horse at the front. When the men from the council came to open up the place after they had gone, I don't mind telling you—it was terrible."

"What was it?"

"Well. They let me in to take a look, and the place was full of rotting food and dead things and flies and the smell...well, I had to hold my house-coat up to my nose. And do you know what they found in the scullery?"

"What?" Mum said, moving closer, and dragging on her cigarette.

"It was dead, poor thing!"

"What was dead?'

"A cat. A dead cat, for the love of God!"

"A dead cat?"

"You heard right. A dead cat. It was flat and hard like it had been dead for weeks."

"How did it die?"

"No one will ever know. The men from the council said those gypsies probably left it in there, poor thing. It took them weeks, cleaning this house out and repainting it. And wallpapering every room. Those roses on that paper are quite nice though, aren't they? A beautiful red."

"That explains it!"

"Ooo-er! What's that?"

"The man from the rent office implied that I brought those lice with me."

"Lice?"

"Yes, lice! I found them in his bedroom. I'm not having it, Joan. They're sending a fumigator round tomorrow to deal with it. It's an infestation."

"Ooo-er! I don't like the sound of that, but it's no surprise really, is it? So they're sending a man round? Where's your husband, if you don't mind my asking?"

"Och. It's a long story."

"Ooo-er! Is there a short version?" Joan laughed.

"He went out for a packet of Woodbines and never came back."

"And left you with three kids?"

"And left me with three kids."

"They're all the same. Men. Well, Fred isn't. He's my husband, but lazy? I should say he's lazy. He painted my kitchen, and he didn't even clean off the cobwebs first. He just painted right over them. It's a shame about that one," Joan said, nodding at me.

"What about him?"

"Well. A boy needs a father. There are more things you need to know. The woman opposite has four children and no husband. Those children run around naked and poop in their front garden. The man living next door to her says he drilled a peephole right through the bedroom wall. It wasn't difficult. The walls are paper-thin. Anyway, he spies on her to see what she's up to and lets us all know. Do you know she sleeps completely naked! Imagine that! I could never sleep with no clothes on. It's not healthy. Ooo-er!"

"Go on," Mum suggested, lighting another cigarette.

"He says she lets the children play on her bare bosom! Imagine that! What else? Oh, yes, behind us is a German woman. Her husband is a bus driver. She met him when he was stationed as part of the Frontier Control Service on the German border with Belgium. Ooo-er, do you know something?"

"What?"

"She undresses some nights with the light on and no curtains. I'm always telling Fred to stop watching her. Ooo-er, it's not right, is it? He should not be watching her."

"Why is she undressing in the window, for God's sake? Doesn't she have any curtains?"

"Oh, she has curtains right enough. But the Germans are like that. No shame."

"I suppose."

"And just up the road are the Dumbys. Old Man Dumby is deaf so don't bother talking to him. Although he does say he can lip-read. He keeps rabbits, but he had too many so he tried to gas them, but we have all been converted to natural gas. It's not poisonous, you know. So don't go putting your head in the oven if you want to kill yourself because it won't work!" Joan laughed. "Anyway, he held them underwater until they drowned. We all went to watch. Their little mouths were wide open as they tried to get air, poor things. And their eyes bulged out of their sockets. Ooo-er!"

"He drowned them?"

"Yes. And if you see someone on the back of a Vespa scooter with a big bum, excuse me, hanging over the back—that would be me. And I do have a problem with my housecoat on the Vespa. It catches the wind. Like a sail. Imagine that! And that can be dangerous because it makes the scooter very difficult for Fred to control."

"That sounds really dangerous."

Joan Housecoat is completely bonkers if you ask me. But at least she's not spying on us.

26

Being nosy is not the same as spying but it is very similar. Mum should never have told Joan that we've lost the kettle. That's just the excuse a nosy woman needs to keep coming round with a pot of tea and stick her nose into business that should not concern her, especially when she's got nothing better to do. And especially when there's a van outside our house from the council and a man with buckets and hoses is coming up the path.

"Are you the woman with the lice or the blocked drains?" the man asked.

"Blocked drains?" Mum replied.

"Lice or drains?"

"Ooo-er! She's got lice!" Joan replied.

"Lice," Mum replied.

"OK. Lice it is, then. Did they tell you I have to spray this brown liquid over the floors and halfway up the walls and you can't stay in the house afterwards because it's toxic?"

"No."

"They never tell anyone. Don't know why I bother asking. I'll make a start then."

"We don't have anywhere else to go," Mum said.

"No one does. You know this is going to make a mess of your lovely new wallpaper, don't you? Those red roses will be brown by the time I've finished. It would be better if you had blocked drains."

"Ooo-er! She doesn't have blocked drains. She's got lice!"

Mum told Joan to go home. Enough is enough and you have to be firm with a nosy person or before you know it they'll know all your business and they'll be telling everyone in the street.

I followed the man from room to room to watch him spray everything and he was right because there was a brown stain halfway up the walls when he finished. And he was having a cigarette with Mum when we heard the screaming.

"Aieeee! Aieeee!"

"What's she screaming about?" he asked.

"What's wrong, Joan?" Mum asked.

"Lice! Lice! They're crawling all over my airing cupboard!"

"That happens. They're running away from the poison. Quite intelligent really," the man replied.

"Get rid of them!" Joan shouted.

"Not today, love. I'm down to do one case of lice and one case of blocked drains. That's my lot for today. You'll have to go to the office and see when they can fit you in."

"But there's lice in my airing cupboard!"

"Like I said, if you had blocked drains I could help you," he replied and pulled out his notebook. "Look. Blocked drains and a case of lice. And I've already done this woman's lice."

"But I can't sleep with lice!"

The man came back the next day to do Joan's lice. I'm glad it's the summer holidays and I don't have to go to my new school yet or there would be a lot of explaining to do. Mum has put chamomile lotion on the bites on my face and body and that's just to be expected because some of those lice don't die the first time you spray them. But they will die eventually now that both houses have been sprayed and we are semi-detached.

My face is very white. Margueretta says I look like a ghost.

27

Mum found the kettle in the oven. No one knows how it got in there but it's obvious to me. Something is going on. If Dad was here, we would get the metal stepladders from the scullery and go up into the attic together. I'm sure Margueretta's right. There's something terrible up there and that's why Mum keeps saying she will go into the attic but never does. Something really bad is going to happen.

And another thing. I've been staring out of my bedroom window every single night and not once have I seen that German woman getting undressed in front of the window. Mum says you can't believe a word that Joan says and I'm beginning to think she's right, although I have met Old Man Dumby and he let me stroke his rabbits. But I can't be sure if he drowned any of them. You have to speak very slowly to his face so he can lip read. Now that I know he can read my lips, I might ask him about the drownings and the bulging eyes next time I see him. Then again, I might not.

Mum has to leave the house a lot because we have black floors downstairs. That's the thing with black floors. You can't be around them for too long or you will go stark staring bonkers and anything could happen. If we had the money, we would cover the floors with yellow lino because yellow is my mum's favorite color. Yellow would remind her of the sun and she would be happy every day instead of sad. Orange would also be good.

I don't get sad because I am a happy boy. That's why people rub my hair and smile at me, especially when we are at the launderette and I am helping Mum put the dirty clothes in the washing machine. As soon as I am bigger,

Mum says I will be going to the launderette all on my own and that will be a big help for her when it comes to the weekly wash.

Margueretta beat me again today. She waits for Mum to go out. It's the same every day and I should know that just because we don't have a cellar for her to lock me in, I still should not have been born and everything would be better if I was dead.

She gets me down on the floor and sits on me. I'm very small for my age and I only have myself to blame because I stopped drinking milk, except on my cornflakes, and I can't expect to grow up big and strong if I don't drink my milk. She sits on my stomach and digs her knees into my shoulders. Then she twists the little bit of hair that's right above my ears until my eyes water but I never cry. And she makes a big glob of spit on her lips and slowly lets it fall into my face. I screw my mouth shut tight. I don't want my sister's spit in my mouth. I don't like the way it smells. And when she lets me get back up, I run and hide. The coal bunker is the best place to hide because no one knows I am in there. But it's very dark in the coal bunker and there are spiders and beetles and slugs in the corners. One day I am going to clean out all the dirt and insects and make the coal bunker into my secret house. And I will put my robot back together and get some new batteries.

I want to be happy tonight. I should be happy tonight but I am sad. I had to come out of the coal bunker eventually when Mum kept calling my name.

"Oh, there you are. It's your dad! I've been looking for you. Your daddy!"

"Daddy?"

"Yes! For you!"

"Where is he?"

"Oh, he's not here. He sent you something."

"What is it?"

"A postcard. Addressed to you! From your daddy!"

"A postcard?"

It's a postcard with a picture of Scottish Soldiers in their kilts.

POSTMARK: July 21, 1965
Dear Wee Johnny,

Trust you are looking after Mum, as you are the man of the house now. Are you doing a good job? Yes! I thought you would.

Lots of love and good luck, and I hope to see you soon. Keep your chin up.

Your loving Daddy
XXXXX

Mum says that I am the man of the house how because I am seven years old. I'm going to keep the postcard under my pillow. I'm going to keep it there until Daddy comes home. It has five kisses. Five is a lot. Five is more than four. I will give him five kisses when he comes home.

28

t is best to hide under the blankets when there's a thunderstorm and press your pillow round your head as hard as you can. Thunder makes your blood pound in your ears like the ocean. The problem with thunder is you can't see it and it makes things shake and feels like it's right over your head and will suffocate you like a giant black cloak of seaweed. And lightning makes your bedroom light up suddenly in the dark and you might see something that should not be there. I've seen lots of things that shouldn't be there.

Thunderstorms make you want to go to the toilet in the middle of the night. And it was a huge thunderstorm in the middle of the night that made me want to pee. That's how I ended up in the toilet, pushing out the pee as fast as I could and looking at that green rubber handle and waiting for it to twitch and turn into a face dangling there. And the lightning flashed through the window and lit up the toilet and made a long shadow of something that was bigger than me, something that shouldn't be there. And I stared at the rubber handle and the thunder cracked and made my legs wobble and I never waited to finish peeing when the lightning came again.

I just ran. I didn't even flush the toilet. I ran back into my bed and put the blanket over my head and waited. I waited and waited under the blanket but there was no more lightning and no more thunder. Just the rain coming down against the window and the wind blowing in the tall weeds in the garden below.

And that's when it began.

It started like a small dog whining and getting ready to howl. Then it howled long and high and cried and the howling turned into a scream. And the scream came again and again. I think it was a girl's voice. Yes, a girl. And I knew where it was coming from. Anyone would know.

It was a girl.

Screaming in the attic.

There was just the rain and the screaming. The rain on the window and the screaming in the attic. And even though I knew I shouldn't do it—I couldn't stop myself. I pulled the blankets down away from my face and stared up at the ceiling, up at the attic door right above my bed.

I stared at the door and waited. Mum told me not to stare at that attic door. Sooner or later, something would happen. The screaming stopped. And right at that moment, I saw it.

The attic door jumped up.

It jumped up and came back down with a thump.

29

This morning, I told Mum about the screaming and the attic door and she said it was all nonsense and I am a boy with a very vivid imagination and it's no wonder I heard things, being woken up in the middle of the night with all that thunder and lightning.

"Anyway," Mum said, "you need a hobby. So I've enrolled you in the Cub Scouts."

"What?"

"I've enrolled you in the Second Garden City Cub Scouts. It will be good for you. They do things like make knots and go camping."

"I don't want to make knots. Or go camping."

"You don't know until you try it. You will be an Owl."

"An Owl?"

"Yes. They have packs. You're in the Owl Pack. I think it was owls. Or it may be the Hawk Pack. Anyway, it's birds of prey. They have a motto and everything."

"You can make camp fires," Margueretta said, jabbing me in the stomach. "And perhaps you'll burn the tent down!"

"Well, it's tonight. You have to be sworn in, and they said to polish your shoes and take a clean handkerchief."

"We haven't got any shoe polish. And I haven't got a handkerchief!"

"We'll have to improvise. I've got one of your nana's old hankies. You can take that."

Cub Scouts did not start well. I knew this would happen because Mum just doesn't listen to me and when I said we did not have any shoe polish, she completely ignored me and gave me one of Nana's old hankies. I am a disgrace to the whole history of scouting and an insult to the memory of Baden-Powell. He's the man who invented the scouts. Things will have to improve dramatically if I ever expect to become a Leaping Wolf.

And it wasn't just my shoes. I had to show my clean hanky to Akela, who is our leader and a symbol of wisdom and authority. He asked me if I thought it was a joke. It might well be a clean hanky but the lace around the edges and a pink *A* embroidered on the corner was a further insult to the good name of scouting. I told Akela that my nana's name is Alice. He said this is not the Brownies.

I was therefore lucky to be sworn in with another new boy who just happens to be a spastic. I don't know exactly what is wrong with him but his eyes dart about in different directions and he rolls his head around and his tongue hangs out. It doesn't lash around but there are a lot of similarities to Pop. Akela is only letting the spastic into the Cub Scouts on a trial basis because a spastic can be very disruptive to knot practice and could not be trusted to make a campfire. Also, he was not able to repeat the Cub Scouts Promise due to a severe speech impediment and the problem with his tongue.

As a new member of the Owl Pack, I need to start at the bottom and learn the difference between a granny knot and a reef knot.

Right over left, left over right makes a knot both tidy and tight.

The more experienced Cubs will be doing the bowline knot because they are on *B* of the *A to Z of Knots*. I should expect to catch up somewhere around *F*.

Our Owl Pack has a leader, and we are required to hoot for him whenever he sees a need for bonding. One hoot is not enough, and we should all try to hoot in unison, which helps to build a team spirit. Obviously, the spastic is not able to hoot either on his own or in unison because he does not understand the idea of bonding. He therefore shrieks after each hoot.

"Hoot, hoot! Hoot, hoot!"

"Aieeee! Aieeee!"

"Hoot, hoot! Hoot, hoot!"

"Aieeee! Aieeee!"

"We have to initiate the two new boys!" shouted our leader.

"Hoot, hoot! Hoot, hoot!"

"Aieeee! Aieeee!"

"Who do we want to go first?"

"Spastic! Spastic! Spastic!"

"An excellent choice, Owl Pack. The spastic did not repeat the Scout's Promise. He must therefore have what?"

"Sandwich! Sandwich! Sandwich!"

"Another excellent choice!"

Owl Pack Leader produced a sandwich from behind his back.

"Eat it! Eat it! Eat it!"

At first it did not seem to be much of an initiation ceremony to have to eat a cheese and lettuce sandwich made with medium sliced white bread. But then the spastic bit into the big fat slimy slug that the Owl Pack Leader had hidden in the lettuce. I think the spastic was enjoying the attention because he never spat it out.

"Hoot, hoot! Hoot, hoot!"

"Aieeee! Aieeee!"

"You! Poor boy with a girl's hanky! Do you have a sister?"

"I've got two sisters," I replied.

"Have you ever seen them naked?"

"Nope."

"Useless! We will initiate you next week. Right. Owl Pack, who's got a story for me?"

"I have, Owl Pack Leader!"

"Go on! Go on!"

"I saw my brother wanking!"

"No! About girls. Only girls! How many times do I have to tell you, moron! Naked sisters. I am not a homo! I am *not* a homo! Is that clear? No homo stories! I am *not* a homo."

"I saw my sister in the bath, Leader!" shouted another Cub Scout.

"That's better! Detail. Tell me detail! I *need* detail!"

"There's a hole in our bathroom door."

"A hole in the door! Outstanding! Why didn't you tell me before? Now that's a detail. A hole in the door! More! Tell me more! More! More!"

"I saw her getting undressed."

Owl Pack Leader was rubbing the front of his shorts very quickly, up and down.

"Then she took off her knickers!"

Rub, rub, rub.

"And? More! More! Detail! Detail! Don't stop! Don't stop!"

"I saw everything. She had hair down there. A black triangle of hair!"

"Pubic hair! Outstanding! More! More! Pubic hair! More! Old Henry is getting really hard now!"

"And big pink nipples! She had big pink nipples!"

"Yes! Yes! Yes!"

Rub, rub, rub.

"And then she bent right over!"

"Oh, yes!"

"And I saw her bum!"

"Oh, yes! Her bum! Her naked bum! Was it a big round bum?"

Rub, rub, rub.

"Yes. A very big, white, round bum. Completely naked. Bent over!"

"Arhhh! Hoot! Hoot! Hoot! Arhhh! Arhhh!"

Rub, rub, rub.

"Yes! Yes! Yes! Yessssssss!"

Leader was sweating, and his face was very red.

"Leader?" asked another scout.

"Yes?" Leader replied, panting.

"Can we fart into the hurricane lamp like we did last week?"

"Yes. But take your pants down and bend over so that it makes flames! I want to see blue flames coming from your naked arses!"

"What shall we do with the spastic, Owl Pack Leader?"

"That's right. I forgot about him. Bring him to me!"

"Aieeee! Aieeee!"

"Tie him up! Use him for knot practice! Now get going with those bowlines!"

Next week we will be doing the clove hitch. With twenty-four letters to go, the spastic is going to be tied up a lot. And our Owl Pack Leader is looking forward to *H* when we can do the hangman's knot.

"Hoot, hoot! Hoot, hoot!"

"Aieeee! Aieeee!"

30

Mum will absolutely not tolerate me dropping out of Cub Scouts just because the spastic ate a slug sandwich and was tied up with seventeen bowlines and one granny knot. It was therefore pointless to mention the Cub Scout who told us about spying on his naked sister through a hole in the bathroom door while Owl Pack Leader rubbed his shorts until he hooted. Cub Scouts will teach me the importance of bonding and how to work with other boys in a team and if that means I have to have a new hanky then Mum will get me a new hanky. There is also a special fund for poor boys to get their green Cub Scouts pullover, a scarf, and a woggle. I will thank Mum when I am older.

I will also thank Mum for bringing me up in a good God-fearing Christian household and sending me every week to the Methodist Church Sunday School with Miss Peabody. Miss Peabody is a spinster, which means she has never been married and is now too old to find a husband and has therefore devoted her life to the Women's Institute and saving our souls for Jesus. And Jesus wants me for a sunbeam. He also wants Emily.

Akela is prepared to overlook the incident with Nana's hanky, as he is aware that I am a good Christian boy and go to Sunday School every week and say my prayers every night. I could teach some of the other boys a thing or two about religion and the Bible and the importance of keeping God in your heart. And the Ten Commandments.

Akela thinks the most important commandment is to honor thy mother and father. He asked me if I honor my mother and father and I said I do but no one knows where my father is because he hasn't been seen since Churchill's funeral. He said I should focus on the other commandments for now.

When you are religious, it helps to memorize the Bible, as you never know when you might be in need of a scripture and you can't always expect to have the Bible to hand. We have been learning the Twenty-third Psalm in Sunday School as Miss Peabody says it can comfort you, particularly in times of betrayal, agony, and death.

> *Yea, though I walk through the valley of the shadow of death,*
> *I shall fear no evil.*
> *For Thou art with me,*
> *Thy rod and Thy staff they comfort me.*

We also sing it because that helps you remember the words. It lifts our joyous hearts up to Jesus to sing together. And Miss Peabody plays the piano, which she cannot do in church because she is not note perfect, and that shouldn't be a surprise for a woman of her age and eyesight, and anyway, that old piano is out of tune.

> *The Lord is my shepherd, I shall not want.*
> *He maketh me down to lie.*
> *In pastures green, He leadeth me,*
> *The quiet waters by.*

Miss Peabody has memorized everything in the Bible, and she can quote from it without even opening it. She can also sing hundreds of hymns without a hymnbook.

Mine eyes have seen the glory of the coming of the Lord!

She is passing on her love of the scriptures to us so that we might also see the glory of the coming of the Lord. For instance, this week she told us all about the Last Supper and the Twelve Apostles and how one of them betrayed Jesus. His name was Judas Iscariot and he betrayed Jesus to the Romans for thirty pieces of silver, which was a lot of money back in those days. And Peter, he was another apostle, denied Jesus three times as the cock crowed and that's also a betrayal because he must have known that they would crucify Jesus and he only did it to save his own life. Betrayal is the worst thing.

"Would any of you betray Jesus for thirty pieces of silver?" Miss Peabody asked us.

"No!" we all shouted back, and Emily even jumped to her feet when she said it, so I know she meant it. Emily loves Jesus as much as I do.

Raymond Jones did not say no like the rest of us. In fact, he didn't say anything. But I know he would have betrayed Jesus because he told me he wants a new bike. He didn't look so sure when he heard what happened to Judas. Judas bought a field with his thirty pieces of silver and then he tripped and fell into a ditch and his guts burst and spilled out and he died. And that's what you get for betraying Jesus. I don't know what happened to Peter.

And it's because they betrayed him that Jesus died on the cross. They nailed his hands and feet onto the wood instead of tying them on with rope. That is a very cruel thing to do because it's painful enough just being cruci-fied, especially when you haven't even done anything wrong. King Herod made them do that to Jesus because people said he was King of the Jews and King Herod was jealous because he was the king and you can't have two kings or there's no point in being a king. And they crucified Jesus along with two thieves but they tied their hands and feet onto their crosses with rope and did not nail them on. They also broke their legs so that they would die quicker. I'm not sure why you die quicker if your legs are broken. And it took Jesus quite a long time to die because they did not break his legs so one of the Roman soldiers stuck a spear in his side to make him bleed to death. Now that we know all the details of how Jesus died, we should not discuss it with anyone. We should just focus on the Holy Spirit.

Once, I hit my finger with a hammer in the garden trying to put a nail in a piece of wood, not in my hand. And I screamed and cried and Nana rocked me on her lap and sang Danny Boy quietly to me.

> *But come ye back when summer's in the meadow...*
> *And I shall hear though soft you tread above me,*
> *And then my grave shall warmer, sweeter be.*
> *For you will bend and tell me that you love me,*
> *And I shall sleep in peace until you come to me.*
> *My wee Johnny boy.*

Nana said you have to have the Gaelic melancholia to appreciate the sadness of that song. Mum said a four-year-old should not have been given a hammer and nails to play with in the garden. Nana said I was just trying to build a wee hoose for her. Mum said I'm lucky I didn't lose a finger or worse.

We are too young to have known betrayal. You can't really know betrayal until you are a grown-up and have first experienced what is called loyalty. You have to be loyal first and then you can betray someone because if you weren't loyal to them in the first place and you say bad things about them behind their back then you're just being nasty to someone and not betraying them. We are too young to understand loyalty and therefore cannot have known betrayal.

Miss Peabody, on the other hand, says she knows betrayal all too well, and that is why she has never found Mr. Right.

31

The first thing we saw was that black Hillman Minx coming up the road to our house. We didn't know who the two men were inside it, but Joan had already met them while we were at the Co-op. She asked them why they were knocking on our door because she saw them from her front room window. But they never told her, and they laughed and said they would come back soon enough. And Joan said it wouldn't be long because we've only gone up the road to the Co-op to get a tin of baked beans and a bag of sugar. Joan knows everything we do. I'm beginning to think she is spying on us and not just nosy.

And we had just finished our beans on toast for tea when I was looking out the front room window and I saw the car coming back like Joan said it would. And the two men got out and they were laughing and they had their arms around each other's shoulders like they were trying to hold each other up.

Mum sent us to our rooms at first. And then she called for us to come downstairs when she let the men into our house. She called my name, over and over, and I grabbed my postcard from under my pillow and I ran down the stairs, two at a time. I took my postcard with me to show to Uncle Jack. But mostly I took it with me to show my dad, even though he knew about it because he wrote it.

Uncle Jack and Dad were both really happy and laughing and making jokes to each other and Dad rubbed my hair and asked me if he could have some of it because he is losing his. He always says that. And he bent down and kissed me and his moustache is very prickly and I thought it might even

THE BOY WHO LIVED WITH GHOSTS

have cut my lip but it didn't. And he had tears in his eyes when he said he loved me and missed me and did I miss him? Yes! He knew I did.

Mum said he's a fine one to talk, leaving his children like that, without a word. But he ignored her and lifted Emily up in his arms and hugged her and she cried and she held on to him and wouldn't let go. And Margueretta seemed shy, like she didn't even know him, but she still kissed him. And then she cried too.

Dad suggested we should all go out together because this is supposed to be a happy time and we shouldn't be crying like that when we should be so happy, together again. But Mum said no at first and certainly she wasn't going to let Dad take us out on our own in that Hillman Minx, wherever he might take us, and maybe never see us again. And especially not when he's been drinking with Uncle Jack and can hardly say his words or stand up. Then Mum agreed to go with us.

So we all went to the pub together in the black Hillman Minx, but we didn't pretend we were in a police car.

I played on the swings in the pub garden with Emily and God knows you have to be careful where you step because the landlord's got a bloody big dog and it shits like an elephant all over that garden. And Dad brought us each a bottle of hubbly-bubbly and some cheese and onion crisps. He even brought Margueretta a shandy, which is made from beer and lemonade, because she is almost twelve and one of these days she will be a teenager and before you know it she will be a woman with her long blonde hair and pretty green eyes and it's amazing how quickly they grow up. So she could have a shandy. But I just had a bottle of lemon-lime hubbly-bubbly, the same as Emily, even though I am the man of the house.

Margueretta wouldn't let me have a sip of her shandy. When I am almost a teenager, I will drink shandy. And when I'm a grown-up, I will drink beer and whisky like my dad. And I will go to see a man about a dog and never come back.

We stayed out in the garden until all the hubbly-bubbly was gone and it was dark and freezing cold and there was one light in the garden on the back of the pub—just a single light bulb, making long, thin shadows across the garden.

Margueretta always gets angry when she has to be a babysitter because we're not her bloody brats. And that's always dangerous because she already flicked the back of my ear four times and pulled the side of my hair and said I was a pig. She also said she was going to get some dog shit on a stick and wipe it on me.

So I was really glad when Dad came out of the back door into the garden with Mum right there, running after him.

"Don't talk to me about responsibility!" Mum shouted at him.

"Och, don't be like that Emily," said Dad.

"Don't tell me what to do!" Mum replied.

And Uncle Jack came over and looked at me.

"John. Do yoush want your father back home?" he said.

But I just stared down at my empty hubbly-bubbly bottle.

"Of course he want'sh me back, don't you Johnny?"

"Don't bring the children into this argument!" Mum shouted.

"But Johnny need shis daddy, don't you Johnny?"

"A real man wouldn't beg to come home," said Uncle Jack.

"Whatsh that? And whatsh d'you know about being a real man?" Dad shouted back.

"You kilty! Don't tell me sh'about being a real man! Fucking bagpipes, that's what shou are!"

"Ha! You cockney piece of shite!" Dad yelled.

That's when Uncle Jack broke his beer bottle on the wooden trestle table and held the ragged end up in the air.

"Come on! Come on! I'll put this in yer Scottish face!"

Emily grabbed my arm, and then she bit off the rim of her glass. And she gripped that piece of glass between her top teeth and her tongue.

"Oh, for the love of God!" Mum screamed. "Now look what you've made her do!"

Dad said he was sorry and Uncle Jack put the broken bottle down and said he didn't mean to frighten the children and he was sorry too. So we all looked at Emily and she still had the broken glass in her mouth and little bubbles of purple blood seeped out of the corners of her lips and ran down her chin.

And I noticed the smell and I looked down at my shoes—all covered in dog shit.

That's why the black Hillman Minx has gone, and I'm back in my room. I've left my shoes at the back door. I will have to use a stick in the morning to get the shit off. But I can still smell the dog shit because I think it is on my socks.

At least Emily didn't swallow any glass.

32

I heard the screams again last night—just as I was falling asleep. Mum says it's just a dream but I know when I am awake and I am awake when I hear the screams. And I know where the screams are coming from. Anyone would know if they had to sleep right under the attic door. I still can't stop myself from staring at it. Something is trying to get out.

Mum says I tell too many stories, just like my dad. She says I will grow up exactly like him. Well, I don't want to grow up like my mum because she is losing her mind. She says it's the black floors but I think there's something else that she's not telling any of us. I've seen someone standing behind me—someone who should not be there. I don't know who he is and when I turn around he's always gone. Maybe he stands behind my mum too. And maybe Mum has told Margueretta what it is but no one would just sit on the sofa and cry for no reason the way Mum does. And I don't know why black floors would make her cry even if they are very black and we don't have money to cover them up.

That's why Mum has to get out of the house. Mum leaves me and Emily to be looked after by Margueretta. It makes her so angry. When people get angry their faces go all red and sometimes they hit people. Margueretta hits me. She throws me down on the floor and sits on me and she digs her long nails into my neck and screws up bunches of my hair in her fists and pulls until it comes out by the roots. Her favorite thing to do when she is angry is to slap my face because that's how girls fight and she says I am a girl.

She also likes to give me Chinese burns, which you can do by twisting the skin on someone's wrist in opposite directions until they scream for you to stop. And even if they scream for you to stop, you don't have to. That's the thing with Chinese burns. You can twist and twist while they scream and scream and you don't stop because you're having so much fun.

Twist, twist, twist.

Sometimes she holds her hand over my nose and mouth because when you do that the person can't breathe and it makes their eyes pop out like marbles. You have to take your hand away eventually or the person will die from suffocation and you will be a murderer. So she always takes her hand away just in time and that means I can gulp in the air but then she puts her hand back just when I'm starting to breathe because that is not expected and just when I think I can breathe again, I can't. That makes her laugh. It makes me feel like there is boiling water in my stomach.

But Margueretta says I'm right. There is something dead in our house: it is a ghost of someone who is stuck in this world because they should not have died. It is God who should decide when you die. Then he sends the Angel of Death to come and get you and there's no point in refusing to go because it's the way of all things mortal. When it's nearly your time, the Angel of Death knocks inside the walls and whispers your name and then when you die it stops. But if someone murders you then it is against the Ten Commandments and is not God's intention and so the angel won't be there to take you home. And you could wander around for years waiting for the angel to come for you. That's what Margueretta says.

And she says there is a child entombed in our attic. Entombed alive up there. I wouldn't want to be entombed alive because I'm scared of tiny spaces. But I'm also scared of really big spaces like the inside of a cathedral because they reach up so high and I feel too small for the space, which is the same feeling as being crushed into a small space, even though it's so big. You shouldn't have really big spaces on the inside. They should be outside. The worst thing would be if I was locked up in a pipe that was only just wide enough for my body but reached up into a black space where I could not see the end. A black space that goes on forever.

I think that is what it must feel like to be entombed alive in the wall of an attic.

33

Some people have bacon and eggs and bread in their kitchen cupboards the whole time and they can just make a dinner whenever they want— even if they aren't hungry or it's not even dinnertime. I think that's why Joan Housecoat is such a big woman. She has a lot of food in her house and she's always cooking, when she's not looking out of her front room window.

I've seen all the food. I saw it today. Her cupboard is actually full of food.

I was sitting on the front doorstep with Emily after school because we don't have a key. If we had a key, we would only lose it and then where would we be? Someone would find it and break into our house and steal everything and we wouldn't be able to complain to the police because they used our key, so don't ask again.

So we were sitting on the doorstep in the rain and the next thing we knew, Joan Housecoat was standing there saying we looked half-starved and she should know a thing or two about being half-starved because she grew up between the wars and once had to eat turnips for dinner for a whole week and she doesn't mind if she never sees another turnip as long as she lives. That's all behind her now that she has a fully stocked larder.

And just like that, we were sitting in her warm kitchen with magnolia walls and spider webs and a big paraffin heater and lots of jugs and kettles and pots and steam. And she was frying bacon and eggs and buttering thick slices of white bread and pouring mugs of tea, all for me and Emily and we didn't even have to ask. And she told me to slow down and not to eat so fast, but I couldn't, and she laughed and said that anyone would think it was the first meal we'd had in days. And after the bacon and eggs, she gave us more bread and butter and jam and a chocolate McVities biscuit and Emily scraped her fingernail on the chocolate and licked it and looked at me and smiled and licked it again. I ate mine in two bites.

"Where's your mum?"

"Don't know."

"When's she coming home?"

"Don't know."

"How old are you now?"

"Seven."

"You should not be sitting on the doorstep in the dark and rain at age seven. Where's your big sister?"

"Don't know."

"Would you like another chocolate biscuit?"

"Yes, please."

"Well. If your mother doesn't come home soon I will have to fetch the police. It's not right. Ooo-er."

That's why we are in disgrace. It is completely wrong to go off with some woman and eat her bacon and eggs and bread and tea and chocolate biscuits when our sister was already on her way home with a packet of rice and an Oxo cube for tea. And our mother was simply at the Methodist Church Young Wives Club.

"I need my time too, you know. I need my time with adult Christian company. And some solace with God. I need to get away too. And now I have to come home to this disgrace."

And the time flies when you are enjoying yourself with the Gospels. She would have been home soon enough after our sister was here with the rice and the Oxo cube for our tea.

"And what if a total stranger came and took you away? If Old Man Dumby came over here right now and offered you a sweet would you go off with a man who has drowned innocent baby rabbits with his bare hands until their eyes bulged out? I sincerely hope not! I could be sitting here weeping in the desperation of a mother's grief because her two children have been strangled and drowned and murdered by some madman and now my children are sitting at the feet of God. And God only knows what I have done to deserve this."

Mum is right. It's not like we were even getting wet because the front door has a porch. Granted, it is leaning to one side because the wood is all rotted and it could collapse with the next gust of wind, but that's not the point. And it may have been really cold with the howling wind and rain but we could quite easily have huddled together for warmth. So we must never let this happen again or we may not be so lucky the next time and we could be strangled and drowned and murdered.

And quite rightly, we should be sent to bed without any tea but that is not possible because we have already gorged our gluttonous selves on the greasy excesses of some nosy, interfering woman who should not be kidnapping someone else's children and definitely should not be calling the police to say that we had been abandoned on our own doorstep. Now the whole street will know.

And if we want to go and live with Joan Housecoat in that hot steamy kitchen of hers and feast ourselves on bacon and eggs and bread and tea and chocolate biscuits for dinner every night then we should go now and knock on her door and tell her. But we should not expect to see our loving mother or sister ever again. We might want to think long and hard about what we have done.

Gluttony is a deadly sin.

Enough said. We are forgiven.

I'm in bed now. We now have a paraffin heater but only for the front room, so it is freezing in my bedroom. I can scratch the ice on the inside of the window if I want to but I never lick it because it is black. I have to get undressed really quickly and then dressed again before I freeze. Tonight, I put on pajamas, woolen bed-socks, a sweater, scarf, and two sheets of the *Daily Mirror*. Mum gave me a hot water bottle but mine leaks, which is fine at first but in the morning it's cold and clammy and I get the horrible feeling I have pissed myself.

With all of those clothes on, I mostly have to roll into bed. And it is a good thing that Mum does not tuck my blankets in cozily around me at night or I would never be able to get out in the morning.

34

Now that we have been forgiven for our disgraceful gluttony we can focus our thoughts on the Harvest Festival, which is a time to give thanks to God for providing us with a plentiful harvest so that we will not starve to death in the winter. It is also a time for us to stop and think of people who are worse off than we are and to make donations in church for the poor people of our parish so that they may feel the blessed love of Jesus and the righteous gift of the Almighty's charity.

I looked with Mum in the larder this morning to find something to donate to the poor people of our parish so that they will not starve to death in the winter. But there was only a bottle of vanilla essence and an old tin of Tate and Lyle's treacle with the lid rusted shut. There was also a small jar of those silver balls for decorating fairy cakes but Mum said we would have to make a sacrifice. We will donate the Ritz Crackers. She was hoping to keep them for a special occasion but it was the Ritz Crackers or a tin of baked beans and we need that for Sunday tea. Nana bought those crackers two years ago and Mum is very sorry to see them go but the needy must be fed.

As the man of the house, I will be going to the front of the congregation to donate our Ritz Crackers to the poor people of our parish. I asked Mum where all the poor people of our parish are and she said they're out there somewhere and I asked her why they weren't in church praying to God for food because Jesus will feed them like he did with the five loaves and two fishes. But apparently that is just symbolic and I should realize that even Jesus could not feed five thousand people with five loafs and two fishes. Our donations for the Harvest Festival are the physical representation of God's charity and thus a clear indication that His work is being done on Earth by we, His loyal servants.

But if the poor people are in the congregation that means they will be making donations for themselves, which does not make any sense at all. And if they're not in church, they should be ashamed of themselves. I don't see why they should receive God's righteous charity if they can't even be bothered to go to His holy house of worship and pray for salvation like the rest of us.

Mum says I am making this far too complicated and I should pay attention to the service. I have therefore decided to watch all the people who are making donations to see if they look poor and are therefore making donations to themselves.

We will sing, "We Plough the Fields and Scatter," as everyone goes up to make their donations. It is only right that Belinda should go up first because she is the reverend's daughter. She's in my class at school and I am in love with her and I am prepared to overlook the fact that she has blue veins showing through her skin, because she also wears a clean dress to school almost every day.

She has placed a tin of Jolly Green Giant corn by the potatoes and cabbages that were already on the table. Belinda can't be poor because she is the reverend's daughter, and the tin still has its label on it. Poor people buy tins with the labels missing because they are half price but they don't know what's inside them until they open them up for their tea and find they've got a tin of black prunes, which is completely disgusting but what can you expect for half price.

Next up is a bony-looking girl who is carrying two potatoes. I think she could be poor because two potatoes are not a very generous donation for the poor people of our parish. Her dress is too small for her and she also looks hungry and she is eyeing up that tin of corn. Yes, she could be poor.

Now we're all leaning forward because an old lady in a purple hat with a feather is putting a basket of fruit on the table. Bananas, oranges, apples, and grapes. She is definitely not poor. We only get one orange a year and that's as a treat at Christmas. And I have never even tasted grapes.

An old man in a tweed jacket is making his way to the table. The congregation is gasping but I can't see what's in his hand because it's hidden by his jacket. There, he's putting it down. My God! It's a tin of Fray Bentos braised beef! He's turning around and smirking. No one could top that. Even the reverend has raised his eyebrows.

There's a whole family that the usher has missed. He deliberately ignored them and they stared down at the floor. They haven't even got a donation so they either forgot or they are the poor ones and they can't afford to make a donation in which case it all makes sense. If you are the poor of the parish you should go to the Harvest Festival and thank God for his charity but not make a donation to yourself.

It's my turn. My heart is thumping because Belinda will be watching me. I can feel my cheeks turning red. Now where do I put the Ritz Crackers? There. Right beside the Jolly Green Giant corn. They look good together. I even touched the tin that Belinda touched.

Belinda is smiling. She is in love with me.

The reverend says that the strongest liquor that should touch our lips is the wine of the Holy Sacrament. Those vile public houses are dens of iniquity and the abuse of alcohol has ruined many fine men and destroyed their families. Jesus weeps for those sinners who would sooner drink than see their own children fed. It is in this time of need, this time when need is felt the most, that we should feel the pain and sorrow of others who suffer the unnecessary hunger in their bellies whilst others feast. God provides enough food for us all but he cannot change the wicked ways of man where gluttony takes the place of sharing.

"Mark my words! We will all be equal in the end. We are all equal in the eyes of God! And to Him we shall return. Thank you all for your generous donations. The hungry bellies of our parish will be fed tonight. Yes, there will be no hunger tonight. God Bless them. Amen."

"Amen."

Our church sermon will end later than usual today, at half-past one. Some of the congregation will have to run across the road to the pub because last orders are at two o'clock.

35

could not believe that she was kissing me. Then she spoiled it by putting her tongue in my mouth but I pushed it back out with my tongue. She smells like soap and I've heard a rumor that she has a bath more than once a week. If I marry Belinda, I will change my underpants every Sunday, even if they aren't dirty.

I wish I had known she was going to come round to our house this evening with the reverend. Surely Mum must have known but she said it was a big surprise when the reverend was at the door. It was after we finished our beans on toast and Mum was having a cigarette and saying she hoped the Ritz Crackers are going to a good home, disappointed as she was to see them go. And we were just sitting down for a good sing-along to *Songs of Praise* when they knocked.

"Go into the kitchen, Johnny. I need to talk with the reverend."

That's how I ended up alone with Belinda in our kitchen. And when she kissed me the second time and put her tongue back in my mouth I left it there because it felt good and she pushed it round my teeth like she was looking for some food. It's called a French kiss and that's because the French do it all the time even with complete strangers. I will French kiss with Belinda until I am at least forty. I wish I'd cleaned my teeth today.

And then the reverend made us jump by coming into the kitchen with a big cardboard box. Mum and Emily were right behind him.

"Do you say your prayers, John?" the reverend asked.

"Yes, every night."

"Good. And do you pray for your mother, John?"

"I do."

"And do you pray for your sisters?"

"I do."

"Do you feel the hunger in your belly, John?"

"Sometimes."

"It will bring you closer to God. The hunger opens your mind. It is the feasting that brings us closer to the Devil. The gluttony, dressed up as feasting while others starve. It makes us weak and then the Devil can work his wicked ways. Be glad you are not feasting, John. Is it any surprise that gluttony is one of the deadly sins?"

"No."

"Feel the hunger. Feel that hunger! God will provide, John. Do you know that?"

"I do."

"And while we hunger, we feel the pain of others, the pain of those less fortunate than ourselves who starve on the African plain or in the vile slums of Calcutta. And as we feel that pain, we feel the Holy Spirit entering into us, His children."

"Yes."

"Let us hold hands together and give thanks to our Lord, the Father."

So we said the Lord's Prayer together, me, Mum, Emily, the reverend, and Belinda. Margueretta does not believe in God anymore because she is almost twelve and she hears voices and I'm sure one of them is the Devil. I held Belinda's hand and even though we should have had our eyes closed so we could concentrate on God the Father, I opened mine and so did Belinda, and she stuck her tongue out at me.

We didn't open the box until they left. Mum said it would be rude, like looking a gift horse in the mouth. But she was very happy when she saw the Ritz Crackers in the box and I was really happy when I saw the tin of Jolly Green Giant corn. Emily clapped her hands and asked if we could have some for supper but Mum said that would be gluttonous because we have already eaten our beans on toast for tea. There was no tin of Fray Bentos braised beef but there was a banana and a cabbage.

"I tell you something," Mum said, "This is quite a feast. We will share the banana."

And she sliced up the banana and we had three slices each, sprinkled with sugar.

"Things are going to get better now, John. This is a sign. And do you know something?"

"What?"

"You are a good boy, Johnny. God knows you are a good boy. You deserve more. Tomorrow you will go with me."

"Where?"

"You'll see. The reverend helped me with a plan. God will always provide, Johnny. God will always provide."

36

I hope Belinda did not notice that I hadn't cleaned my teeth. Anyway, it's too late now and she was the one who put her tongue in my mouth and wiggled it around, not me. Still, she smiled at me when she left so I think she didn't notice.

I brushed my teeth this morning. Mum said I had to look my best as the man of the house because we were going to see a woman called Mollie who would explain the reverend's plan and all would become clear.

It wasn't far to walk from our house to Mollie's house. But I do think Mum should have explained that Mollie is a midget and she's smaller than me.

We had to go into Mollie's kitchen when we got there because the doctor was in the living room syringing her husband's ears.

"Eech! Don't mind the birds," Mollie said. "They're chaffinches. Robert breeds them. That's why he's having his ears syringed. He can't hear them anymore."

There was a huge wooden birdcage against a whole wall of the kitchen and the bird chatter meant I couldn't hear a word Mollie was saying to Mum. But I could hear that she started every sentence with a loud screech, like someone had stepped on her foot. I thought she was doing it for the chaffinches but Mum thinks it is a nervous habit.

And the other thing Mum never explained was that we were going to meet a little black girl called Folami who is three years old and doesn't talk.

Mum said she wasn't even sure herself because the reverend arranged it all and there wasn't much detail.

"I haven't seen you in church," Mum said.

"Eech! No. I don't like to go out much. Neither does Robert."

"How does the reverend know you?"

"Eech! He always gets involved with the fostering of children. There are always needy cases and he knows who has a good home in the parish."

Mum says that fostering means looking after a child like they are your own even though they are not yours. Mollie is fostering the little black girl and she is obviously not her own because she is a different color. Folami's real mother lives in London and she's having another baby soon and it will need to be fostered too.

"You know something, John?"

"What?"

"I'm very proud of you. You were very well behaved at Mollie's. You didn't say anything about her being so short or her nervous problem."

"Mum?"

"Yes, Johnny."

"What is the plan? Exactly?"

"We are going to foster troubled children. I am going to create a refuge for troubled children and people will pay for us to take care of them. It was all the reverend's idea. He's always looking for a good home for children in need."

"What are troubled children?"

"Well. Children from broken homes and children with problems, I would think."

"What sort of problems?"

"I don't know, exactly. I expect we will know when they arrive. So the first one will be Folami's brother or sister. We don't know if it is a boy or a girl because the baby isn't born yet. So what do you think of the plan?"

"It's good. Where will they sleep?"

"That's just a detail. Boys in one room, girls in another. Are you excited?"

"Yes."

"Yes, God helps those who help themselves. Mind you, I will need a lot more help from you now that I'm starting the refuge-for-troubled-children. You know what?"

"What?"

"I think you are old enough now to take the dirty washing to the launderette on your own every Saturday."

"Oh."

"And you know what else? I think we should open the tin of Jolly Green Giant corn to celebrate!"

Emily said we should open the Ritz Crackers too but Mum still wants to keep them for a special celebration. Especially now that we've got them back so unexpectedly.

37

Something terrible has happened but I'm glad. I wasn't the first one to wake. No one would be able to sleep through that terrible sound. It was a howling scream that wouldn't stop. But this time it wasn't coming from the attic. This time the scream was coming from out on the landing. Out by the toilet.

Mum was there with Emily when I ran out of my room. And Emily had her hand over her mouth like she wanted to scream and Margueretta was standing by the toilet door in her gray nightshirt, barefoot on the wooden boards. Her face was covered with snot and she was the one doing the all the screaming.

"It's in there! It's in there!" Margueretta shouted.

"What's in there?" Mum shouted.

"It's in there! Don't go in there! It's evil!"

"What?"

"It wants to kill me!"

"What wants to kill you?"

"It's going to kill me!"

"What's going to kill you?"

"There's something in my room!"

I waited by the toilet when Mum walked slowly up to Margueretta's bedroom door and pushed it open. Light from the landing bulb shone into the room. I could see the bed, dresser, and blankets on the floor. Mum stepped into the room and looked around.

"There's nothing here."

Mum doesn't believe in ghosts but she's wrong. She'll know soon enough.

"I can't go in there," Margueretta pleaded and pulled at her nightshirt.

"Get back to your beds," Mum said softly.

I looked at Margueretta's face and the snot was running down her lip. She wrung her hands in front of her while she pressed them against her stomach. For a moment I wanted to feel sorry for her, but I hate her. Anyone would hate someone who beats him every day. God will punish her.

"What did she see?" Emily asked.

"Nothing. She had a bad dream. It's just growing pains. She's twelve years old. The same thing will happen to you."

Emily glanced at me. The same thing will happen to her. That's because girls are very sensitive. It's their own fault. I would never stand on the landing screaming. I would chase that thing out of my room with my robot if it had new batteries. And if I hadn't taken it apart.

"Now go to bed, all of you. We need some sleep."

"I can't go in there," Margueretta shouted.

"There's nothing in there!"

"That thing wants to kill me! It spoke to me! It wants to kill me tonight! It said so!"

"Well. You can sleep downstairs on the sofa. I'm sure it won't follow you down there, young lady. Now let's get some sleep. I'll leave the landing light on, just this once."

It's obvious that this would happen. Margueretta doesn't believe in God, which makes her one of Satan's children, and she didn't hold hands with the reverend and say the Lord's Prayer with us. She just stayed in her room like she always does. So if there is something evil in our house, and I'm sure there is because I have heard it, it would know that she couldn't pray to God for help. She is now lost to the Devil. She is lost to the Devil for all Eternity and I'm glad.

THE ATTIC

Now I know for sure. I will get the stepladders from the scullery and go up into the attic just as soon as possible. I'm going to find what it is that is screaming up there. We don't have a torch but I will use a candle. And I will take my robot with me just as soon as I have put it back together.

38

Mollie came around with a cat. It's a stray but she can't keep it because it might attack the chaffinches. We've called her Misty and she will eat scraps of food because strays don't care what they eat since they are starving. She's also a bit lopsided because she's been savaged by a dog. But cats don't really have nine lives. That's just a myth. If a cat had nine lives then Boots would not have died when she was run over by a bus outside the public library.

Misty has already arched her back and hissed at the scullery and she won't go upstairs. That's because she can sense what is going on in our house. Even though cats don't have nine lives, they do have a sixth sense. And Misty knows there is something evil living in this house and I will be keeping a close eye on her to see if she arches her back again.

It is also really lucky that Mum went to the Co-op to buy some Kit-e-Kat and found that they were having a Fish Week. She said it's not a fresh-fish week because they don't have a cold counter so it is a tinned-fish week, which is just as well as we don't have a fridge.

"They had all kinds of exotic fish in tins and jars," Mum said.

"Fish week? I don't like fish. What kind of fish?" Margueretta replied.

"Well, they had jars of jellied eels. Oh, I love jellied eels. Reminds me of the seaside when I was a girl."

"Yuk."

"And pickled whelks."

"Double yuk. Tell me you didn't buy any bloody whelks. Please say you didn't buy any whelks. They're just giant snails for God's sake! Only primitive people would eat giant snails."

"Of course I bought some whelks. But you don't have to eat them because I have a surprise for tea."

"What is it?"

"We'll know soon enough."

"I don't care. I probably won't like it."

Mum lifted a tin onto the kitchen table and it was half the size of a beer barrel.

"Hand me the tin opener."

"There's no label on the tin," Margueretta said.

"I know," Mum replied.

"So how do you know what's in it?"

"I don't. That's why it's a surprise."

It took Mum forever to open the tin with our rusty old tin opener. We all sat round waiting for the surprise. Mum told Emily to get the big bowl, the one we use for making bread pudding.

"One, two, three. Here goes!"

It almost filled the mixing bowl when I helped Mum to slither it out. I thought I saw those massive eyeballs swivel around the room, looking at each one of us in turn. And then at the cat.

"Oh, good God!" Mum said.

"That's a...what in God's name?" said Margueretta.

"We will all eat well tonight!" Mum exclaimed. "It's so huge! Even the cat will have some!"

It had a wild look in its eyes that said, "Who the bloody hell put me in here?"

I think it had been canned in its own slime. Or that might have happened after they closed the lid on the thing. I'm sure it must have been alive when they put it in there.

"Holy Mother of Christ, would you look at it?" Mum shouted.

It was dead, of course. I mean, a giant gray octopus with suckers all over its tentacles could not survive in that tin, even in its own slime. My two sisters ran out of the kitchen. Mum turned to me.

"Well, your sisters are obviously not starving, eh? Fetch the bread knife, Johnny!"

"Are you going to eat it?" I asked.

"Of course! What do you think?"

"I'm not eating that."

"Well you're obviously not starving either!"

"So you are going to eat it?" I asked again.

"Maybe I will have some later," Mum replied.

So she sat the whole creature in the cat's bowl and it stared across the kitchen with glassy eyes while its huge tentacles hung over the side and onto the kitchen floor, like it was taking a rest before eating the cat.

"Well, at least the cat will have a feast tonight!" Mum announced.

We ate dry bread and a cup of beef stock for dinner. I'm sure the Co-op manager deliberately took the label off that tin.

39

We have not seen the cat for two days. Mum threw the octopus away this morning. She said she should have sliced it up and it was probably too tough for the cat to eat. Anyway, she had to throw the octopus away because we have visitors coming today and you can't have visitors in your kitchen with a bloody great octopus staring at you from the cat's bowl.

The visitors are not from England and they would never understand about tins with no labels.

"We are from Lagos. The Yoruba tribe. Which is the largest of over two hundred regional tribes in Nigeria!" the black man said.

The two black people standing in our front room were very, very tall like Zulus but in real clothes and shoes. The woman was holding a baby and they all smelled of olive oil and mothballs and they said Lagos was the capital of Nigeria, which is in Africa, and they come from the Yoruba tribe. I could not picture where it was on the map because Miss Jones only went as far as G for Greenland, which is actually full of ice and not very green.

It was when the black woman went to kiss me on the cheek that I noticed something horrifying, really horrifying. I don't know how Mum could not have noticed. The black woman had white patches on her legs and that could only mean one thing.

She had leprosy.

Miss Peabody said it is all explained in the Bible when Miriam caught it and they called her unclean and Aaron saw she was white as snow, which is what happens when you catch leprosy. And it's incurable.

Then the black woman handed the baby to my mum.

"He's only six weeks old. His name is Akanni. That's Yoruba for *our meeting brings gifts*," the black woman said.

Gifts? They have brought us the gift of leprosy. You lose all your feeling when you get leprosy and then rats come in the night and start eating you and you don't even know that they're biting pieces out of your face and then you get up in the morning and look in the mirror to comb your hair and see that your nose is completely missing. And you're wondering what happened to your nose. The next night it's your ears.

"What do you think?" Mum asked, nodding to the baby.

I looked for any white patches. So this is what Mum meant by troubled children. Children troubled with leprosy.

"It will be good for you to have a little brother!" the black man said.

I stared at the black man's face for signs of the incurable disease. But all I could see were two scars on his cheeks.

"They're tribal markings," the man said. "They were made when I was a young man."

"Take good care of our little boy, now," Akanni's mother said, and she burst into tears.

And that started Mum crying because it doesn't take much to start my mum crying these days.

"I will treat him like my very own son! My very own son!" Mum said, looking at the baby and then at me and then back to the baby.

Then the black man started crying too and that made Emily cry because she is very sensitive.

"We can't visit very often," the black man said.

They had some tea and biscuits before they left. I whispered to Mum about the Ritz Crackers but Jesus returned them to us for a reason and we will know soon enough when we should open them. Now is not their time.

"It's only me!" Joan Housecoat shouted through our letterbox after the black people drove away.

"This is our new baby," Mum said.

"Ooo-er!"

"We just got him. He is the first of our troubled souls in the refuge-for-troubled-children."

"Troubled children?"

"Yes. We are now a refuge-for-troubled-children."

"Ooo-er! He's just like a real baby, isn't he?"

"He is a real baby!"

"Yes, but…he's different, isn't he?"

"In what way?"

"Well, he's black."

"He is black."

"Yes, that's what I said. I saw those two black people come in here. What are you going to do with him?"

"We're fostering him."

"Ooo-er! Does that mean he's staying?"

"Yes, I just told you. I'm starting a refuge-for-troubled-children. Right here in this house. It was the reverend's idea."

"I hope he doesn't cry. These walls are paper-thin, you know. What will you call him?"

"He already has a name. It's Akanni."

"Akanni? No one will understand that, now will they? And they won't be able to spell it. You should give him an English name. Like George or Arthur. A good English name."

And the baby started to cry and Mum looked in a big bag that the black people left behind and pulled out a nappy. She laid the baby on the sofa and started to change him.

"He's got quite a large you-know-what, hasn't he?" Joan said as she arranged her bosom under her housecoat.

"Yes," Mum agreed, "it does look bigger than his was at that age."

"Ooo-er! They all do, you know. I mean black people. Black men. They have bigger ones."

So we all stared at the black baby's willy until Mum covered it with a clean nappy. And so far, there is no sign that the baby has leprosy.

40

Now Mum is saying that the screaming in the attic is just the new baby that I can hear. But for Christ's sake, the screaming sounds like a girl and not a baby. I think I know the difference. Anyway, Mum is going mad because she says the black floors in our house make her think of the eternal darkness and we should be sure to say our prayers every night and pray for her salvation in particular. I think the eternal darkness is a place you go to when you die but it's not Heaven because that place is very bright. And it's not hell because that place is full of fire and brimstone and is therefore also quite bright.

If you do not believe in God then you cannot go to Heaven to sit at His feet. I think you just stay in your coffin where they buried you, even if you are a child. I don't want my mum to die but if she does, she will go to Heaven because she has saved us from being orphans or begging on the street.

The reverend said he is very pleased with the progress at the refuge-for-troubled-children and now we are even closer to God. But Mum cried this morning. She said we shouldn't be overly concerned about her crying and it was just the worry about everything and it's hard to be on your own with all these kids to look after, especially now that we have another mouth to feed in the refuge. She says if we don't save some money then we will have no heating in the winter and even though it's almost summer now we still have to worry about those things or soon it will be winter and we will bloody freeze to death in our own beds.

And the other thing that made her cry was that German woman behind our house. She said that since my mum has a black baby, our father must therefore be a black man. Joan Housecoat told the German woman that it was a lie because she saw the two black people who delivered Akanni and anyway if my mum had a baby with a black man then it would be coffee-colored and not black. And we would be coffee-colored too and not white. Joan said the German woman is only saying that because she is a bloody Kraut and she should get back to bloody Germany where she belongs and not come over here after the war telling people they have black fathers after all the terrible things the Germans did, like bombing her mother's house and all that trouble with the Jews.

My mum showed Joan a picture of my dad, the one with him in his bus conductor's uniform. Joan said he was very handsome and obviously not at all black. Mum said he was more handsome when he had hair and yes, no one has ever suggested he was black. Not that there is anything wrong with being black but it does not make sense to be called black when you are clearly white.

"And another thing," Mum said to us, "Akanni does not know he is black because he is just a baby. In fact, he will not know he is black until someone tells him. So don't tell him."

"He will see it when he looks in the mirror," Margueretta replied and curled her lip up, the way girls do when they are nearly teenagers.

"That's not the point," Mum replied.

"So what is the point?"

"The color of your skin doesn't matter. People don't come up to you in the street and tell you that you have green eyes now do they? Or blonde hair. They tell you you're black because they want to make something of it. Just like that nosy bloody German woman behind us."

I like having Akanni in our house. When he grows up he will be my little brother. I hope he grows up soon because Mum keeps all the dirty nappies in a bucket under the sink and she says that she can't keep washing them by hand and soon I will be able to help her by taking them to the launderette along with all the other dirty washing. There are dozens of flies buzzing all around the bucket and Margueretta says that's disgusting because then they land on our beans on toast.

"And I have a surprise!" Mum announced.

"Oh, God. What is it this time?" Margueretta asked. "Is it another bloody octopus?"

"Enough of that language, young lady! No. It is not an octopus. We are going to rescue another child already. Isn't that amazing!"

"Another one?"

"Yes. We are moving on to the next stage in the refuge-for-troubled-children."

"God, not that again."

"Well, young lady. Where would you be if it weren't for this roof over your head? Eh? You would be out in the elements without protection. There are children out there who need our help."

"Yeh, yeh. What about your own children? You always say that charity begins at home. Well, what about us? We need bloody help!"

"I'll ignore that remark. I've made the arrangements for another foster child. It's a girl this time. Her name is Ngozi. She's a very troubled little girl. She's only three years old, and she can't talk."

"Can't talk?"

"Yes. But I will have her chattering away in no time. No time at all."

"This is madness."

"And she has another problem."

"What?"

"She's still in nappies."

"Still in nappies? At three years old?"

"Yes. She's still in nappies."

We are going to need a bigger bucket.

41

ome nights I fall asleep and stay asleep. But other nights, the dark nights, I fall asleep and then it wakes me up. I crunch my knees up to my chest and hold the pillow over my ears. Sometimes I just pretend I'm in a rocket ship far away in outer space because it's silent in space. Space is a vacuum—you can't hear anything and no one can hear you.

But I can hear it tonight.

I think it's a dead girl. She sounds like she is screaming the way she would have screamed at the very end of her life. Like her very last breaths had to be pushed out in the blackness so that someone might hear before it was too late. But no one heard. And then she died.

She still screams, alone in the attic. Dead and alone.

Jesus made a dead man come back to life once. His name was Lazarus and he was dead in his tomb for four days and Jesus made them roll back the stone and told him to come back out and I think the dead man was very confused because all the people were supposed to be at his funeral and he was still dressed in his funeral shirt. When he came out people said it was a miracle.

Miss Peabody said in hot countries people have to be buried very quickly or they will be eaten by flies and maggots. I'm not sure what Lazarus died of but if it was something bad like leprosy then I don't really like that story. When you are dead you should stay dead or you will be walking around with rotting flesh hanging from your bare bones. Especially if you had leprosy and your face had been eaten away or if you were being eaten by flies and maggots. Flies and maggots crawling all over your face and body.

If I was there when Lazarus came out of his tomb, I would not have touched him. I would have run away.

This isn't a hot country but you still rot when you are dead. You still rot until you are just a skeleton. A dead person should stay dead. And she shouldn't scream in the attic, above my head. She shouldn't try to open that attic door that's right above my head.

She should stay dead and silent. Not dead and screaming. Night after night.

42

have to learn the value of money. Mum says it's not money that is the root of all evil—it is the *love* of money. She says you should never love money above all else because nothing is greater than God and that's why Jesus cast the moneylenders out of the temple. But I think it's only poor people who say you shouldn't love money. That's because they haven't got any money to love.

If I had money, I would cover the black floors for my mum and buy her yellow flowers every day. She can't take the strain anymore and it's no wonder with the refuge-for-troubled-children and Margueretta saying there are people or things inside this house that want to kill her. I wish they'd just get on with it.

If we had money, we would all go on holiday together to get away from it all. But we don't. So it's a good thing that Nana sent Mum a postal order to pay for me and Emily to go away on a summer holiday to London. I have never been on a holiday but Willy Tucker at our school went on a holiday once. His mum said he was going to the Isle of Wight to see his dad who has been missing for six months. When they got there they went to a place called Parkhurst, which is actually a prison. I think his dad is a burglar.

We're eight years old so we can travel on our own now and we are going to stay with our Auntie Dot on Tulse Hill, which is near a place called Brixton where Nana lives. And we shouldn't worry that we've never met our Auntie Dot before because she's almost family. But she isn't our real auntie.

"Your Auntie Dot lives in the attic. So make sure you ring the bell until she hears you!"

Wow! This will be my chance to see inside an actual attic.

We rang the bell by taking turns to press the button because we have never seen a doorbell before. Two black men answered the door.

"Who you looking for?"

"Our Auntie Dot!"

"Big Dottie?"

"Auntie Dot."

"She is al'de way to the top of dose stairs, mind de gaps, until you get to a place in de top where dat sunshine be shining in like you is outside wid de birds. Closer my God to thee. Amen."

"Our Mum said she lives in the attic."

"Ah. That's what I jes said! She is al' de way to de top like she is livin' in a t-ree house, don' cha know. What bee-you-tiful children you is. Such shiny happy faces!"

When we got to the top of the stairs, we knocked on a small door and it swung open out across the broken staircase and I had to grab hold of Emily so she wouldn't fall through the balustrade and break her bloody neck.

"'Ello me darlings! My, you're a sight for sore eyes! Don't worry about those fucking darkies, they're just Jamaicans. I'm only living here on a temporary basis. Jamaicans don't have no choice on account of being black, which they cannot help, can they? Same as the Irish."

Auntie Dot looks like a man. When she bent down to kiss me, her cheek was all bristly like my dad's. And she is wearing a man's uniform with trousers and a waistcoat but they look like they were made for a much smaller person. And Auntie Dot is a very, very big person.

"Well, don't just stand there. Come in! Come in!"

I wanted to run back out and I was only one step inside the attic. Emily was blocking my way, not that she meant to. So I just threw my hand over my nose and mouth and tried not to breathe. But you have to breathe eventually or you will faint and God knows, it was like opening my nostrils and letting a thousand cats piss in them.

"You'll get used to the smell, me luvvies! It's the cats. I take them in. Strays mostly. Can't see them starve or get put down. Never could. I was a stray myself once. This is my cat refuge. Can't turn any of them away from the refuge."

It may not be hers, but there was a shaving mug and a razor on the mantelpiece and this could mean that she is a man. I don't know why we would call her Auntie if she was a man. I will have to look for other clues. The room does have a window but it's taped up with brown paper and that makes things darker than they should be.

But everywhere we looked there was only one thing to see. Cat hair. Cat hair covering the sofa, the armchair, the carpet, the table and the television. Cat hair covering the cat hair. And more cat hair on top of that.

And just then, the cat hair moved and a huge black cat jumped onto the furry TV and squatted down right there to take a piss.

"Ooo, you cowson! Get the fuck off of there! Fucking Nora!" Dot shouted, hurling a shoe at it.

As we moved, cat hair floated around us, disturbed by our entrance. Emily already had a light covering. She pulled one from her mouth. It was black.

"Have you met Lassie?" Dot asked.

A large mound of cat hair broke free from the sofa and lollopped over to us.

"She's an Alsatian. Make yourselves at home. I'll go and make dinner. You must be starving!"

We were starving. Mum made us some Shipham's Salmon Spread sandwiches to eat on the train but in the rush to catch the bus to the station we left them on the kitchen table.

"Sit yourselves down!"

Emily's got a weak stomach, which is why she wanted to be sick. I know she didn't like the smell and I told her not to look at the pile of cat turds in the corner next to the stack of Beano and Dandy comics with the open box of nut clusters on top. I said she should just push her hand over her nose and mouth, the same as me. She said she could still smell it.

Dot came back into the room with two large plates of sausages and mash.

"Eat up! Eat up!" she said, and pushed the plates into our laps.

"But, Dot," Emily gasped.

"What?"

"I can't eat this!"

"What's the problem?"

"There's cat hair all over this plate and food."

"So?"

"Cat hair! There's cat hair all over the food!"

Dot looked at the plate. She brushed away one or two of the hairs. Several hundred remained. More were floating in the air, waiting to land.

"I can't eat this," Emily repeated.

"What's wrong with you?"

"It's disgusting. The food has cat hair all over it."

"You kids don't know how good you've got it. 'What the eye don't see, the heart don't grieve.' Don't you know that mushrooms are grown in shit? Didn't you ever eat mushrooms? Well, you're eating shit. So a few hairs won't hurt you."

"And there's something like a flea crawling across my plate," Emily said.

Emily was absolutely right. A flea was making its way towards the shelter of a sausage. It would have jumped but its legs were glued together by the grease. Dot wiped the flea onto her finger.

"It's a flea alright! Extra meat! Do you want HP Sauce?" she laughed. "Can you still smell the cats' piss?"

"Yes."

"Told you. Your nose gets used to it. Now those Jamaicans, they complain all the time about the smell. They're fine ones to talk! They make a terrible smell with all that foreign cooking. Jamaican jerk chicken they call it. Disgusting I call it. Bloody stink. The woman underneath said they've got a big brown bulge on their ceiling. She says she's afraid she'll be sitting down to *Z-Cars* one night and it will burst and all that cats' piss will land on her head."

"Where are we sleeping?" Emily asked.

"Here. Right here. One on the sofa, one on the armchair. The telly's not working. The fucking cats keep pissing on it. So we'll roll Lassie over in a minute and you can help me crack the fleas on her. I'll show you where they hide. In her armpits and around her tits, mostly."

I know Emily was just trying to create a distraction from cracking the fleas, but it was a mistake to say she wanted to take a look around the rest of the attic. If she had stayed on the sofa, as I suggested, then she would not have seen the big bowl of cats food on the kitchen table with the pile of maggots making their way out of the bowl and across the empty sausage wrappers. She would also not have seen the colossal cats' toilet in Dot's bedroom or the terrapin called Jimmy who eats live maggots.

"Go on, Emily. Just pick up some maggots and feed him."

It was entirely her own fault.

43

have not scratched so much since they cut my hair off to make me look like a movie star. Auntie Dot said we complain too much and it is just something we will get used to.

"Trust me, those fleas would rather be on a dog or a cat than crawling up your legs! They are not human fleas, you know. You would know it if they were human fleas because they would be sucking your blood as well as biting you. But they're not are they?"

She also told Emily to stop being so hysterical.

I am thinking about Auntie Dot. When we get back to school, we will have to write an essay about our summer holidays called, "What I Did On My Summer Holiday," and some of us will get to read it in front of the class. Last year I just made things up because we have never been on holiday. So since this is our very first holiday, I will have to remember every detail so that I can write it all down. So I am thinking about everything that is happening. And I will describe Auntie Dot very carefully.

I am pretty sure that she is a woman but I have to take into account that she wears men's clothes and she shaves. But in my essay I will say she is a woman because she does wear red lipstick and she refers a lot to her massive but accommodating bosom.

She also uses some of the best swear words I have ever heard like, "Jesus fucking H. Christ what in the bleeding hell are those black cunts cooking this time?" And, "Fuck me, that stinks like a bleeding sailor's arsehole!"

Thluuuuuuump!

That's the sound of her lifting her bum off the sofa and doing massive farts so that all the cat hair blows up into the air. But I probably will not include that in my essay. Actually, I won't include those swear words either.

I must observe other details.

She smokes Kensitas cigarettes and sometimes she smokes more than one at once. She reads the Dandy and Beano comics because she likes the pictures. And she eats chocolate nut clusters by sucking all the chocolate off and leaving the nuts because she said nuts make her fart. She then offers the nuts to me and Emily. Obviously, we do not eat them as that would be disgusting, but she means well.

Yes, she does mean well. Take this morning, for instance. We were all sitting on the sofa together scratching and Auntie Dot said she couldn't get any time off work so she would take us to work with her, which was a very nice thing to do or we would have been left on our own in the attic with the cat hair and fleas and the nut clusters, even if there was plenty of sausages and mash left over from last night. So that's how we found out that Auntie Dot works for London Transport at the Stockwell underground station and those clothes she is wearing are her uniform.

When we got to the station, the first thing she did was to take us to see a secret tunnel that was even more exciting than that time I put my finger in the back of Nana's old valve radio and touched the live terminal. We met some more Jamaicans who were hiding down in the tunnel from dangerous passengers. We had a nice cup of tea with them and they told me never to work on the underground because it's too dangerous.

"We come all de way from a hot place in de Caribbean wid sand and banana trees. Ha, Lordy! We come here to better ourself. Ha! Praise de Lord, you is bee-you-tiful kids wid de faces like de shining sun."

They also did not expect to be called wogs and niggers when they are British Citizens just like the rest of us. If they had known then what they know now they would have stayed in poverty because at least it was warm and there wasn't a bunch of violent thugs trying to avoid paying their tube fares. They don't get paid enough to get punched in the mouth for a sixpenny ride.

That's when Auntie Dot pulled a train grab-handle out of her knickers.

"Some fucking drunk tried to punch me in the mouth because he hadn't paid his fare so I whacked him on the fucking head with this," Dot said, holding her weapon in the air.

"Dat is de right ting to do, ole Dot. De right ting."

"Well, he sued me, the fucker. But the London Transport Workers Union defended me, and I won the case. I love the Union. But they said it was a dangerous weapon, and I was not to keep it down my knickers."

"Lordy! No way should dat ting be down a woman's knickers. But dat has not stopped you, Dot!"

"No fucking way! It's staying down my fucking knickers as long as I want!"

"You are de example to us all, Dot. A wonder to be beholdin'."

Dot put her weapon back in her knickers. We couldn't spend all day chitchatting with the Jamaicans so Dot took us to see a stain on the tracks where a woman killed herself last week by jumping in front of a train. Dot said it was very thoughtless.

"No one would jump in front of a train if they saw the fucking mess it makes!"

She has to clean it all up along with the fire brigade and the head always gets chopped off so someone's got to pick it up by the hair.

"God forbid some fucking bald man doesn't jump! We'd have to pick up his head by the ears! We have to make sure we've got all the main body parts in the bag. They get caught in the wheels. We count them. Two arms and two legs. Feet and hands. The last thing you need is to put someone in their coffin and find that a foot is missing. Or a hand."

We can't go back tomorrow because the Station Manager said it was not appropriate for two small children to collect tickets and sweep the station platforms while Auntie Dot was having a cup of tea with the Jamaicans. We were only trying to help. He said we could fall in front of a train or get kidnapped. I think he was just jealous because people were giving us money to help our poor, widowed mother.

But the really amazing thing about today was when we were walking back home to Dot's attic after eating our fish and chips, we saw a dead man lying in the road. He'd crashed his scooter into a lamppost. Auntie Dot said not to look but we did look and so did lots of other people. Purple blood was oozing out of his head and nose and it made a puddle round his head and he looked like a saint on a stained glass window in church with a halo and I told Auntie Dot about that and she said it was a very nice thing to say and she rubbed my hair. And she said to try not to think about the dead man but that's all I can see when I close my eyes. His face was really white and that made the purple blood seem darker and the black of the road seem blacker.

People say that blood is red but it's closer to purple. And it turns brown when it dries.

Auntie Dot says he had a white face because his soul had left him. Your soul is a part of you that lives forever and that's why it's alright for your body to be buried when you are dead. You don't need your body in Heaven but it's best to imagine someone inside their body or else they will just be a bright light and that's not an easy way to remember someone when they are dead. It's also best not to think about someone being dead inside their coffin, especially if he killed himself by jumping in front of a train.

I have been thinking a lot about Auntie Dot and all the things that we have seen already on our holiday. I am going to write all the little details about our Auntie Dot but also the dead man with the purple blood lying on the black road who will become a bright light in Heaven. That was the most interesting thing and I will say I thought he looked like a saint with a purple halo around his head, lying on the black road.

I wish Mum was here because this is the best holiday anyone could have and I am sure that no one could ever have a day as exciting as this one.

44

was completely wrong. There are much more exciting things than seeing a dead man. We couldn't stop scratching so Auntie Dot dropped us round to Nana's flat for a break. And that's where we met Auntie Dee who had a holiday surprise for us.

Auntie Dee is another woman who is not our real auntie. She also wears a uniform but her uniform is from the Salvation Army because she is saving souls for the Stockwell Citadel. She is a very brave Apostle of Christ because she takes her tambourine into the public bar at The Castle every Saturday night and promises eternal happiness for the righteous or endless punishment for the wicked. Nana says that most people settle for endless punishment and order another drink. It's very dangerous being an Apostle of Christ in the public bar of The Castle because a man smashed her tambourine right over her head, which was not easy to do because she was wearing her Salvation Army hat at the time.

> *The sun has got his hat on, hip, hip, hip, hooray.*
> *The sun has got his hat on, and he's coming out to play.*
> *Stand up, stand up for Jesus, ye soldiers of the cross!*
> *Hold high his royal banner, it must not suffer loss!*

Auntie Dee sings God's praises all the time because an idle mind makes work for the Devil. And she keeps her grandson Danny with her constantly because he is only five years old and he is special because he was sodomized in the back bedroom by a boy called Arnold when they were only supposed to be playing snakes and ladders. And even though it has made Danny special to be sodomized, he now lives with Auntie Dee because he does not want to be sodomized again.

Nana said I should not ask when I wanted to know exactly what it means to be sodomized and I don't know why they told me that he was sodomized if I can't even ask what it means. All I know is that there is a place in the Bible called Sodom and God burned it down with fire and brimstone.

Auntie Dee said she had a holiday surprise for everyone and if we were good and loved Jesus, she would tell us all about it.

45

We are going on the Salvation Army summer daytrip to Littlehampton. It will be sun, sea, sand, and salvation because our souls will be saved by the righteous songs that we will sing on the bus. And Danny is going with us because he has been sodomized and he is special. Also, Jesus wants him for a sunbeam.

For one thing, God knows it would have been better if we had had tickets. There were nearly two hundred bloody people trying to get on our double-decker bus outside Clapham Junction tube station. And those riff-raff, who have never been to church or even opened a Bible, didn't listen to a word when Auntie Dee told them that God's son died for them on Calvary so that they might be saved from mortal sin and eternal damnation. And if you want my opinion, it was very disrespectful when that man stole her brand new tambourine.

Rattle, rattle, rattle.

And another thing. It would have helped if there were more Salvation Army people there to control that crowd of riff-raff and not just our Auntie Dee and a small old man with a whistle who said he was the captain. It was lucky for him that someone snatched his whistle away from him before that other man pushed it down his bloody throat.

That's when a fight broke out.

"We've got as much right as you to be on this bus!" squealed a woman, dragging a dirty, wild-eyed boy behind her.

"When did you last go to fucking church?" another shouted.

"May God strike you down for that language!"

"You ain't set foot inside a church since your ol' man died! And that was in 1945!"

"Don't you bring my dear, departed Harold into this, you fucking old cow!"

And once they broke the fight up, it wasn't much fun driving to the seaside because it should only have taken two hours but we kept having to stop so that the dirty wild-eyed boy could be sick and he was sick seven times including once on the bus. I held my breath and moved to the other side. And his mum slapped him every time he was sick, which made him scream, and Nana said no one should blooming well have to listen to that screaming on a Salvation Army bus to Littlehampton.

Also, we had to stop every time we came to some bushes because the grown-up ladies said they could *not* just stick their bums out the back of the bus to pee like some of the men suggested.

So, it took over four hours to get to the seaside and not two and as soon as we got there nearly all the grown-ups went into a pub called the Marine Hotel and Nana said she didn't know why they came all the way to the seaside just to go into a pub when there were plenty of pubs back in Clapham. Not to mention the ten crates of beer that had already been drunk on the journey.

We did not sing any righteous songs on the way to the seaside because Auntie Dee was too angry about her missing tambourine. She was also very unhappy that an old man called Cecil kept taking out his teeth to show her that he could pop the caps off of beer bottles with them because no one thought to bring a bottle opener.

"If you stare out to sea," the captain said, "you will be able to experience the eternity of the Holy Spirit."

Auntie Dee agreed that she felt closer to God than she did in Clapham.

I tried not to look while Auntie Dee was getting undressed with a towel around her. That towel was nowhere near big enough. That's why she ended up sitting down to do it and asked Danny to help shield her but all he could do was point at things that no one should be seeing. It was completely mesmerizing. But the captain just stared out to sea.

And we were not at all happy when the captain told us to get dried and dressed after only an hour.

"It is my responsibility to get all of you back to Clapham before dark. We should have arrived here hours ago! This has not been the experience that it should have been."

The captain said he would leave without the grown-ups because they wouldn't come out of the pub. I thought it was a very good idea when the captain got the driver to start the engine and he revved it up and even moved forward a bit and that nearly started another fight when everyone came running out of the pub, still holding their drinks, screaming for us to stop.

"And another thing," the captain shouted, "We will not be stopping this bus forty-two times on the way back to Clapham. If you need to go, you will just have to do it in a bottle. Or out the back of the bus. And that's final!"

"I'm not sticking my arse out the back of no bus just for you fucking men to have a good look!"

It was the woman with the wild-eyed child. Then she slapped the boy to show us she meant it. I don't think she's right. It would be dangerous for a woman to try to pee out of the back of a bus. But for the men to have a good look at her bum, they would have to swing out of the back deck to do it. Anyway, I think the men are too busy drinking all the crates of beer they brought with them from the pub. And this time, they've got a bottle opener so Cecil doesn't have to use his false teeth.

We were only as far as the turn at the end of the esplanade when Auntie Dee smiled at me and started to sing a righteous song, even though her tambourine was still missing.

> It's an open secret that Jesus is mine,
> It's an open secret this gladness divine,
> It's an open secret I want you to know,

It's an open secret,
I love my Savior so...
But the grown-ups joined in with their own song.

*When I went home on Monday night as drunk as drunk can be,
I saw a horse outside the door where my old horse should be...
Ah, you're drunk,
You're drunk, you silly old fool,
Still you cannot see,
That's a lovely sow that me mother sent to me...*

You can seek Him, find Him, share this secret too...

*Ah, you're drunk,
You're drunk, you silly old fool,
Still you cannot see...*

Jesus said unto her, I am the resurrection, and the life:
He that believeth in me, though he were dead, yet shall he live...

*And as I went home on Saturday night as drunk as drunk could be,
I saw two hands upon her breasts where my old hands should be...*

"Stop the fucking bus or I will piss myself, do you hear!" shouted the same woman who said she would not stick her bare arse out the back of the bus to piss just to have a bunch of drunken old men peering at her drawers.

"Really! I am reciting from the Scriptures," said the captain. "Jesus saith unto him, I am the way, the truth, and the life..."

"And I'm saying I will piss right here in this seat if you don't stop this fucking bus!"

"Watch and pray that ye enter not into temptation. The spirit indeed is willing but the flesh is weak…"

"And another thing! The driver says he needs to stop. He's thirsty, and he needs a fucking beer!"

This is the best time ever. I never want to go home to our haunted house again. I want to stay here forever.

46

When we got back home, we were still scratching so Mum put some white powder in our clothes. I asked about it and she said it was for humans but the container had a picture of a dog on it.

And I got a gold star for my essay.

Two more black people came to our house today as we are now welcoming another troubled soul to the refuge-for-troubled-children. I looked closely at them but I don't think they have leprosy. I think this is on account of them coming from a completely different tribe.

"Where are you from?" Mum asked.

"We are from the Igbo tribe! Igbo! Yes, we escaped our country a year ago," the black man replied.

"What did you escape?" Mum asked, leaning forward and lighting a cigarette.

"Oh, it's complicated," he replied.

"Go on. Go on," Mum said.

"Well. There was a lot of political unrest," he began, "and then, earlier this year, my tribe seized power in Nigeria. There were riots. Almost thirty thousand of my tribe were killed."

"Thirty thousand? Good God!"

"Yes. My brother and auntie were killed, God rest their souls. You see, Nigeria is a country that was created by you!"

"Me?" Mum replied.

"Well, not you personally. The British. Nigeria wasn't a country before the days of the Empire. We got our independence from Great Britain in 1960. That's when the real trouble began."

Mum took a long drag on her cigarette. "Really?" she said, moving in even closer.

"There was no recognition of the terrible tribal differences between my tribe and the Yoruba and Hausa-Fulani. Or the fighting that would start over the rights to Nigeria's oil supplies."

This was a bloody sight more interesting than the last two black people. All they did was cry but these people actually came from a warring tribe. Death, destruction and terror. I really wish I hadn't taken my robot apart.

"This is the start of a civil war. Many more will die. Perhaps millions by the time it is over."

"Millions? Die?"

"Maybe."

"So, let me see," Mum asked. "You are at war with another tribe?"

"Yes. Back home in Nigeria."

"Which one, did you say? Which tribe are you at war with?"

"The Yoruba. Mostly the Yoruba. They are an evil people. And very tall."

"Very tall?" Mum asked.

"Yes. Very, very tall. I'm sure there will be genocide before this is done. But we will fight to the death. And I will send money home to our brave soldiers."

"Genocide?"

"Yes. Genocide."

Mum bounced Akanni on her knee.

"So please take care of our little girl, Ngozi. She cannot talk..." the black man said.

"And she still has to wear nappies!" the black woman added.

"Don't worry," Mum said. "We'll have her chatting away in no time. And potty trained."

I looked at Ngozi and snot was running down from her nose and she was licking it from her lip. Then she frowned and looked away.

She shit herself. I am glad she is a girl and will be sharing a bed with Emily in the refuge-for-troubled-children.

47

Mum has denied it but she is avoiding the truth, if you ask me. Even I know what has happened. We have fostered children from two warring tribes, one with a definite case of leprosy. It is a civil war in which thousands have already died, maybe millions. As the man of the house I have a right to know some things. I accept that I am never going to know what it means to be sodomized but this is under our own roof, for God's sake. I need to know all about genocide.

"But what exactly is genocide, Mum?"

"Well, John, that's really a grown-up question."

"You always say that. But what is it? As the man of the house, I need to know!"

"Ha! It's something that happens in wars when one group of people massacre another group because of who they are."

"Because of who they are?"

"Yes. Like the Nazis in World War Two. They massacred five million Jews. Or it may have been six. That was genocide."

"Oh."

"We should learn more about their ways," Mum said.

"The Nazis?"

"No! The Nigerians."

To help her learn more about their ways, Mum has bought a book called *Teach Yourself Yoruba*. It had to be specially ordered from the bookstore but I do not understand why she would want to learn how to speak Yoruba when those first two black people only come here every three months, and the other two are from a different tribe with a different dialect. And they are at war with the Yoruba so it may not be very nice if you spoke to them in Yoruba.

"*Ek'abo!*" Mum exclaimed.

"What?" Margueretta replied.

"*Bawo Iowa?*" Mum continued.

"You've lost your mind! I'm not listening."

"*Ek'abo* means welcome! *Bawo Iowa?* How are you?"

"Who cares?" Margueretta laughed because she is now an actual teenager and teenagers hate their parents and their mothers in particular but also their younger brothers.

"You'll be laughing on the other side of your face when I am speaking to Akanni's parents in Yoruba when they come over!"

"They speak English, for God's sake!"

I could see Margueretta's point because even though we are now a refuge-for-troubled-children and we could foster more children from the Yoruba tribe, it is more than likely that their parents will speak English unless they have just arrived here from the war on a boat. But I hate Margueretta so I took my mum's side.

"I want Mum to learn Yoruba!" I shouted.

"No one cares what you want!" Margueretta replied.

"Well, John is my helper," Mum began, "And he is going to help me today, aren't you John?"

"Yes!" I beamed.

"Yes. He is my helper!"

"I am!"

Mum smiled at me, and I smiled back.

"He's going to take the nappies to the launderette for me. And he's taking Akanni and Ngozi with him to give me a break, aren't you?"

This is my own fault. I like to help my mum because she cries a lot and it's very hard bringing up five children in this dreadful cold house with the black floors and a child screaming in the attic and hardly enough money to keep us from bloody well starving to death or freezing solid in our own beds. And every time you turn around there's another bloody mouth to feed and Akanni is getting bigger and that means he's eating even more and he's tall for his age because the Yoruba are a very, very tall people.

And even though Mum said she would have Ngozi chatting away in no time and potty trained, she is still wearing nappies. And Akanni is eating solids. Now we have two nappy buckets under the sink and there were some terrible things floating in them this morning.

There is a very old Hotpoint top-loader washing machine in our backyard that Mum got from the Methodist Church jumble sale. It's in the backyard beside the coal bunker because Mum says it is possessed on account of it hopping all the way across the kitchen when it was on the spin cycle. And leaking most of its tub of dirty water all over our kitchen floor every time she used it, which is not very helpful, even if it was only once a week and probably explains why it was only two shillings in the Methodist Church jumble sale.

But it's my own fault that I ended up taking Akanni and Ngozi with me to the launderette with the buckets of nappies in the tray under the pram. Mum emptied some of the fluid out of the buckets so they wouldn't splash around too much.

I was hardly out of the garden gate when an old lady came up to me and looked in the pram.

"How old is your baby?" she asked.

"He's just twelve months old."

She peered around the pram hood.

"Oh my! It's a pickaninny! A little black pickaninny!"

Then she looked at Ngozi who was hiding beside me.

"Really! What on earth did we fight a war for? Pickaninnies indeed! In England! Bring back the Empire!"

THE BOY WHO LIVED WITH GHOSTS

It's not surprising really. There are only three black children on our council estate and two of them live with us. It must be quite a shock for old ladies to suddenly see a little black face for the first time when they were expecting to see a shiny white face with blond hair and blue eyes looking back at them. It's just like Mum said. People don't say anything about the color of your eyes but they have a lot to say about the color of your skin. It doesn't matter if we ignore it because everyone else shouts, "Nigger!" and, "Sambo!" and, "Wog!" and, "Fucking darkies!" I never heard any of those words before we became a refuge-for-troubled-children.

I headed straight for an empty machine when we got to the launderette.

"Are those with you?" said a woman who was obviously in charge.

She nodded at Ngozi and Akanni and I could feel my cheeks get hot and red and all the women in the launderette turned and stared at us.

"I said, are those with you?"

"Yes."

"Are you washing their clothes?"

"Nappies."

"Their nappies?"

"Yes."

"You can't wash them here. You can't put *their* clothes in these machines."

"Not clothes. Nappies."

"Or nappies. You'll have to take them back with you. You can't use these machines," she said and stood in my way so I couldn't get to the empty machine.

The other women just stared at me and all I could think about was taking the two buckets of nappies back home and Mum would not think I was her little helper anymore and Margueretta would laugh and Mum would probably cry because she would have to wash all those nappies by hand.

And then the woman shouted at me.

"Wait!"

I turned around.

"You can wash them in there!"
I looked at the machine. It had a sign on it,

Use This Machine For Oily Work Overalls Only
—May Cause Soiling —
Management Not Responsible

48

It's freezing cold now and we still don't have any heaters in our bedrooms. I'm quite sure that we will freeze to death in our beds. They will find us stiff as boards and our hot water bottles will be blocks of ice and they will carry us out like that cat they found in the scullery.

Our only paraffin heater has to stay in the kitchen so we can dry the nappies. Normally we hang them on the washing line in the backyard and prop it up with an old branch from a tree. But when we hang the nappies out in the winter they freeze solid and don't even begin to dry and you don't want to run out of nappies with two children shitting themselves like donkeys.

I told Mum about the woman at the launderette and she said that some people are ignorant and the worst thing you can be in this world is ignorant because knowledge frees us and ignorance traps us. The only way that some people can feel better about themselves is by looking down on other people instead of looking inside their hearts and finding God. Mum told me to say a prayer for that woman tonight and at first I did not want to because she made me feel bad in the launderette even though I hadn't done anything wrong. But I did pray for her and it made me feel better because I asked for Jesus to go into her heart and free her and I know that will happen and she will wake up one day soon and not care which washing machines black people use.

I should never have asked for that glass of water right before bedtime. And the worst thing about the cold is that it always makes me want to pee in the middle of the night. And I was about to get up to pee when the screaming started right above my head. It was coming from the attic as it always does. It's almost two years since we moved here but we still haven't been in the attic.

It makes me shiver when I hear the screams. It's a shiver that comes from deep inside you and makes your head feel hot and cold at the same time and then you can't even think.

But tonight it was different. Just as suddenly as it began, the screaming stopped. But I still needed to pee.

So I climbed out of bed and felt the terrible pain of the cold and wanted immediately to get back under the blanket. But I had to pee and the only other alternative was to wet the bed and blame it on the hot water bottle leaking, which I have done before, but we don't have any clean blankets and its too cold for the pee to dry and so I will have to get into a wet bed tomorrow night and I will be really angry with myself.

So I kept moving, slowly in the dark, and found the bedroom door handle, and the door creaked ever so slightly as I pulled it open. It was a shock when I saw a light shining across the landing. We never sleep with the light on because we don't have money to waste on those things, like we are millionaires for God's sake.

So I looked to see where the light was coming from and my bladder hurt with the sudden pain that shot through it, seeing that light. I stopped for a moment and didn't breathe and waited to hear something or someone.

And there was nothing. Not a sound.

I could go back but I would have to piss myself because it was too late to hope that I could hold it in all night, not now that the pain in my bladder was made worse from the light that shouldn't be there.

The toilet door was closed. No, not completely. Just enough to let the light out. The light was coming from the toilet.

It moved easily when I touched it. Just the slightest movement, as I pushed the toilet door. The bare light bulb was there, brightly lighting the toilet. And nothing. Nothing in there except the toilet bowl and the cistern with water droplets all around it. Black mold on the boards around the bowl.

And the handle on the end of the chain, swinging there on its own. Swinging from nothing.

Swinging, swinging, swinging.

I pushed the pee out and it rattled the water in the toilet bowl and it felt like it would never stop and I shook the last drips away and turned to the door. I couldn't move, of course. Who could? The toilet door was moving inwards on its own. Slowly, ever so slowly, the door was opening towards me.

There it was.

In the doorway of the toilet, standing on the landing in the half-light in its gray-white gown, it was staring at me.

And then it opened its mouth and screamed. But nothing came out. I knew it was screaming because its face was screwed up and its mouth was wide open as far as it would go. And still nothing came out. Wider and wider it opened its mouth until it seemed that its whole face was just a giant mouth. And it was screaming in silence.

Screaming silently in its gray-white gown.

And then it was gone.

The handle on the end of the chain was still swinging.

Diddle, diddle dumpling, my son John,
Went to bed with his trousers on,
One shoe off, and the other shoe on,
Diddle, diddle dumpling, my son John.

49

have been trying all morning to get Mum to listen to me but her mind is on something else, as usual. She says I have an overactive imagination and there is not a ghost of a child living in the attic who came down last night and tried to scream in my face but had no voice. I know very well that I saw a girl making a silent scream in the door of the toilet. And I saw it with my own eyes and I was not half-awake in bed dreaming, which Mum said I was, because I was in the bloody toilet for God's sake and it was so bloody freezing that no one could be half awake.

This is getting worse. Something terrible is going to happen.

I cannot talk to Emily about it because she is very sensitive and she is easily frightened and she has already told me many times that there is something with a big face that comes into her bedroom and sits on her legs in the middle of the night. Anyway, she is more upset about Ngozi sleeping with her in a nappy that sometimes leaks than anything else now. I don't blame her.

Mum's still trying to learn the ways of the Nigerians so now she's got a book from the library called *African Glory: The Story of Vanished Negro Civilizations*. She wants to understand more about why they are always at war with each other. And she's been to see the reverend because he always comes up with a plan. In our case, it needs to be a plan for dealing with warring tribes and genocide.

"*Ek'abo!* Hello!" Mum said, holding *The Story of Vanished Negro Civilizations.*

Joan Housecoat was holding the other book.

"*Teach Yourself Yoruba.* Ooo-er! You're much braver than me. I can hardly speak English!"

"*Bawo Iowa*? How are you?"

"Ooo-er! Very well, thank you! Ha, ha!"

"It's easy really."

"It is, isn't it? Well. Didn't you know they were from warring tribes?" Joan asked.

"No, of course not. How could I? I mean, the fighting started last year but I never saw anything on the *BBC News* about it. Did you?"

"No. It's all about those Rolling Stones with their drugs and that Marianne Faithful woman with the Mars bar. Ooo-er!"

"I know. Imagine that!"

"Hmm. Do you know where he put it? Sticky. Ooo-er! So what are you going to do?"

"About what?"

"About the warring tribes?"

"Well. I know exactly what to do."

"You do?"

"Yes, I do. I spoke to the reverend. He says we are all the same in God's eyes."

"What?"

"God does not see the color of our skins. Or what country or tribe we come from. We are all equal in the eyes of God. We will all be equal on the Day of Judgment."

"Ooo-er! Imagine that."

"So I'm going to have an open house."

"An open house? What's that?"

"I'm inviting them all to tea."

"Who?"

"All of them. The Igbo and the Yoruba. Yes. I'm inviting them to tea and then they can see they are just same. Well, almost. But those Yoruba are very, very tall."

"Ooo-er! Won't that be nice? Can I come too?"

I knew the reverend would have a plan.

50

It does not matter that Misty is not house-trained. If she takes a shit in the scullery it doesn't worry any of us, because we don't use that room except to keep the paraffin cans and the broom and some of Grandpa's rusty old tools that no one has used in years. And if Misty takes a shit in the kitchen, we leave it to dry up and then you can kick it under the sideboard or scoop it up with the coal shovel and throw it into the backyard by the coal bunker. Mostly, I kick the turds under the sideboard. I looked and there are a lot of turds under there, which is probably no surprise because a cat's got to take a shit almost every day.

Cleaning up cat shit is not something that a teenager would ever do. Margueretta says we live in a midden, which is a place where they dump all the rotten food and garbage and excrement. And apparently, she was born for better things but it's easy to say that when you are thirteen and don't even wash the dishes because you have delicate skin. But every day she still beats me with her fists and her nails and she spits in my face until it runs down my cheeks and makes me scream, "Submit! Submit! Submit!"

Mum says she had better watch out because one day I will be big enough to hit her back and I have a lot of pent up anger from five years of being beaten every bloody day. And Mum is right. I will hit her, and more, just you wait. Tonight I promised myself that one day I will kill her.

Margueretta hears voices inside her head. She told me. She said the voices tell her to do things to herself and to me. But I know that there are only two people who talk to you inside your head and they are God and the Devil.

And you would know if God was actually talking to you because it is very rare and it would make you want to join a monastery or become a saint and have a stained glass window made with a picture of you in a white robe holding a dove and looking up to Heaven. But Margueretta does not believe in God so I know what that means. Yes, it means it is the Devil who is talking inside her head.

She says that the sight of a running tap makes her want to scream if it looks like a single tube of water that never splashes. And there are colors that talk to her and make her want to cut herself and bleed. I know that is not normal because a running tap is just water and not something that would make you want to scream. And I've seen blood and I know it's not really red but it's purple but it doesn't make me want to bleed if I see the color purple on a carpet or a wall.

I think that's why she beats me. She beat me again today.

We came home from school and we had to wait on the doorstep because Mum was gone with Akanni and Ngozi. She was at the Young Wives Club at the Methodist Church again and sometimes she starts talking and forgets that she has other children who need to get inside the house because they are still not allowed to have a key or they will lose it and then someone will break in and steal all of our valuables.

Margueretta let us in and there was a note on the kitchen table for her. I saw it. It said to make risotto for tea for me and Emily. And by the note was a packet of rice and an Oxo cube because those are the ingredients for risotto.

Emily asked what we were having for tea so I whispered that I thought it was risotto because I had seen the note. I whispered it because I could see that Margueretta was in a very bad mood like teenagers get into sometimes and I didn't want her to hear me but she did hear me. And she screamed and she said she wasn't our servant and she threw the bag of rice across the kitchen and it burst and spilled on the black floor.

"Not risotto! Not risotto! You are eating fucking cat food for tea!"

Emily screamed when Margueretta grabbed me by the hair and pulled me off the kitchen chair and across the floor by the turds and rice and up to the cat's bowl. And Emily cried when Margueretta pushed my face into the Kit-e-Kat, what was left of it, dried up and stinking of dead fish. And she told me to lick the plate but I wouldn't and she said I was filth and should never have been born and she wished I was dead and she screamed for me to lick the plate. But I wouldn't. So she twisted my hair until my eyeballs popped out and I couldn't close my eyelids and I couldn't cry because you have to screw your eyes up to cry.

Then she let go and I looked at the floor and I could see hair around the cat's bowl but it wasn't cat hair. It was my hair in clumps.

But I never licked the Kit-e-Kat.

And she ran out of the kitchen and screamed all the way up the stairs and I couldn't hear everything she said but some of it was about me being vermin and filth and that I should die and she will kill me.

But all I said was risotto. I think we're having risotto for tea.

And Jesus says we must love our enemies and pray for those who persecute us and he asked God to forgive them when they nailed him to a cross and crucified him. I pray for Margueretta every night. I pray that God will bless her and keep her safe from harm. But I never heard God or Jesus say you should love the Devil and forgive him for his sins because the Devil is the Devil and you can't change him. He is evil. He is original sin. And I know the Devil has come down from the attic and is inside her head.

As I walk through the valley of the shadow of death I shall fear no evil.

51

My daddy is losing his hair and he wants some of mine. He always says he wants some of my hair and it makes me laugh because anyone would know that you can't give your hair away even if you wanted to. My daddy has a moustache and when he kisses me it's prickly and spiky and it hurts so he always kisses me gently on the cheek.

"Come here, wee Johnny, come here. Come and sit on my knee, wee laddie. My Lord, you are looking so big now and so grown up! And all that hair! Can I have some of that hair?"

He shaves every morning in the kitchen and I sit on the chair and watch him and when he is done, he wipes his face with the towel and buttons up his shirt. He always smiles, especially at me, and he winks his eye and puts his head to one side and winks again. One day, he says, I will be a man like him and I will shave with my own boy sitting beside me.

He has to see a man about a dog a lot and that's alright because it is something that I will understand when I'm all grown up and have a little boy of my own, don't you know. And Margueretta never dares to touch me when Daddy is here because I am the apple of his eye and I have the same name as him. He will slap her if she so much as touches me.

He is going to teach me to play the piano one of these days and when his boat comes in he will buy me a bike and it won't even be a second hand bike. And at Christmas he will put up a tree as tall as the ceiling and sing "White Christmas" like Bing Crosby and everyone will join in.

"Do you love your daddy? Do you?"

"I do! I do!"

"But how do you know you love me?"

"Because I do!"

"And have you missed me?"

"Yes."

"I said I would come back. Didn't you believe me?"

"I did."

"That's good! And I love you! Let's sing a song shall we? Would you like that?"

"Yes!"

Would you like to swing on a star?
Carry moonbeams home in a jar?
And be better off than you are?
Or would you rather be a pig?

He touches my nose when he says pig but he doesn't think I am a pig because he knows I am his little boy and he smiles when he touches my nose. Then he swings me by my arms high up in the air and around and around because I am swinging on a star and I am still small enough for him to swing me above his head.

"What do you want to play?"

"Cops and robbers! I want to play cops and robbers, Daddy!"

"Then we shall play cops and robbers!"

"Can I go for a ride in your new car?"

"Yes! And we shall pretend it is a police car!"

"Yes!"

Margueretta leaves me alone now. She's scared of my dad. There are five kisses on the postcard. Five. That's a lot. One, two, three, four, five. Yes!

My daddy kisses me and tucks me in every night.

It's dark in my room but the moon is shining through the window and I can just about read the words on my postcard. And I have the picture of him in his bus conductor's uniform because Mum doesn't want it anymore.

I like to make up stories in my head about my daddy. Pretending he's here.

I know he's not really here but he will come back for me very soon. Very soon, I hope.

52

don't think it's just the black floors that make my mum cry. She cried a lot yesterday. Mum always tries to find something at the butcher's on Saturday so that she can make a Sunday dinner. We don't have money for beef or chicken or anything fancy like that because everyone knows you have to be rich to eat chicken every week. Our butcher knows we always come in at the end of Saturday when he's getting ready to close the shop because you can find all manner of bargains at the end of the day in a butcher's, which is especially helpful if you have a dog to feed. Mum never tells the butcher that we don't have a dog.

But yesterday he didn't have the ox heart that Mum usually buys and I must admit I was a bit relieved because last week I ended up with a mouthful of arteries and they are very rubbery and difficult to chew and if you swallow one whole it can get stuck from your mouth to your throat and choke you. And he didn't have half a sheep's head because Mrs. Arnold, that Irish woman with the nine kids who claims she is a Catholic even though she never goes to church, bought the last one. And the pork belly was far too much money, thank you very much.

"That's a pity," the butcher said. "That pork crackling is a wonderful thing with some delicious applesauce."

And when we got home with the rag end of the mince, which was more suet and sawdust than meat, Mum threw it down on the kitchen table and sat in the chair and wept. I watched the butcher's paper as the purple blood from the mince soaked its way through. I waved the flies away but they kept coming back the way flies do.

I put my arms around her shoulders as best I could and she said, "Oh, Johnny, oh Johnny, oh Johnny," in between sobs and I don't like it when she does that because it makes me want to cry too. And everyone knows, for the love of God, I am the man of the house now but I'm only nine years old and I just don't know how to make money so my mum will be able to afford pork belly.

I think Mum is ashamed. She's ashamed that the butcher thinks we are shopping for food for our dog. I know I feel ashamed.

But she found a recipe where you make the mince into flat pancakes and fry them in the pan and they are called rissoles and we ate one each with roast potatoes and turnips. I didn't tell Mum that I was still hungry because I knew there was no more food left and she would give me that sad look.

We don't have a fridge so I looked in the larder with Emily and we found the same vanilla essence and the packet of Ritz Crackers but they are still waiting for a special occasion. And there is a box of cornflakes but we've run out of milk because we only get one pint a day and there's just not enough to go round.

There's another reason we always run out of milk and it's not because Akanni drinks it. Teenagers drink coffee but we can't afford real coffee, so Margueretta drinks something called Camp Coffee. It's a brown liquid in a tall bottle and it has a picture on the label of a Scottish soldier in a kilt sitting with his coffee cup outside his tent. And beside him is an Indian soldier in a turban with a tray with a bottle of Camp Coffee and it says, "Ready, Aye, Ready!" because it's very easy to make if you have hot water or milk. So Margueretta takes all the milk that's left in the evening and makes a cup of Camp Coffee with it. And no one even stops her and she laughs when she sees me watching her drain the last of the milk into the pan because she knows that in the morning when we get up for school there will be no milk for our cornflakes and that's that so stop moaning and groaning and get to school or you will be late.

So I prayed to Jesus to help us. And Jesus answered my prayers. Right there and then he spoke to me. He told me to sell my stamp collection.

Not just my stamp collection but anything else we can find to sell. So I searched the house and found some things that someone might want to buy. There is the five-shilling piece, called a crown and dated 1888, which my Grandpa left me, but Mum said it would be a terrible sin to sell it because he loved me even though I was only two when he died and he is now looking down on me from Heaven and will know if I sell it. There is also a pocket-watch chain but no pocket-watch because Dad pawned it and now it's gone, like everything else we owned, down his throat.

We also have two oil paintings painted by my Great-Uncle William—they are of Scottish Highland scenes. And I looked at all of Grandpa's and Pop's war medals but Mum says they are all common medals because no one was brave enough on our side of the family to win the George Cross or anything that would be very valuable to a collector. I asked Mum how come we still have Pop's war medals because they were on his chest when I saw him in the coffin. Mum said that was just for display purposes and Nana took them off him before they closed up the lid and buried him with Grandpa for all Eternity. I do not understand why she didn't leave them on his chest if they aren't worth anything. No one else wants them.

But we will sell my stamp collection and the oil paintings and we will be eating pork belly every Sunday.

53

Mum said it was a disgrace, the way that woman spoke to us. How does she know anything about fine bloody art anyway, working in a junk shop in Portsmouth? And to say that the frames were worth more than the pictures, even though the frames were badly damaged in several places, was very insulting to the memory of my Great-Uncle William, God rest his soul, who must have spent hours and hours painting those Highland scenes. And what if they were painted on boards and not canvas? All artists have to start somewhere.

So that woman offered us ten shillings for the two frames and said we could keep the paintings.

At least the man at the stamp shop knew about stamps even if he did look at Mum and me as though we did not belong in his shop.

"We've got a Penny Red!" I told the man.

"There were more than twenty billion Penny Red stamps issued," he said.

"What if it was a Penny Black?" Mum asked.

"It would be worth a fortune. But it's not black. It's red. Absolutely worthless."

He said that the whole collection was damp and smelled moldy and we would be well advised to keep it in a place of constant temperature and low humidity and in about fifty- to a hundred-years' time it might be worth something, which it certainly is not right now. No, not even my complete page of British Honduras stamps arranged in order of value.

We are therefore worse off now than when we started as Mum refused to sell the frames and we had to pay our bus fares. It also rained on the way back and the stamp collection is even more damp.

Mum said to keep my chin up as we always have the refuge-for-troubled-children even if the reality is that we would need to foster at least six more children to have any hope of getting out of living from hand-to-mouth and Jesus knows there's nowhere to put that many troubled children even if we could find them.

At least it's warmer now that the summer is almost here and we don't have to pay for paraffin so that's helping with the food budget. But we are going to have to buy some extra food because the tea party at the refuge-for-troubled-children is on Saturday and we have to put on a good show for all the Nigerians, Mollie Midget, Robert, and Folami—and Joan from next door even though she is not family. Well, none of them are family, but according to Mum, it will seem like one great big happy family under the eyes of God.

We do not have any china for the tea party but fortunately Ready Brek cereal had a coupon on each packet, which could be exchanged for a melamine plate or bowl or a cup and saucer. We collected a complete set during the winter. You can also eat Ready Brek with hot water if you don't have any milk, which is very helpful when your big sister has drunk all the milk. The good thing about melamine is that you can drop a dish and it will not break—ever. This is very useful in our house, especially today.

I knew there was going to be trouble this morning when Margueretta came into the kitchen wearing lots of eye make-up and a ribbon tied around her head, singing a song about going to San Francisco with flowers in her hair.

"It's the Summer of Love! But you wouldn't know anything about love, would you?"

"Watch your mouth! And get that muck off your face!" Mum replied.

"Oh, don't be so aggressive. Don't you know there's a place in San Francisco where you can get free food, free drugs, and free love? We're not your generation. We're renouncing the material world..."

"Och! That's a good one. Material world, is it? We're as poor as church mice, if you hadn't noticed."

"You start wars. We make love. Everything is free in our world. I would go to that place in the Golden Gate Park if I could…"

"Well, you can start by going back upstairs and taking that ridiculous makeup off your face, young lady. You are thirteen years old, and while you are under my roof, you will not be dressing up like a common tart!"

"I'm a woman! In less than two years, I will be free from this filthy midden—free from you and the stench you leave behind you! You vile woman!"

"You foul-mouthed, ungrateful little madam…you've got a lot to learn, and you will—the hard way. You want to try feeding and clothing five kids without…"

"Without a man? Well, you'll never get a man, dressed like a tramp! And when did you last take a bath?"

"What did you say? What did you say?"

"I said…oh, it doesn't matter. I don't have time for these petty arguments anymore. I only have time for love."

"Well, I can assure you that I don't have time to talk to you. I've got a tea party to get ready for…"

"Oh, yes…the warring tribes. I suppose it is the Summer of Love after all. So you're brokering peace while a war rages thousands of miles away. Are you expecting to win a Nobel Prize? I'll have to call the *Portsmouth Evening News*…"

"Shut your mouth, Margueretta! Shut your bloody mouth and get up those damn stairs, or I'll take that dish cloth and wipe that muck off your face myself right now!"

Mum started to move towards the sink where the dishcloth was lying and I know I wouldn't put that thing anywhere near my face because it's a dirty gray color and has been used to wipe up everything that anyone could spill in this kitchen for as long as I can remember. That includes the nappy bucket and the cat's bowl. Which is probably why Margueretta picked up the Ready Brek cup from the draining board and held it over her head like a weapon.

"Throw that cup, and it will be the last thing you do in this house!" Mum shouted.

That's how we found that you can also throw a Ready Brek melamine cup at someone and when they duck, it can hit the wall and bounce on the floor—and still it will not break.

54

absolutely did not mention the leprosy. Mum is of the opinion that it's just dry skin. Dry skin is white and therefore shows up more on black people than on white people and it's nothing that some Pond's cream couldn't cure. This may make sense to her but I think she is just covering up for them. They've got leprosy.

Mum said she thought the tea party went really well, all things considered. I admit that I did ask Mum why it is that black people have such white teeth and she said that it's just a contrast with their dark skin and their teeth are no whiter than ours and I should not embarrass her by asking questions like that so loudly in front of them. But I absolutely did not mention the leprosy even though it has now spread to that woman's arms.

Mum put the Ritz Crackers in the center of the kitchen table. Their time has come, in the name of peace and the Summer of Love. She surrounded them with two plates of cucumber sandwiches, a packet of McVitie's digestive biscuits to have with the tea, and a Swiss Roll.

Mum had already chosen the music for the tea party. I think her choice of the Jim Reeves LP, "Distant Drums," was good because we only have three other LPs, and Mum didn't think Gustav Holst's "Planet Suite" would be very appropriate to warring tribes because Mars is the god of war. And the sound track from *South Pacific* is too racy with all those men trapped on an island thinking about women. And we all agreed that "Puff the Magic Dragon" is really only for children.

The Igbo arrived first and then Mollie Midget and Robert with Folami. And Mollie said that Mum must be a mind reader because Jim Reeves is her absolute favorite and it's very sad that he's dead now, God rest his soul, and she knows all the words to most of the songs on that record, and especially to "Distant Drums." So she sang along to the whole LP.

"Eech! 'I hear the sound...of distant drums.' Eech! 'Far away...far away...'"

And Mum was particularly careful not to say any Yoruba in front of the Igbo because that would be inconsiderate but I knew she was excited to say something in Yoruba when Akanni's parents arrived, especially because Akanni's mum was wearing her full tribal costume.

"Ek'abo! Bawo Iowa?" Mum announced.

"Mowa dada, Ese!"

I was very pleased with my mum because she had no one to teach her those words, except from a book, and Akanni's parents obviously understood them because they answered her in Yoruba.

"What a wonderful costume!" Mum said.

"Ah, yes. It's traditional," Akanni's mum replied.

"I've been reading all about African traditions! What is that cloth?"

"Well, this is a special cloth. It is hand woven...an alaari asho oke cloth. It is the traditional cloth of the Yoruba people."

"Och, that's wonderful! I will get a photo of you later. Come into the kitchen and meet Ngozi's parents. I'm sure you will like them."

"Peace and love," Margueretta whispered and made a strange gesture with two fingers.

This is when things started to go wrong.

No one said we were not to eat all the cucumber sandwiches and Ritz Crackers and there really wasn't enough to go round especially when Joan Housecoat ate far more than her fair share before the Yoruba even arrived. We had not started on the Swiss Roll, however.

Mum introduced them to each other and asked wasn't it wonderful that Akanni's Mum had worn her tribal costume for such a special day? And they just stared at each other and the Igbo especially stared at the tribal costume. Then the music came to an end, and Joan Housecoat said it was far too quiet.

"Ooo-er! Did you know each other when you lived back home in Nigeria?"

"No. We lived in the Southeast. There are sixty million people in Nigeria, you know!" replied Ngozi's father.

And he stared at the tribal costume again and stood up and asked if there was more tea.

"We need more music! Music soothes the savage breast," Mum announced.

"Make love, not war," Margueretta added with a smirk.

"Shut up!" Mum replied, under her breath.

I had to move quickly. I had already hidden it behind the sofa. I had been practicing for weeks and Mum said it would be a very good idea even though Margueretta laughed at me. It was my David Nixon Junior Magic Box. Mum bought it at the Methodist Church jumble sale and the instructions were missing but I managed to work out how most of the tricks were done—a sleight of hand can deceive the eye.

"I will now do a magic show!" I announced.

"Oh God, how embarrassing," Margueretta said.

"Ooo-er! I've never seen a magic show!"

I started with the special David Nixon disappearing egg trick. No one could work out where the egg went and everyone clapped. I had to do it again because Joan said she didn't really see it the first time because she did not have her glasses on. Everyone clapped again.

"Eech! That's amazing. Eech!"

Then I did the trick where you appear to be cutting a rope in half and then, as if by magic, it is joined back together again.

I saved the collapsing stick trick to last. It's all done with my five-in-one magic wand.

"He only knows three tricks," Margueretta said loudly.

"It was seven tricks!" I protested because I had in fact done five tricks with my five-in-one magic wand.

"Leave him alone," said Mum.

Everyone clapped again and Mum put *South Pacific* on the record player even though she said she wouldn't. It's a very racy record.

"Eech! Another one of my favorites! Eech..." The midget woman sang:

> *Bali Ha'i may call you, any night, any day...*
> *Here am I your special island...*
> *Come to me, come to me...*

"Eech!"

"Gather round! Gather round! Time for a group photo!" Mum announced, holding Nana's old Browning camera.

"Peace and love. Well done, Mum. I think you've brokered peace!"

"Watch your mouth, young lady!"

"Peace out. Make love, not war."

"Joan, could you take the picture, please? You don't need to be in it. You're not family."

55

Ngozi is no longer living with us in the refuge-for-troubled-children because she will not be sharing a roof with an evil people who are guilty of genocide, even if Mum did manage to get her to talk and she is now potty trained. The Igbo came back a week after the tea party and took her away. And the Igbo do not wish to be called Nigerians anymore because they are now from the breakaway state of Biafra.

They agreed that it was obviously not my mum's fault that they came from warring tribes.

"Well, it is true that the *BBC Six O'clock News* only started reporting the conflict when our Republic of Biafra was proclaimed by Colonel Odumegwu Ojukwu, may God make him victorious. But a war is a war, and Ngozi cannot stay," said Ngozi's father.

Ngozi put her fist in her mouth and started to cry.

"You can't stop her talking sometimes. Quite the chatterbox, she is," Mum said and started to sob.

"You are a gifted woman!" Ngozi's mum replied, and then she started to cry.

"And she's mostly dry at night, but she does have the occasional accident. Don't you, sweetheart?"

Ngozi nodded and made a frightening low-pitched squeal, like the noise an animal would make just before being clubbed to death.

It's true that Ngozi is no longer in nappies but the other day she did an actual shit in her bed and Mum had to scoop it out with toilet paper. I had to take the sheets to the launderette and I still have to wash them in the machine for oily overalls because even if I don't take Ngozi or Akanni with me that bloody woman knows I am washing things for black people and despite my prayers, she still does not seem to have Jesus in her heart.

"You have worked a miracle with our little Ngozi! She is like a different child! A totally different child, I say!"

"Take good care of her, please, please," Mum wept.

Ngozi held onto Mum's arm and looked up at her, bottom lip turned up and tears streaming down her little shiny cheeks.

"We will. We will. We will take such good care of her."

"She's a good little girl. Aren't you, sweetheart?"

"Thank you for everything! She's going to another foster home next week."

The good news is that before they left, Ngozi's dad gave Mum five pounds for a gas fire to be fitted in our front room so that we do not have to freeze to death next winter. And if we want to foster any other children in the refuge-for-troubled-children, they will now be warm and it would be wise to ask where they come from, unless they are white, as there is a full-scale civil war going on in Nigeria.

"God bless our soldiers!"

Things are looking up. One less mouth to feed, and we will not freeze to death next winter.

Mum is continuing to teach herself Yoruba and she says I would do well to learn a foreign language because I should go to live in another country one day as this country's going to rack and ruin and the weather is terrible. And I reminded her that I have been learning French for two years with Madame Auclair.

I did not, however, tell Mum that Madame Auclair's knickers fell down last week. It's her own fault because she is so fat and her knicker elastic broke when she was walking up the driveway into school. I am very happy that her knicker elastic broke because I do not like Madame Auclair and she does not like me. She says that I will never learn French and I told her that I never wanted to learn French in the first place and I hope I that I will never live in France or any other country that speaks French.

"You doe nat know 'ow lucky you air. I am ear az part of zis special project to get you all out of diz trageek poverty. Franch will become the lingua francas of ooll modern societies. Zis country is doomed. Zat ees why Monsieur de Gaulle said, 'Non!' It will always be, 'Non!' You had better zink about zat, Dominique Mitchell!"

Madame Auclair gave us all French names. She deliberately calls me Dominique because I said it sounded like a girl's name when she first suggested it.

When her knickers fell down, I was playing Jerries and English with my best friend Danny, and he was a German as usual but the English were winning, and Madame Auclair screamed and shouted for all the girls to gather round. We could see her knickers lying at her ankles. This could mean only one thing: we needed to move in close and maybe see a French quim. Or at a minimum, a French arse.

"Fuck, we could see her French arse, for fuck's sake! We might see her fucking pubes too!"

Danny likes to say "fuck" more than any other word and he can use the word "fuck" to mean any word he doesn't know.

Danny is my best friend because we want exactly the same things. We want money and we want to see girls naked. But we can never agree on which one we want the most.

We have not seen a girl completely naked as yet but we are getting close to seeing the quim because Danny has persuaded Cindy and Mandy to do handstands with us over by the bushes. We hold their legs for them so that they can stand on their hands for as long as possible with their dresses over their heads while we stare closely at their knickers, looking from different angles to see if we can see the quim. We try to do this most playtimes but we still haven't seen anything beyond a gusset.

So this was our big opportunity. We moved in for a closer look at Madame Auclair's knickers.

"Aieeee! Mon Dieu! Aieeee! Come close! Girls! Come close! Zut alors, mes enfants!"

We watched her closely because Danny said she would have to pull her knickers up and that always means you will get to see at least an arse. There was a small gap in the circle of girls and we made our move.

We could see Madame Auclair wriggling her ankles.

Wriggle, wriggle, wriggle.

But she stepped out of her knickers and never even took her stiletto shoes off.

"I don't fucking believe it! Fuck that! She's fucking stepped out of those fucking great knickers. Fuck!" Danny moaned.

"You have such a très jolie robe, Madame Auclair."

"Merci, Maxine. Merci très beaucoup."

Maxine was not *Tracy's* real name.

And Danny was waiting for a really big gust of wind.

56

Danny dropped his pencil on the floor seven times in our French lesson. He kept saying, "Zut alors!" That is what you say in French and not, "Fuck me, I've dropped my fucking pencil on the floor again," if you've accidentally dropped your pencil on the floor right under Madame Auclair's desk.

"Did you see anything? Anything?" I asked.

"Not a fucking pube. The desk is in the fucking way," he whispered to me.

"She might have her knickers back on."

"No fucking way! Those knickers were fucked. Didn't you see them? She's naked under that dress. I know it. Her quim is completely fucking naked."

"She might have a spare pair."

"Fuck me, that's funny! No one has a spare pair of knickers, you idiot! She's only got two pairs. One on and one in the fucking wash. Just like the rest of us!"

Danny was lying. We have to get changed for physical education in our classroom, girls and boys together, and that's how we all know that Danny has no underpants at all. The first time we all got changed together he took down his trousers and his willy was there for all the girls to see. Of course, the girls all crowded round for a closer look while I tried to shield him.

"Go on, have a fucking look! I don't care if you see my fucking cock!" he said and wiggled it at them.

Some of the girls gasped.

Danny says his plan is to let the girls see his cock and then he can ask to see their quim. It is a simple trade.

"You've fucking seen mine so now let me see yours!"

So far this has not worked. But he keeps trying. He has even offered Mandy a private viewing.

Danny says it's better to have no underpants at all because then you know you are never wearing any and you therefore know you are naked under your trousers. If you have only one pair then you might be wearing underpants and you might not and then the girls will not know whether they are going to see your cock or not. Although Danny did accept that this could create quite a bit of anticipation from the girls at PE time. Two pairs, however, is ideal because then you've got one pair on and one in the wash but that can also be a problem because one wet fart early in the week and you will have to sit on it for days.

That's what happened to Gary Gibly today. We were getting ready for our swimming lesson and luckily we have actual changing rooms at the swimming pool or the girls would have seen what we saw. When he hung his underpants on the hook we could all see that huge thing poking out like a ferret. It was dried up, of course. He said he did it on Monday when he thought it was just a fart and now it's Thursday and he is going to have to live with it until the weekend or not wear any pants at all. I've never heard of someone farting an entire turd. It will be quite a shock for his mum when she comes to do the weekly wash.

Danny loves swimming lessons and so do I because it means we don't have to have a bath that week. The only thing we hate about swimming is Mr. Hudson. He's our class teacher and he slaps us for no reason at all and everyone knows that a slap on a wet leg really stings.

Mr. Hudson likes to supervise the girls getting undressed in their changing room because he is an old pervert and likes to help them with their knickers. Danny says he wishes he could help the girls with their knickers because then he could see all the quims he wants. That's why Mr. Hudson spends so much time in the girls changing room.

"He doesn't fucking get any you know what from Mrs. Hudson."

"Any what?"

"Shagging. No shagging. Fucking old pervert. I'm desperate for a fucking shag, I am."

"Yeh. Me too."

I am not sure what a shag is.

We've also tried standing behind the girls in the swimming pool when they are practicing their leg movements for the breaststroke but we haven't seen anything worthwhile because the water gets all frothed up. And recently, I have been paying particular attention to Viola Pinkerton because she has got actual breasts. But Danny says they are not real breasts and the only reason she's got them is because she is so fat. Her mum works in a cake shop.

It would be a lot better if I could actually swim because then I could show off and the girls would be amazed and want to watch me. They are not amazed by my three strokes of doggy paddle in the shallow end. I therefore decided it was time to make my move. I would push away from the side and do the breaststroke. This was a huge mistake.

I sank immediately and swallowed a lot of water. And that's when I realized something terrible. Gary Gibly was practicing his leg strokes right beside me.

His stinky bum was being washed clean by the water I had just swallowed. I could die.

57

I don't know if it was Gary Gibly's shitty bum or the sardines on toast for tea that made me throw up. Mum said I needed to go and lie down and stop being so dramatic. That's easy for her to say. She's not the one who has swallowed Gibly's crusty turd. I really could die.

The room is spinning round and round and I've noticed that if I open my eyes in the pitch black in the middle of the night I can see tiny creatures floating in the air. They only come out at night. I don't think they can harm you but it's best to keep your eyes shut tight and keep the blanket over your head.

Sometimes a week passes without a single sound and it's easy to believe that the screaming has stopped forever but then it starts again and a nasty pain shoots down through my stomach. Tonight it is making we want to throw up again.

It's not quite so scary, because Akanni sleeps in my room now. He sleeps in a box bed that folds out of a wooden cupboard. It has a really thin mattress and when he pisses himself, which happens a lot, it runs straight through the mattress and bounces off the floorboards with a sound like a machine gun. He left some Lego under his bed last week. I'm not playing Lego anymore.

Akanni never wakes up when the screaming starts in the attic. Sometimes it starts like a howl, like someone who is pretending to be a ghost. And then I know it's not someone pretending to be a ghost because it turns into the sound you would make if you were being murdered and it's hard to pretend you are being murdered. But still, Akanni never wakes up.

There is something really bad in our house. I think it is going to get worse. Much, much worse. Margueretta says that the thing from the cellar in our old house has finally found its way back to us and is living in the attic. She also says that it speaks to her in the night and tells her to kill herself. Or kill someone else.

And if she doesn't, that thing will kill her.

She said there are other things I should know. The water must never be allowed to run from a tap when she is in the room. Under no circumstances can it be allowed to look like a glass tube. And there are voices in her head that are not hers and they wait for her and they say very bad things. She hasn't told me all the details but they are voices of evil. One of them is the Devil.

I need to be sick one more time.

58

Auntie Dot is so much fatter than I remember. She was only supposed to be visiting for a day but she is going to stay for a week. That's why she didn't bring a change of clothes but it doesn't matter because she never changes her clothes anyway. And as for washing or having a bath, I overheard her telling Mum that she was on her "monthly" and a woman should not wash during her cycle for fear of infection. I asked Mum about this and she said it was not important for me to know and Emily would know when her time comes because it is the blight all women were born for.

Auntie Dot will, however, have to buy a razor and some shaving soap or she will become the bearded lady.

"You can sleep in the front room, here on the couch," Mum said to Auntie Dot.

"Thanks, ducky. You're a real sweetheart. And this is a real palace! A real fucking palace, if you don't mind my saying! I can even watch telly in bed."

There could be a problem with Auntie Dot watching our telly in bed. When we could afford it, I went with Mum to the Radio Rentals shop to ask about renting a television and the man there said it would be fine but he could not rent a television to a woman.

"It is the rule because, unlike men, women don't have jobs, and a telly is a very expensive piece of electrical equipment, and we need to know that the rental payments are going to be made. And no, Mrs. Mitchell, a woman cannot sign a rental contract."

So Mum asked Robert to sign the contract. At first he said no and then Mollie Midget said he had better sign it if he wanted to continue to keep those damned chaffinches in the kitchen. And he said it would now be his personal financial responsibility and will keep him awake at night. So he would therefore only sign for the cheapest telly rental they had. This turned out to be a Ferguson Type 306T black and white telly with a screen the size and shape of a small frying pan.

Our Ferguson takes about seven minutes to warm up before it shows a picture and it keeps blowing its EY86 rectifier valve. I know all about EY86 rectifier valves because the Radio Rentals repair man is here a lot. And he told me that those valves are getting harder and harder to find and our telly belongs in a bloody museum. We must not, under any circumstances, turn the volume up above four. And we should not watch any programs with loud music or keep it switched on for longer than four hours each evening.

So Auntie Dot should not watch telly in bed.

"Those are lovely orange curtains, ducky," Dot said.

"They're fiberglass. I got them from the Littlewoods Catalog. They're fireproof."

"Fireproof?"

"Yes, fireproof."

"So I don't need to worry about smoking in bed then! This really is the height of luxury! Telly and a fag in bed! Now listen, ducky. Have you ever been on a diet?"

"None that worked. Other than starvation! And we've all tried that."

"Well, I need to go on a diet and not soon enough. I can't get my arse in these fucking London Transport trousers any more. I've complained to the Union. And then there was last week. My foot went right through the fucking floorboards in the bedroom. Course, they were rotted, but that's not the point. No, I'm as fat as a bleeding, pregnant elephant."

"Sounds like a diet is the only way then, Dot."

"I tried that grapefruit diet from the telly, but I can't stand grapefruits. Too blooming bitter. So I was thinking I might go on an apple diet. Is there a fruit and veg shop around here?"

"Yes. Just up the road."

Dot came back from the shop with a whole box of Cox's Orange Pippin apples.

"I will begin my diet tomorrow. Nothing but apples. Nothing. Do not try to tempt me."

"You'll fade away!"

"I know. But needs must. I'm the size of a London bus. And look at these bloody tits. They're like carrying around two giant fucking watermelons, and I'm never going to have any use for them at my age, am I?"

"Well, that's right enough!"

"Right, you kids come here. And you, Margueretta."

"Uh?" Margueretta replied.

"We're going to roll Lassie over and crack some fleas, poor girl. This is a holiday for her too, you know."

"Disgusting!" Margueretta replied.

"Emily, you get the ones under her back legs. John, you do the front legs. Margueretta, get the ones round her belly. And make sure you crack them or they'll jump right out of your hands and back onto her."

Margueretta ran out of the room and didn't come back so Dot told me and Emily that whoever cracked the most fleas could have an apple. I won the apple.

And all this evening I've been thinking about whether to do something. At first I thought about doing my David Nixon magic show for Auntie Dot but I think I have a much better idea. It's not a magic trick but it is a trick. I bought it at the U-Need-Us jokes and novelty shop on Arundel Street while Mum was at the Portsmouth Magistrates Court getting a divorce from my dad, which is not something a small boy should witness.

My trick will make everyone laugh, especially Auntie Dot, because she always says she loves a really good laugh. This will be a really good laugh. She will be talking about it for years.

And it will be so much better than anything I could do with my five-in-one magic wand.

221

59

Auntie Dot had four apples for breakfast this morning along with two mugs of tea and three Kensitas. After reading the *Daily Mirror* and having a good long fart, she made an announcement.

"Listen everybody. I have made a decision."

"What's that, Dot?" Mum replied.

"I'm going to cut down that jungle in your front garden. You can't even see the front of your fucking house from the path! You could lose a child in there! It will also be just the right exercise I need to go along with my apple diet."

"Well, that would be nice, but we haven't got a lawn mower."

"What about some garden shears?"

"No."

"Scythe?"

"No."

"A knife?"

"Only the breadknife. And it's serrated."

"Scissors?"

"Just my sewing scissors."

"Well, beggars can't be choosers. I'll use your sewing scissors, then."

Auntie Dot settled down on the path by the front door and started to clip at the weeds with Mum's scissors. I would have to make a move soon as this was the ideal opportunity, while Dot was distracted. Yes, the ideal opportunity because she had two open packets of cigarettes and one of them was on the floor beside the couch with just four cigarettes left in it.

I just know for sure that my Exploding Cigarette Bomb trick will make Dot laugh more than anything in her life. There is a diagram on the packet showing the tiny bomb being pushed up the end of a cigarette. And there's a picture of a man in a smoking jacket with an exploded cigarette dangling from his mouth.

He is saying, "Gasp!"

Auntie Dot will definitely gasp.

Mum has been supplying Auntie Dot with mugs of tea and she has smoked one cigarette after another from the open packet beside her. Mum even made Margueretta lend Dot her transistor radio for the day. And Auntie Dot is singing along to the music.

Silence is golden, but my eyes still see. . .golden, golden. . .

"Fuck these weeds are full of fucking nettles and brambles! 'How many times will she fall for his lines?'"

. . .golden, golden, but my eyes still see. Still see. Still seeeeeee!

"Cowson, that fucking thistle!"

Pushing the bomb up the end of the cigarette in the packet by the couch was really easy. Now I just had to wait for her other packet to run out, which shouldn't be long. Then we will have such a laugh.

"Johnny! Get my other packet of fags, there's a love. Jesus Christ, these apples are tasteless."

"You'll be tightening that belt on another notch soon!" Mum suggested.

"I will. Fucking fading away at this rate. How many apples have I had today?"

"I think it's about seventeen, Dot."

"What time is it?"

"Half past eleven."

"Fuck. I'll limit myself to six apples for lunch, then."

I ran back with the second packet of cigarettes. Dot took one out and lit it. Nothing. Ten minutes later, another one. Nothing. That means there are just two cigarettes left.

"Ooo-er! What's she doing there?" asked Joan Housecoat, standing at the garden gate.

"She's..." Mum started.

"I'm cutting the fucking grass. What d'you think I'm doing? Playing fucking billiards?" Dot replied.

"Ooo-er! Only asking. Why don't you use a pair of shears or something like that? It'll take you a month of Sundays to cut down that jungle with those scissors. Ooo-er!"

"If I had a fucking pair of shears that's what I'd be fucking using. Now, unless you've got any other stupid fucking questions, I've got work to do."

Dot took another cigarette from the packet and lit it and threw the empty packet on the heap of weeds. Hang on a minute. There were four cigarettes in that packet and this is only the third one she has lit. I put my hands over my ears. I must have missed one. Now this is it!

"Johnny! Run up to the Co-op, there's a good boy, and get me another packet of Kensitas. Here's ten bob. And buy yourself an ice cream."

It was almost a disaster, but Emily offered to go to the Co-op. Dot took a long drag on her cigarette and I waited. Nothing.

Then I noticed what happened to the fourth cigarette. It was behind Dot's ear. She had tucked the last cigarette behind her ear. So that's the cigarette with the bomb!

"You know something, ducky?"

"What's that, Dot?" Mum replied.

"This is some fucking paradise here. You don't know how lucky you are living out here in the country with this garden and everything. Some fucking paradise, I'd call it. Actually, I will now call it Green Acres. Yes, you now live at Green Acres. And this is me last fag till little Emily gets back. But I'll take another mug of tea, please, me ducks!"

The smoke clouded around Dot's face as she dragged on that last cigarette.

"Oh, I love a smoke. A diet's one thing, but I could never give up me fags. Never."

60

I t is absolutely not my fault that there is no warning on the packet about the dangers of putting a small bomb in the end of someone's cigarette. And there is no mention in the instructions of the chance that half of the cigarette could get stuck up that person's nose and that the rest of the cigarette would catch fire leaving a black patch of smoke around that person's nose and mouth making them look like Adolf Hitler.

I now know for sure. Auntie Dot is definitely a woman because she screamed and screamed like a little girl.

"I could have been fucking blinded by that fucking cigarette. Fucking blinded! The fucking quality of those Kensitas has gone right down hill. I'm switching to Guards from now on. Fucking almost blinded for Christ's sake!"

I've hidden the other five bombs under my bed. And I'm saying nothing.

Mum has left with Akanni and taken Auntie Dot round to Mollie's to have a cup of tea and calm down. So, I've switched the old Ferguson on so that it can warm up in time for *Steptoe and Son*, which is my favorite program on the telly.

"That was terrible what happened to Auntie Dot, wasn't it?" Emily asked.

"Yes."

"She could have been blinded."

"Yes."

"I like it when Auntie Dot is here. She makes me laugh," said Emily.

"I know. It feels safe when she's here. Here with Lassie. I feel safe."

"What are you watching?" Margueretta asked as she came into the front room.

"*Steptoe and Son*. It's just started."

"Well, I don't want to watch it! I'm switching it over."

"But you were listening to your radio," I protested.

"Radio? What business is it of yours what I was doing? If I want to watch the telly then that's my choice and there's nothing you can do about it. I've noticed you have far too much to say for yourself while Auntie Dot is here. Well, she's not here now is she? Want to make something of it?"

"We were watching *Steptoe and Son!*"

"Shut your little mouth. Actually, I'm going to shut it for you!"

So, she shut my mouth with her hand tight across my face so that I couldn't breathe. Then she held me down on the floor and sat on me and bounced up and down on my stomach and slowly dripped a big glob of bubbly spit into my face.

"Got anything to say now, little boy?"

"Get off him!" Emily shouted.

"Let's see if I can make the little boy cry! Ha, ha! Crybaby! Crybaby!"

She twisted that little bit of hair that sits right above my ears again. She twisted and twisted but I wouldn't cry.

"I know what will make you cry! A Chinese burn! Yes! A Chinese burn! That always works."

She grabbed my wrist with both hands and began turning my skin in opposite directions until I screamed for her to stop.

"Submit! Submit!"

"I'll tell you when to submit! Ha, ha!"

"Submit! Submit!"

"Get off him!" Emily screamed.

"Ha, ha! Ha, ha!"

And the front door opened. It was Mum and Akanni and Auntie Dot.

"Those fucking chaffinches! I couldn't hear myself fucking thinking!" said Dot.

"Well, at least Robert can hear them now," said Mum.

"Right. Where are my fucking apples?"

Margueretta jumped off me as quick as she could.

"What's going on in here?" Dot asked.

"Margueretta was beating John up," Emily replied. "She does it all the time."

"What?" Dot replied.

"I was just playing!" Margueretta said.

"She spat in his face and twisted his wrist to give him a Chinese burn. She does it all the time," Emily shouted.

"Did you know about this?" Dot asked my mum.

"Well, I've tried to stop it, but I can't be here all the time."

"Tried to stop it? Tried to bloody stop it? Well, you should fucking try harder!"

"But she's out of control..."

"She's a damned bully..."

"I've tried..."

"Tried? You! Margueretta! Get here!"

Auntie Dot grabbed Margueretta by the throat and threw her onto the sofa, and Margueretta screamed, and I laughed, but only inside.

"You fucking touch him again, and I will kill you with my bare hands! Do you understand?"

Margueretta looked frightened for the first time ever.

"I said do you fucking understand, you pathetic little bully?"

"Yes."

"Yes, what?"

"Yes, Auntie Dot. Yes, I understand."

"Right. Now, Johnny, come here for a hug. You will never be bullied again, OK? I fucking hate bullies more than anything. Everything will be all right now. If she so much as looks at you, you tell me, and I will beat her to within an inch of her fucking life!"

I love Auntie Dot more than anyone, more than anything. She is my pretend dad, even if she does have a grab-handle for a willy. This is the happiest day of my life. But Auntie Dot is leaving tomorrow.

61

t's dark. Dark. So very dark. The shilling ran out in the electric meter and Mum is gone. I don't know where she is. I never know where she is. We haven't got another shilling to put the lights back on and take the darkness away.

She came from out of the darkness and held me silently by the throat until I couldn't breathe. If you hold someone tight enough around the throat it stops the air and then you pass out and then you die. She let go before I died but I couldn't talk. The only sounds that would come out of my mouth were croaking, rasping grunts.

She said I sounded like a pig, grunting on the floor.

A pig, a pig, a grunting little pig. Grunt, grunt, little pig. Grunt, grunt. Piggy-pig. And she laughed at the grunting little pig. A pig is an animal with dirt on his face.

Grunt, grunt, grunt.

His shoes are a terrible disgrace.

Lying, grunting on the floor in the dark.

62

There is only one thing left to do. I am going to run away from home and Danny is going with me. We are going to live in the wild and kill animals to eat and sleep in a hidden shelter, which we will make out of branches and leaves and bracken. And we will steal milk and eggs from farms and make small campfires to roast a rabbit or a chicken, which we will shoot with a bow and arrow.

I told Danny that I am running away from home because my sister is trying to kill me and he said he was planning to run away from home too because his big brother keeps wanking on his bed. He told him to wank on his own fucking bed but he keeps doing it on Danny's bed.

I said we needed to make a plan but Danny said there was no time like the present.

"That's what my fucking dad always says. Mind you, he's got a bad fucking back. My mum says he hasn't had a job since before I was born. So he just sits around fucking smoking. It's no wonder he says there's no time like the present. He's got fuck-all to do."

We drew some diagrams of shelters and tried to think of things we would need but we decided that it might be better to just run away and then steal the things we need on our way to the woods. So our first stop was the Co-op but this did not go well. For a start, it would have been better if we had agreed on who would steal food and who would steal essential supplies such as matches and candles.

When we ran out of the Co-op, Danny had a packet of pork sausages, a packet of bacon, and some Swan Vesta matches. I had a packet of Trebor

Polo Mints and some Black Jack penny chews. I also had some dog biscuits but that is only because they were on a display by the front door as we ran out and obviously not because I thought they were essential supplies. And the reason we were running out the door and not walking is the manager saw Danny putting the bacon down his pants and he was trying to catch us but we were too fast for him. Danny thinks this is good news as it means that we are now fugitives and will be wanted by the police. So Danny is on the run and not just leaving home because his brother keeps wanking on his bed.

On the way to the woods, we found a small metal pot that was lying by a ditch, which we will use for boiling water or making a rabbit stew. Danny said it was a good decision to just steal things on the way and we didn't even have to steal this pot because it was just lying there for anyone to pick up. But at this point, we haven't got anything we can use to kill any animals like a bow and arrow. But we've got the packet of pork sausages and the bacon so we will be able to have a feast tonight around our campfire and shelter.

"Fucking you know what?"

"What?"

"We should become Blood Brothers. I saw it on a fucking episode of Bonanza."

"Blood Brothers? OK."

"Fucking brilliant. Here's a sharp stone. Slash your wrist and I'll slash mine and then we can bind our fucking wrists together with a vine and become fucking Blood Brothers forever."

He made me go first and I admit I only made a small cut on my finger and did not slash my wrist but he wouldn't do the same even though it was his idea in the first place. He did eleven practice strokes and then said he was thirsty and we should find a stream for some water to drink. It was only because he fell over and cut himself that we were able to bind my finger to his knee and swap our blood.

I am now a Comanche Blood Brother but I am not impressed with Danny. This has wasted a lot of time and it is getting dark.

"Let's start a fire."

"Fucking brilliant. Let's make it under that fucking tree and we can make a fucking shelter by that bush there!"

"Do you want to make the fire first or the shelter?"

"Fire, of course! I'm fucking starving! Fucking bacon and fucking sausages. Yum, fucking yum!"

We will not be cooking any bacon or sausages. It is best if you can find some dry leaves and twigs to start a fire and that is best when it has not rained the night before. And Danny suggested setting fire to the whole box of Swan Vestas to make a huge blaze that would light the wet twigs and leaves, just you fucking watch.

So we don't have any matches now.

"Only one fucking thing for it!"

"What?"

"Fucking eat the whole fucking lot raw. Here's a fucking sausage. Fucking eat it and then I'll fucking eat one."

We also had the mints, chews, and the dog biscuits. So we ate the mints and chews. And dog biscuits don't really taste of anything but they help to fill you up while you dare each other to eat a raw pork sausage.

63

am very disappointed that no one called the police. No one even noticed I was missing even though it was dark when I got back home. We ate the raw pork sausages and they tasted of meat, all slimy and sticky, but they didn't taste a bit like sausages. Then Danny said he didn't feel very well and he vomited the sausages and dog biscuits back up and we went home.

I told Mum that I was now a Comanche Blood Brother and she said I could get blood poisoning and not to be so bloody stupid swapping blood with a boy like Danny who comes from a poor family and doesn't even have any underpants. And then she said that what happened with Auntie Dot was extremely humiliating for her and I should learn how to defend myself and fight back.

Soon I will be ten years old but Margueretta will be fourteen and she towers over me and my arms don't reach her face when I try to punch her in the mouth because she holds me away with her arms and I just swing wildly at her. One day, my arms will be longer and then she will be sorry.

So, as I am now going to have to stay in this house with my sister who wants to kill me and the ghost of someone who keeps screaming in the attic, I need a rapid escape plan. I have been practicing jumping out of my bedroom window but there is a lot of dog shit and nettles and brambles down there and I should only do that in a real emergency. I therefore need to sleep with a knife under my pillow but there's only the bread knife and Mum would soon notice if it was missing when she goes to make our beans on toast for tea. And I am supposed to have a penknife for Cub Scouts but Mum says I will have to wait until Christmas, which is less than two weeks away, but not to get my hopes up.

As a matter of fact, I am not getting my hopes up. I do not want a penknife for Christmas. I have been looking at the Littlewoods Catalog. It's very boring expect for two sections: toys and women's underwear. I always start with the women's underwear and definitely not the pages with those fat old ladies wearing nighties and dressing gowns and housecoats. There are three whole pages of women in their bras and knickers so I stare at those pictures really closely and sometimes you can see a nipple through the material but mostly it's gussets. Absolutely no quims. Then I turn to the toys. There is only one thing that I want for Christmas and that is a Dan Dare Radio Station. It costs £5 19s 6d. Mum says that is more money than she has ever known so I'm definitely not getting a Dan Dare Radio Station for Christmas and don't even ask.

Danny said he is getting a new bike for Christmas but I know he is lying as he still does not have any underpants. But the good thing is the girls don't look anymore when we get changed for PE because they are bored looking at his cock, even when he wiggles it at them. But today we saw something amazing.

Mandy was sitting on the floor getting undressed for PE and Mr. Hudson was putting his hand on her breast, because she now has breasts, so she didn't notice me and Danny staring at her knickers. We have asked her if we could touch her breasts but she always says no and Danny even offered her a bite of his Fry's Turkish Delight bar but she still said no. Mr. Hudson doesn't even ask—he just slides his hand inside her vest and touches them.

Today she was wearing really baggy knickers that I think must be her sister's. I have been trying with Danny to see inside her knickers for months with all those handstands down by the bushes but we still haven't seen a thing. But today was different. Today we saw the quim. It wasn't a whole quim, just a glimpse, but we saw it. And it was a bit of a shock. It was hairy. Danny is always talking about pubes but I did not know what he meant. Now I know—a quim is hairy.

Danny pulled out his Parade magazine picture, which he carries with him at all times, and showed me the naked girl in the picture but she did not have any hair between her legs.

"Fucking look at that! Not a fucking pube in sight! Fucking useless!"

Danny let me keep his Parade magazine picture because he said it was fucking unacceptable that they didn't show any pubes and anyway his dad has got a lot more where that one came from. His dad keeps them at the bottom of his chest of drawers under his socks.

So we have come up with a trade. Danny will show me his dad's Parade magazine pictures and I will give him something that he wants. I suggested a look at the women's section of the Littlewoods Catalog but Danny said that's just for homos and he wants to see my big sister naked and I said that's impossible and he said there must be a way.

"You could fucking do something with a mirror if it was at the right fucking angle!"

"She keeps her door closed all the time."

"Drill a fucking hole in the toilet door and we can spy on her when she takes her knickers down. Yeh. We can fucking spy on her."

I told Danny that everyone would notice a hole in our toilet door and he said to hang a picture over it, like they do in ghost films when they want to spy on someone. This is a completely ridiculous idea because we only have the oil paintings from Great-Uncle William or a small picture of Jesus and the Last Supper, which is hanging in my mum's bedroom. Either way, questions would be asked.

We therefore agreed that Danny could come round to my house at lunchtime and have a drink of ginger beer in return for me seeing his dad's pictures. My mum is brewing the ginger beer for Christmas. She got the recipe from Mollie who brews it every year and gave Mum some yeast and all she had to do was add some ginger and sugar and water.

I will leave the backdoor unlocked so that we can get in and no one will ever know so long as we don't drink too much of it.

64

I am going to have to blame it on the cat. Danny has drunk three whole cups of ginger beer and I have drunk two and Danny says he is still thirsty, which I think is a lie. And at this rate we are going to be late and today is not a good day to be late back to school because Mr. Hudson said we all have to do party pieces in our class this afternoon for Christmas.

"One more cup, that's all, Danny! And when are you going to show me the pictures?"

"Fucking hell, my dad would kill me if he knew I had them. I had to wait for him to go to the bookies. He says you should never back two horses in the same fucking race. You need to place your bet. Mind you, he bets on a lot of fucking horses. Every fucking day. Just in different races, I suppose. And he never fucking wins."

"OK. Just one more cup each."

"Two. Fucking two more!"

"OK. Two. And that's all. Now show me those pictures!"

My hands were shaking as I unfolded them.

"One more fucking cup. Come on. I fucking love this beer. Fucking love it!"

"OK. Just one. And that's it!"

And that's how we ended up being ten minutes late for the Christmas party pieces and ten minutes is enough to make Mr. Hudson have a bloody heart attack and he whacked me and Danny round the head and told us to take those smirks off our faces. Then he told Belinda to continue after being so rudely interrupted.

Silent night, holy night. All is calm, all is bright...

Belinda was singing for us. She seemed more beautiful than ever. So very beautiful.

Holy infant so tender and mild...
Sleep in Heavenly peace.
Sleep in Heavenly peace.

I leapt to my feet and clapped and Danny burped so loudly everyone looked at us. Danny's face was very red and he looked like he was sweating. I must admit it was very hot in the classroom.

Then I noticed that Belinda was frowning at me. I do not love her anymore.

"Sit down, Mitchell, and stop making such a damn fool of yourself! Thank you, Belinda. That was quite beautiful. Now, Gibly. What have you got for us? And for God's sake, tell me you're not going to sing."

"No, sir. I'm going to tell you what I'm getting for Christmas."

"What you are getting for Christmas? That's the best thing you could think of for a party piece?"

"Yes, sir."

"Well get on with it, you clod. We haven't got all day!"

"For Christmas, I'm getting a...Dan Dare Radio Station! A Dan Dare Radio Station for Christmas!"

If I don't get my hopes up, I'm getting a bloody penknife for Christmas and Gary Gibly is getting a bloody Dan Dare Radio Station when he had a bloody great turd hanging out of his underpants like a fucking ferret. You cannot be secret agent Dan bloody Dare with a turd hanging out of your shitty underpants. And how can his mum afford £5 19s 6d for God's sake?

"He can't have a Dan Dare Radio Station! They cost £5 19s 6d!" I shouted.

"Sit down!" Mr. Hudson shouted back.

And for some reason that made Danny laugh and he couldn't stop laughing and that made me laugh and I couldn't stop laughing. But it didn't make Mr. Hudson laugh.

"You, boy!"

He was looking at Danny.

"Get on your feet and give us your party piece!"

"A poem…" Danny said.

"Yes?" said Mr. Hudson, "We're waiting."

There once was a man from Guyana…

Mr. Hudson moved forward.

Who learned how to play the piana,
His right hand slipped,
His fly button clicked,
And out popped a hairy banana!

"How dare you!"

"Hiccup! My dad taught me that one when I was three! Blurp!"

Well, that made everyone in our class laugh except Belinda because she's too stuck up to laugh at Danny. I hate her. I will never let her put her tongue in my mouth again. Even if I have not cleaned my teeth in days.

And even though Danny has told me that poem loads of times before I laughed until I was choking and Danny laughed at me and we laughed together at Mr. Hudson even when everyone else was not laughing anymore because Mr. Hudson was now in one of his rages. And we laughed and we laughed and we laughed.

Ha, ha, ha.

And we laughed.

65

It was Mr. Parsons who caned us. He's our headmaster. Mr. Hudson was in too much of a rage to cane us or else he could have killed us with his bare hands. That's what he said when he dragged us both down to the headmaster's office. Then they gave us a letter each to take home to show our fathers and I said I didn't have a father and they said it's no wonder and to show the letter to my mother.

Danny ate his letter on the way home. He said it was the only certain way to destroy the evidence. Well, he didn't eat the whole letter because it was very chewy but he ate the bit with the address on it and threw the rest in a bush. I told him it was a stupid idea to destroy the evidence because we are supposed to get the letter signed by a parent and bring it back to school and he should have just forged his dad's signature. Danny said he never thought of that because he had a very bad headache.

"It says here you were intoxicated! Drunk! For the love of God, what is going on, John?" Mum said.

"It was the ginger beer."

"Ginger beer? There's no alcohol in ginger beer."

"Oh mother," Margueretta said, "don't be so stupid. Everyone knows that if you ferment something with yeast it makes alcohol. It's called a by-product. And that's why it's called beer."

"You need to watch your mouth, young lady. Well Johnny, I suppose you were not to know. And it is Christmas, and this letter is punishment enough. I will sign it, and you need to apologize to your teacher when you go back."

I did not tell Mum about being caned by the headmaster. And I saved the letter for Christmas Eve, as no one could be angry with a little boy on Christmas Eve.

"Do we have to watch this?" Margueretta asked.

"It's Herb Alpert and his Tijuana Brass. Och, it should liven this house up for Christmas!"

"Herb Alpert is Jewish."

"Jewish? What? He's a Latino."

"Latino? That's just an act. He's Jewish. And the Jews do not celebrate Christmas because they do not believe in the Son of God on account of the fact that they nailed him to a cross and crucified him, you fool!"

"I will not be spoken to like that, Christmas or no Christmas!"

"Well, it's true. Herb Alpert playing "Spanish Flea" is blasphemous if you ask me. If you believe in Jesus, of course, which I do not. And I don't see how anyone who is Jewish could believe in God when they murdered his only son."

"Stop spoiling it. We're not listening to you. Johnny, turn the telly up. We don't want to listen to your sister talking like that on Christmas Eve of all times."

"Well, the story of Joseph and Mary and Jesus in a bloody stable, and the three wise men, and the shepherds is a story for children and simpleminded people, if you ask me," Margueretta added.

"No one is asking you."

"You can't face the truth. What has Jesus ever done for you? I mean, look at this disgusting hovel we live in! It's a filthy, bloody pigsty!"

"Jesus died for you, young lady! He died so that you might live!"

"You call this living?"

I knew I should not have turned the volume up that far. I turned it up to six and Mum was getting angry with Margueretta so she told me to turn it up even louder and I turned it up to eight and that's when it happened. It was like an exploding cigarette bomb only with more smoke.

"We'll never get Radio Rentals out on Christmas Eve," Mum said.

"Well mother," Margueretta began, "it's a Rodgers and Hammerstein television. We shouldn't be listening to anything as *modern* as Herb Alpert and his bloody Tijuana Brass."

"We'll just have to do without the telly."

"Oh, God. This will be the worst Christmas ever. It's your bloody fault."

"This will not be the worst Christmas ever! What do you think they did before there were any televisions, eh? I'll tell you what they did. They entertained themselves, that's what they did."

"Oh, for Christ's sake, tell me he's not going to do his magic show again!"

"We are going to play games. That's what we did when I was a child, you know."

"You can remember back that far? I'm not playing any games."

"You need to get into the Christmas spirit, young lady! We're all going to play the 'Minister's Cat.'"

"Oh, God."

"I'll go first. The Minister's Cat is an *avaricious* cat. You go next, Margueretta."

"The Minister's Cat is an avaricious, *bonkers* cat."

"Bonkers is not an adjective. Bonkers is a pronoun."

"Ha! You should know. The Minister's Cat is an avaricious, *blasphemous* cat."

"How can a Minister's Cat be blasphemous?" Mum asked.

"He thinks Jesus was just a man with long hair and sandals."

"I'll ignore that. Now, Emily, it's your turn."

Emily added *creative*. I added *dreadful*. Mum added *enigmatic*.

"It's your turn again, Margueretta," Mum said.

"The Minster's Cat is an avaricious, blasphemous, creative, dreadful, enigmatic, *faithless* cat."

It's good that X is at the end of the alphabet because there is only *xylophonic* cat and *x-rayed* cat. Margueretta said *xenomorphic* cat, but she didn't know what it meant so Mum wouldn't let it count. We were allowed to pass on Z.

66

Margueretta is going to kill herself, which is a big relief to me. This morning she was in the kitchen by the table and she was holding a knife to her throat and she said if Mum came one step closer she would cut her throat right there in the bloody kitchen. I looked at the knife and it was Nana's breadknife. The only way you could cut your throat with that knife is by sawing it across your neck because it has a serrated blade. That's the best type of blade for cutting bread. We don't have any other sharp knives in our house so if you want to kill yourself by cutting your throat then the breadknife is really the only alternative.

At first, I thought that Margueretta wanted to kill herself because the telly has been broken since Christmas and it is now February. But she wants to kill herself because a voice inside her head is telling her to do it. She also says that something comes into her room when she is asleep in the night and tells her that if she does not kill herself then it will go ahead and kill her itself. It can even come into her dreams like it is real, which doesn't make much sense to me. And there is more than one voice in her head but they aren't people: they are *things* and they are in this house with us but not all the time. But she didn't say anything about a girl screaming in the attic.

Mum told her to put the knife down, like any mum would. And I could smell something familiar in the kitchen, like a smell from a long time ago. I looked around the room but I couldn't see what was making that smell.

Then Mum jumped at Margueretta and grabbed the arm that was holding the knife and pulled it away from her throat. And I was very disappointed that there was only a red mark on Margueretta's neck and not even a speck of blood. I thought it was all over but Margueretta wouldn't let go of the knife and they both ended up on the kitchen floor and Mum got on top of her and held her arms down.

Akanni was standing beside me and he started hopping from one foot to another and then he peed himself, which is unusual for him because he is almost three now and he usually only wets himself in bed at night. So I held his hand and said it doesn't matter but he cried anyway and then he screamed. But you couldn't hear him because Margueretta was screaming much louder. And that made Akanni look like he was just opening his mouth really wide and trying to scream but nothing was coming out. But he was screaming.

And Emily was holding her dress and screwing the material up into a ball and twisting it and she was crying and saying something but I couldn't hear her because of all the screaming.

I thought about helping my mum the way I would if a stranger was attacking her and trying to hurt her. But I was watching that breadknife and wondering if Margueretta would get her arm out of that grip and stick the knife into Mum's throat. And the more I watched as they wrestled on the black floor the more I wondered if someone would die today. Right now.

And then Mum slammed Margueretta's hand on the floor and the breadknife flew under the table and landed by the cat's bowl scattering dried-up turds as it went. I looked at the bowl, all shiny from being licked clean everyday with tiny specks of crusted Kit-e-Kat sitting round the rim. And the small water bowl beside it was empty as always and I wondered how the cat survived without any water.

Mum had to slap Margueretta around the face three times to stop her screaming. I liked that. Mum said they were going to the doctor's because it's not normal to try to kill yourself with a breadknife in the kitchen just because someone or something in your head told you to do it.

"We'll see what the doctor has to say about this, young lady!" Mum shouted as they left.

Margueretta must have known it was the breadknife. She's sliced bread with that knife. She must have known that she would have to slide it back and forth across her neck to cut her throat. And I'm sure that once you've slid that knife once across your neck the shock would make you stop and you'd probably drop the knife. And you wouldn't die from just one cut. But I heard once that there's a vein in your neck and if you cut it you will bleed to death in twenty seconds. Or it may have been twenty minutes.

"What's happening, John?" Emily asked.

"I don't know."

"I'm frightened."

"It will be alright."

"I'm still frightened."

"I know."

I looked around the kitchen and there on the table behind the Ready Brek packet and the empty milk bottles was a bottle of sherry and it was half-empty. I picked it up. Harvey's Bristol Cream. The same smell—the same sweet smell as Nana.

They weren't gone at the doctor's very long.

"Everything is going to be alright," Mum said, coming back through the front door.

"But what did the doctor say?" Emily asked.

"Oh, it's nothing. Margueretta will be fine. Dr. Wilmot said it's not serious."

Mum lit a cigarette, and I could see her hands were shaking. Margueretta just sat silently on the sofa and stared at nothing.

"I don't want anymore talk about this. It's done now. Over and done with. Understood? And the rest of that damn sherry is going down the sink, young lady! I will not tolerate alcohol in this house. And I'd like to know where you got that bottle from."

Margueretta got up, ran from the room and up the stairs, and slammed her door.

"Look, you two. There's nothing to worry about. Your sister is growing up. She's fourteen now, and she's becoming a woman."

"A woman?"

"She's started her period. It's her monthly cycle. That's all."

"What's that?" I asked.

"Women bleed once a month."

"What?"

"Women bleed every month. It's part of God's punishment for the Garden of Eden. It makes us all go mad. Her time will come too."

Mum nodded at Emily.

"Oh."

"It's the blight we were born for. Your sister will be learning all about Dr. White's. Or Tampax. One or the other."

And I watched as Mum's eyes filled with tears and she buried her head in her hands and Emily held her arm. Akanni came over and I picked him up to sit on my lap and he held on tight. As tight as he could.

I have a penknife. It's got two blades and a foldout tin opener and on the other end there is a spike for getting stones out of a horse's hoof. I sleep with it under my pillow and if any of those things come into my room I will be ready for them.

I got it for Christmas.

67

Florie Atkins has been giving me piano lessons for two years now, but she has finally gone deaf. She was hard of hearing when she started to teach me the scale of C major on Dad's piano. By the time I got as far as the E minor arpeggio, she needed a hearing aid, which I had to shout into. But now she can't hear a thing. And we do not have a metronome so she stamps her foot and bangs her hand on the side of the piano to keep time. My piano lessons are very loud.

Mum says I should not worry about Florie being totally deaf because Beethoven was stone deaf when he composed the Choral Symphony. Mind you, he was dead three years later. Florie Atkins smells of onions and perfume and pee and she will be dead soon, just like all the others. I can always tell when people are going to die. They have that smell about them. I will be her last student.

Florie always comes at four o'clock on a Friday, but she didn't come today. And Emily has gone to the Co-op with Mum and Akanni. I cannot go to the Co-op unless I wear a balaclava pulled down over my face, as I am a fugitive wanted for the theft of a bag of dog biscuits.

So now is the time to do it. God knows I've waited long enough. And I had to wait for a time when there was no one in the house because Mum says there is no way I am allowed to go up there because I will fall through the bloody ceiling causing untold damage. But the house is not empty because Margueretta is in her bedroom, listening to her transistor radio. That's what she always does.

The stepladders are bigger than me and made of metal so getting them up the stairs and into my bedroom is definitely the hardest part. Also we still do not have a torch so a candle is really the only choice if you want to be able to see in the dark.

The metal ladders screeched as I opened them beside my bed under the attic door and I stopped for a moment and listened. But there was no sound of Margueretta coming out of her bedroom to see what I was doing—no sound except the radio playing.

The attic door opened by pushing it up. It's just a board lying on a frame of wood. I will have to open it first then light the candle just like I planned. I told Danny and he said he wanted to go up there with me and see the dead child but he's obsessed with seeing my sister naked and it's far too dangerous to have him upstairs in my house this close to my sister's bedroom.

My bedroom looks different from the top of the steps. My bed is right there beside the ladder with the blankets crumpled in a heap. And there's Akanni's box bed with the thin piss-filled mattress and the bedclothes lying beside it. And I can see out of the window into the garden and it's starting to get dark. And there's the German woman's bedroom window opposite. God knows I've stared at that window night after night but I've never seen her getting undressed. Not so much as a bra and knickers.

I'm right at the top of the steps now. I pushed the door and it gave way easily. I knew it would because I've seen it move on its own. Then the stepladders wobbled ever so slightly and I think it's because I'm shaking so much. And I looked up.

The blackness goes on forever like it's too big for the space. I couldn't know it would be like this, no one could. It's a terrible darkness and it feels like it's falling down over me slowly taking away my breath.

Here are the matches, in my pocket like I planned. The candle is flickering with the draft that's coming down from the black space. I hope it will stay alight. I have to stand the candle inside the attic and climb in. I never planned this part.

And something huge is there reaching above my head beside the hole. It's a massive metal tank, gray and stained and crusted with rust and white streaks. I know it's a water tank because I can hear the water dripping inside.

Drip, drip, drip.

I don't want to look at the other things I can see. Long wooden rafters reaching up to nothing. And a flap of something hanging from far above. I want it to be different. I want an orange glow and red bricks and old toys and a chest full of treasure, not the icy black that's wrapping around me.

I'm standing up now, stepping on the joists, holding the candle as best I can. My hands are shaking and it's making the flame of the candle flicker and pop. Everywhere there is the terrible blackness. And the blackness knows that I shouldn't be there.

My eyes are adjusting slightly to the dark and the candle is casting just enough light to see something and nothing at all. I don't know now why I came up here. If that thing is here, it will hide in the corner the way it always has.

But there is a very dim light down between the joists. It's a small vent and if I get at the right angle I can see my bed in the room below. And I'm looking and now I can see another vent and now I realize that's where the sound of the radio is coming from.

Smile an everlasting smile, a smile can bring you near to me...

And Margueretta is singing along. She wants to be a singer or a dancer. Mum says that's just a fantasy.

This world has lost its glory...

I'm going to move over to the other vent. Step carefully. One joist at a time. One joist and one more. This isn't easy, holding the candle. There's the vent. I just need to move a bit to one side and...my God! This is nothing like I was expecting. Jesus, be glad that Danny isn't here with me. I'm looking down through the vent. And my sister is there below in her room. And she is naked.

And I've dropped the candle.

She must have heard that. The candle is out, of course, but there's still the light from the trap door shining in from my bedroom below. Must get back to the door and down the stepladders before she gets dressed and comes after me. One step, two steps, closer, closer to the door.

Great, I'm sliding down from the attic onto the steps below my feet. Thank God I have practiced jumping out of my bedroom window. Down the steps I'm going and I can hear Margueretta screaming. Louder, louder. Need to move faster.

Open the bedroom window. Get ready to jump.

68

should not have gone back for my penknife. All I had to do was climb through my open bedroom window and jump and I would have been safe. But when I turned around from my bed, there she was with her arms reaching out and she had her fingers bent round like a bird's talons and she dug those nails into my neck and screamed into my face and then she slapped me three times and pulled my hair out by the roots and all because I saw her stupid little tits.

And I should not have told Danny.

"So she was completely fucking naked, right?"

"I think so."

"And you fucking well saw everything?"

"No."

"What color were her nipples?"

"Pink, I think. I don't remember."

"We could make a fucking fortune, charging boys to look through that vent and see your sister naked! We will be rich! Fucking rich!"

This is an even worse idea than drilling a hole in the toilet door. For a start, having a line of boys up our stairs and into my bedroom waiting to climb up our stepladders into the attic would be impossible to hide. Danny said that's no problem because his brother would pay a fortune to go up there for a look. But as soon as he sees my sister naked he will probably start wanking up there in our attic and then there is a good chance he will fall though the ceiling causing untold damage. Danny had to agree that it was quite likely.

And anyway, Margueretta has taped a piece of cardboard over the vent.

"Well then, *you* come up with a fucking plan to make us rich! You always say my plans won't fucking work!"

"But your plans always involve my sister being naked."

"People will pay good fucking money for that. My dad always says it's the oldest business in the fucking world, doing it for money. And he should fucking know. He was in the navy."

"Well, I've got a plan."

"Fuck. Now you tell me. What?"

"We don't have a tuck shop at school…"

"That's because no one's got any fucking money."

"Some kids have got money."

"Who?"

"The fat kids."

"Which fat kids?"

"All of them. Like Viola Pinkerton. Have you seen her in the swimming pool? She looks like a whale. But pink. You have to eat a whole week's worth of food every day to get that fat."

"Yeh. But she wants to do handstands with us. I couldn't hold her legs up. No fucking way. Legs the size of fucking tree trunks."

"And then there's Ian Tucker. He's as fat as Billy Bunter. He's so fat he has to get a note from his mum every week so he doesn't have to play football."

"Fuck, he doesn't want us to see his fat belly hanging over his cock. And don't forget Beryl. She's got a bigger arse than a Number 17 bus. My dad always says that a big arse is what a woman needs to keep a man fucking happy. That, and a never-ending supply of Newcastle Brown Ale."

"So that's the plan."

"What plan? Don't fucking get it. What have fat kids got to do with making us rich?"

"We are going to sell chocolate and sweets to fat kids."

"That's the fucking plan?"

"Yep. Fry's Turkish Delight. Cadbury's Dairy Milk Chocolate. Also Rowntree's Fruit Pastels and Maynard's Wine Gums. We're going to sell chocolate and sweets to fat kids."

I got the idea last week when I went to tea with Ian Tucker. The only reason I went to tea with him, and he knows this, is that he has all of the Thunderbirds models and he said I could play with them. Otherwise, there is no way I would go to tea with a fat kid who gets a note from his mum every week because he doesn't want us to see his fat belly hanging over his cock. Anyway, his mum made us a "chocolate tea" because it was a special occasion on account of me being the very first friend he had ever brought home. Everything was made from chocolate. Chocolate spread sandwiches, chocolate Jaffa Cakes, chocolate McVitie's Digestive biscuits, Cadbury's Chocolate Fingers, and Bourneville chocolate drinks. It made me feel sick but fat kids love it.

But when I broke his Thunderbird Two model, the green one with the removable loading bay, he started crying like a girl and told me to get out of his house and never come back. He also said he would not be my friend anymore and I told him I wasn't his friend in the first place and I only came round his house to play with his Thunderbirds. His mum said that I was an ungrateful filthy little brat who did not have any respect for other people's possessions and she was sorry now that she had made Ian's favorite chocolate tea for me to share.

Well, Ian Tucker will be singing a different tune when I show him the Sweet Shop.

"But how do we fucking make money?"

"Easy. We sell the sweets at twice the price we buy them for."

"Why the fuck would anyone pay twice the price?"

"I've thought about that."

The Sweet Shop is made from a cardboard box that I have cut into the shape of a sweet shop with a sign and everything and decorated with pictures of sweets cut out from the Littlewoods Catalog and *Woman's Own* magazine.

I have installed small shelves and miniature lighting. The tiny lights came from Woolworth's and they make the whole Sweet Shop look very realistic.

"Look at this! It's 'The Sweet Shop!'"

"Fuck! It looks fucking amazing!"

Then I showed Danny the secret. I have covered one of the miniature light bulbs with a piece of red cellophane from a Quality Street's chocolate that I had at Christmas.

"Watch this."

I flashed the red light on and off and on and off.

"Fuck yeh. A flashing red light."

"Yep. I will flash this light at the fat kids during playtime and lunchtime and they will know the Sweet Shop is open."

"Why don't you just tell them it's fucking open?"

"The fat kids will see that red light and every time they see it they will start thinking about sweets and chocolate. They won't be able to resist. And they'll pay double."

"But I can only think of four fucking fat kids. We can't get rich with only four fucking fat kids."

"Yes, we can."

"How?"

"We sell them as much chocolate and sweets as they want. No limit."

"What, even if they puke from eating all that fucking chocolate?"

"Yep. Even if they puke. We're not responsible for how much they eat."

69

Some people just don't want to see others succeed. Take Mr. Parsons, for instance. He only comes into our classroom to tell us we are a useless bunch of lazy, good-for-nothing clods and we will never amount to anything in this life because we are stupid, stupid, stupid. Today he asked Gary Gibly what is two minus three and Gary Gibly said it was zero because it was a trick question and you can't have less than nothing. And then Mr. Parsons asked him what weighs more, a ton of coal or a ton of feathers and Gary Gibly said it was another trick question and the answer is the feathers even though he really thought it was the coal. We will therefore all end up as dustmen or on the Welfare.

Everyone knows that Gary Gibly is stupid. Mr. Parsons knows just how stupid Gary Gibly is because he is always bottom of our entire year unless you count Tommy Collins but he is simple and that is different from being stupid. So Mr. Parsons is just showing off by picking on a really stupid boy rather than an averagely stupid boy. And if we are all so stupid then Mr. Parsons is stupid for being the headmaster. And Mr. Hudson is stupid for being a teacher here or he is a really clever dirty old man because he wants to look at girls getting undressed for swimming and touch Mandy's breasts and he knows that we are all too stupid to tell on him.

But I will show them who's stupid. The Sweet Shop has only been in operation for a week and it's amazing how much money fat kids will spend on chocolate and sweets. All I have to do is wait for playtime and then start flashing that little red light. Danny makes all the kids stand in a line and hurries them along when they can't make up their minds. As I suspected, the Sweet Shop works best with fat kids because they are always hungry and they have money to buy cakes and pies and also sweets.

I am sure everyone is really impressed with the Sweet Shop and now Mr. Hudson has sent me to the headmaster's office where he's waiting to see me—no doubt to apologize for calling me stupid.

"OK, Mitchell. Viola Pinkerton's mother was here this morning. And do you know why?"

"No, sir."

"You know very well why she was here."

"I don't, sir."

"So you know nothing about the Sweet Shop?"

"No…I mean yes…"

"Ah! So you do know why her mother was here?"

"No, sir."

"Lies, lies, lies. You clods are all the same. You'd lie to save yourself, wouldn't you?"

"No, sir."

"I'm looking for answers, Mitchell. Answers. Now, did you sell Viola Pinkerton five bars of Fry's Turkish Delight?"

"I don't think it was all in one day."

"That's not the point. What the hell do you think you are doing?"

"Trying to make money, sir."

"Did you know she ate them all yesterday afternoon and was violently sick when she got home? All over the sofa?"

"No, sir."

"You are responsible."

"Me, sir?"

"And Mr. Hudson said you have a flashing red light."

"Yes."

"And you were using it to attract fat children?"

"Yes."

"And you are doubling the price of the sweets? Don't lie to me. Is that true?"

"Yes, sir."

"What did you expect to achieve from this, Mitchell?"

"A profit, sir. I'm using the money to buy more chocolate and sweets. But also bags of crisps and small packets of biscuits. . ."

"You will not make a profit by exploiting fat children! Not in my school. Next it will be gambling and all manner of distasteful things. Sodom and Gomorrah. Jesus drove the moneychangers out of the Temple of God! Out, I say! Out!"

And according to the letter I have to take home to my mum, I offered Mr. Parsons a bribe. That is not at all what happened. When Mr. Parsons complained about me making profits, I thought it was because I was keeping all the profits for myself. So, I thought he meant that the profits should be shared with the school and used for something like the orchestral instrument fund. So I offered to continue with the Sweet Shop and share the profits with him. I did not mean him personally. I meant the school. So it was not the offer of a bribe.

And one more thing. Mr. Hudson confiscated the Sweet Shop and all of its contents. Now, I think that is pure theft because all of the chocolate and sweets were paid for with my pocket money that I have saved for months. He could have let me keep the contents and the lights but he said it was a punishment to fit the crime—whatever that means.

And later today I saw Mr. Hudson outside the Staff Room eating a packet of Rowntree's Fruit Pastels and offering Madame Auclair a Fry's Turkish Delight bar. And there is no tuck shop in the school so I know exactly where he got them.

One day, I will show him that I am not as stupid as he thinks I am.

70

I am disappointed that Margueretta has not tried to kill herself again. The bread knife is lying there beside the bread and most of the time there's no one to stop her from cutting her throat. Mum says she is highly strung and she has no intention of killing herself with the breadknife or any other knife for that matter. That's why we have not hidden the breadknife.

Now Margueretta says that we are all infected with some disease that she will catch if she shares dishes with us. But we only have the melamine Ready Brek dishes so she washes them over and over again even when they are already clean. This is to kill the dangerous germs. And because we put our actual lips on those coffee cups, she has to wash the cup under water continuously for what seems like ten minutes and then she holds it up to the light to see if there are any germs on it and she sniffs it before she will make her coffee. I don't think germs are visible. Or smell of anything.

And when she is running the tap water to wash the cup it is very important that the water must not form itself into a single tube of water that looks like glass. So the water has to splash when it comes out of the tap. She says that all those things are still talking to her and we will all find out ourselves, soon enough, when they start on the rest of us.

Mum said she needs to stop this ridiculous behavior and they even had a fight about it in the kitchen tonight when Margueretta was making her coffee. Mum tried to snatch the clean coffee cup away from her because it is an insult to us all to say that we have germs that she doesn't have. So Margueretta picked up the Camp Coffee bottle and threw it at the wall and it smashed and thick black liquid ran down the roses on the wallpaper and onto the floor and made a small puddle. I think she smashed the Camp Coffee bottle because she knows that the melamine cups are unbreakable. Mum said she could buy her own Camp Coffee now, which is only reasonable. But no one cleaned up the coffee. Misty sniffed at the puddle but she never licked it.

Last week, Margueretta asked Mum to fit a lock on her bedroom door. Mum said no immediately, of course. But when she asked her why she wanted a lock on the door Margueretta said it was to stop something from getting into her room and she said it's something in the house and she's warned us all before but we don't listen and she can't sleep anymore unless there is a lock on the door.

She never leaves that room. She even has a small paraffin heater in there so that she doesn't have to spend time with us. She only comes down now for *Top of the Pops*, especially when Cliff Richard is curling his top lip singing "Congratulations" because she is in love with him. She used to be in love with Davy Jones but now she thinks he is too short.

And because Mum said no to the lock, Margueretta went to Woolworth's and bought a bolt-lock and screwed it onto her door herself. Mum said she would break the door down if she ever finds it locked.

It was locked tonight.

We all woke at the same time because it's hard to sleep when there is a banging sound like someone was being thrown against a door. And it wasn't just a banging sound. There was a terrible screaming and pleading and we ran out onto the landing and even Akanni woke up this time and leapt out of his box bed.

Margueretta's door was closed as it always is and it sounded like someone or something was being thrown at her door over and over. And the screaming. Margueretta was screaming for her life. Mum tried the door and it was locked and she already warned her that she would break it down if she ever found it locked. So she did. The door gave way easily against Mum's shoulder and it flew open with the sudden force and I could see the small bolt-lock broken away from the wood.

Marguereta's face was wet and covered with snot and matted long, blonde hair hung in strands over her eyes. Her hands were bunched up into fists and I thought she was going to hit Mum and then she just stopped dead and her arms dropped to her sides and she stood in the middle of the small room and stared at the floor and small drips of snot fell off her chin.

Drip, drip, drip.

"What in God's name is going on in here?"

I tried to see past Mum and Marguereta into the room. Bedclothes lying on the floor. Nothing unusual there. Dressing table with her transistor radio sitting on top next to a hairbrush. A poster of Cliff Richard on the wall.

She never answered Mum's question. She didn't speak a word. She just stood there in her old, gray nightie, shaking and trembling, staring down at the floorboards.

That's why Dr. Wilmot is here now. He didn't seem to be very happy getting called out in the middle of the night by my mum.

"I've given her a sedative. She'll sleep now. Is there anything at all that brought this on? Anything?"

"Not that I know of."

"Are you sure?"

"We had a row. But that's nothing unusual. She thinks we have dangerous germs that she will catch if she shares our dishes. And she threw her Camp Coffee at the kitchen wall. She also says that there are *things* talking to her."

"What sort of *things*?"

"Water. Colors..."

"How long has this been going on?"

"Oh, she's always in some dream or other."

"No, her concern about catching germs from you. And the voices?"

"Months. Maybe a year or more. She thinks she's too good for this place."

"I've written out a prescription for her. Take it to the chemist in the morning. She should take one a day. We'll see how that goes. We may have to increase the dosage."

"What is it?"

"Valium. I don't know if you've heard of it. Its clinical name is benzodiazepine. We used to use something called barbiturates but this has a much higher therapeutic index. It's also an anticonvulsant. And it's better than barbiturates for treating depression."

"Depression? She's not depressed."

"She is depressed. And we have to get to the cause of it or it will get worse."

"I thought it was hormones. With her periods coming on."

"That's what we both thought. And it might still be hormones. We'll see. Bring her in to see me in a couple of days. I have to go. It's nearly three in the morning."

Mum stayed downstairs and smoked cigarettes after the doctor left. I don't understand why no one asks the right questions. I have been hearing screams coming from the attic for all this time and Margueretta says there is something in the house trying to kill her and she needs a lock on her bedroom door and tonight it is obvious that something got into her room, even though the door was locked, and was throwing her against the door trying to kill her. So they gave her a sleeping pill and no one asked her what happened.

Something is really not right in this house and no one is listening to me. I know I have been up into the attic and there was nothing there but the thing is obviously very clever and it could easily hide behind the water tank or in a dark corner.

And sooner or later it will come back down and try to kill someone again.

71

I have convinced Mum to let me sleep outside in our backyard. We do not have a tent so I am going to sleep in the coal bunker. I have cleaned it out and put a layer of grass in the bottom. There are several problems with sleeping in a coal bunker. For one, some bloody cat crept in through the shovel hole and took a shit on my new grass bed today. I don't think it was Misty because she still likes to squat down in the kitchen to take a shit, mostly under the table. I have therefore wedged the old Hotpoint up against the coal bunker shovel hole. That should keep any animals out.

I told Mum that I have to prove that I can survive like this in the wild so that I can get my Cub Scouts Survival Badge. This is actually a lie and there is no such thing as a Cub Scouts Survival Badge, as far as I know. I do feel guilty about lying but I know this is the only way Mum would let me sleep in the coal bunker and she has even agreed to me having a small campfire to keep me warm and to cook food over. And she has bought me a whole packet of Wall's pork sausages from the Co-op and I can have as many potatoes as I want.

I am going to make things as primitive as possible because in the wild I would only be able to carry the barest minimum of equipment. So I am therefore allowing myself one blanket, my penknife, and some string.

I have not told Mum that this is all part of my secret plan to learn how to live in the wild. I need to make another attempt at running away from home and never return. I have had enough of Margueretta beating me every day but I am also very worried that something terrible will happen to me if I continue to sleep in our house with that thing that wants to kill someone. So I'm hoping that I can prove that I can survive out here. Then maybe Mum will let me build a full underground shelter that I will live in permanently but that will just be another lie because I will actually be living in the wild and will never be seen again. But she will think I am in my underground shelter in the backyard and she won't worry about me being missing for the rest of her life.

Akanni wants to join me because he is now three years old and he wants to copy everything I do. But he's too young to sleep outside in our coal bunker.

Danny also wants to join me but his dad said he is not letting him sleep in a fucking coal bunker.

"That's the first fucking time my fucking dad has cared what I fucking do. But like he always fucking says…you've got to move up in this world or else you're fucking moving down. Sleeping in a coal bunker is not moving up. And he should fucking know."

So I'm sleeping on my own in the coal bunker. It's quite chilly and the sky is very dark tonight but my campfire is keeping me warm and the orange glow from the burning wood is lighting the little area I've cleared behind the bunker. I put two potatoes in the bottom of the fire and they'll be ready soon. But best of all, I made a point on the end of a stick with my penknife and used it to roast a sausage over the flames.

There's plenty of wood for the fire because we have an old broken wooden fence that's at the end of our garden. And it was easy to start the fire because I poured paraffin on it from the can in the scullery. Mum said I was not to use paraffin under any circumstances as I could set myself on fire. So I waited until she was watching the telly. She worries too much.

I've put a candle inside the coal bunker for later because it's very dark in there. It's also quite cold in there. But for now, I'm sitting by my campfire, leaning against the coal bunker, and eating another sausage. I've hooked one of the potatoes out of the fire, and it's cooling beside me. The potatoes are so hot; I could keep one for later and use it to warm my hands inside the cold coal bunker. Living in the wild is better than anything I've ever known. Even better than that time I saw a dead man.

I'm getting into the coal bunker and I'm taking my potato with me. The candle is good but it's so cold in here. I'm trying to sleep in my blanket but I can feel the concrete base under my back slowly freezing me. If I could have my campfire in here, that would work.

It feels like I haven't slept at all but I think I just woke up. I'm sure I just woke up. I'm so cold. I'm getting out and maybe my campfire will still be alight. It is. A few more bits of wood will get it stoked up again and my hands will thaw out slowly.

I can see Joan Housecoat's kitchen window, all steamed up and glowing. They've got a coal bunker too but they use theirs for coal, which I suppose we would do if we had any coal. Their garden isn't overgrown like ours but they hang their washing out on a line like we do. Joan's bloomers are huge, flapping away on the washing line. She has more than two pairs.

The potato tastes good. The skin is burned into a crispy black and it tastes like charcoal. I'm wiping some of the charcoal on my face for camouflage like they do in war films. I don't want anyone to see me. I think I've covered most of my face so now I'm sure no one can see me.

But it does feel like someone is watching me even though I'm all alone by my campfire, beside the coal bunker. I wish Danny was here. He should have told his dad the same lie about the survival badge. But he doesn't go to Cub Scouts. He could still have come up with something convincing because he's a really good liar. I just don't think he wanted to sleep in a coal bunker.

When I run away from home again I am going to ask Danny to go with me, same as before. Being in the wild on your own isn't such a great feeling even though I love my campfire and my potato.

It's strange how the reflection from the campfire makes it look like there is the ghost of a woman in a long, white gown standing beside Joan Housecoat's coal bunker. And it makes the woman who is not there look like she has a yellow face and long, gray hair. If she was there, she wouldn't be able to see me because of my clever camouflage. It looks like she's watching the sparks from the campfire as they float up into the dark night sky—if she was there.

And she looks like she is floating towards me and she's staring at me. And now she's reaching out her arms and howling like a ghost as she comes up to the low fence that separates our gardens. If she was there, she wouldn't be able to get over that fence even though it is very low.

Now she's climbing over that low fence that's only a few feet away from me. And she's wiggling her long fingers on her outstretched arms and floating really quickly towards me. And she's looking at me even though she is not there and no one can see me because of my clever camouflage.

72

I am not ever sleeping in that bloody coal bunker again. That old woman in a white gown floating in the backyard was not a figment of my overactive imagination as Mum said when I woke her up in the middle of the night. She is in fact Joan Housecoat's mother and she is about to die. And that is why she has moved in next door with Joan and she has to be kept locked up because she is a fucking loony and she will wander off into someone's garden and scare the living bloody daylights out of them when all they are trying to do is have a sausage by a campfire and sleep in their coal bunker.

Now perhaps Mum will believe me when I tell her about these things instead of immediately telling me that I have an overactive imagination.

"Ooo-er, her time has almost come, poor thing."

"I know the feeling. I've nursed two of them till they died," Mum replied.

"Two? I can barely cope with one! Ooo-er."

"It's always the same in the end. Have you made arrangements?"

"Yes. I'm going to use the Co-op."

"I used the Co-op with Pop. And Grandpa. The Co-op had a discount on a double plot."

"Ooo-er! That sounds good. But I only need the one."

"I had the same situation. But you can keep the second one for the future."

"Well, that would be Fred. If anyone is going next, it will be Fred."

"Well, there you go. Two-for-one."

"I could never bury Fred with my mother, if that's what you mean! He can't stand the sight of her. Never could."

"Well, he'll never know, will he?"

"He would know. The Co-op account is in his name. Anyway, I came round to ask for a favor."

"Really?"

"Yes. Could you run up to the Co-op for me and get some Dr. White's? The extra large ones."

"Oh, that doesn't sound good, Joan. You poor thing."

"Ooo-er! They're not for me. I dried up years ago. Mother is double incontinent, and I'm going to try to stem the flow at the front with Dr. White's. That's all I can think of. She's leaving wet patches on the sofa."

"It's worth a try, isn't it?"

"Did I see Dr. Wilmot here the other night?"

"It was two o'clock in the morning!"

"Well...I heard his car."

"Yes, he was here for Margueretta."

"I knew it! I heard all that screaming. These walls are paper-thin, you know. Go on. What happened?

"She's highly strung. It's just her hormones."

"Did he give her anything? It sounded like someone was strangling her! I think she needs to take something for those screams."

"She's taking Valium for now. We'll see what that does."

"Valium? Ooo-er! I take that myself. It's good for your nerves. Everyone around here takes it. You should try it yourself. They call it the happy pill."

"I might just do that. My nerves are shot to pieces, I don't mind telling you."

"Well, I'm not surprised, really. Bringing up four kids—and no man in the house. You're a blooming saint, that's what I say. A blooming saint."

"I've had enough of it, Joan. I'm getting a job. A full-time job with the Civil Service. I worked for them before I was married. It's all arranged. We can't live like this anymore with no money for anything. And I need some time for myself before I lose my mind. So I've also joined some evening classes."

"Evening classes?"

"Local History on Tuesdays. And Old Time Dancing on Thursdays."

"Old Time Dancing. Now that sounds alright to me. What sort of dancing is it?"

"The Gay Gordons, foxtrot, waltzes. All the old favorites. You have to have a partner to enroll."

"A partner? What, a man?"

"Yes. So Mollie is going with me. We'll take turns at the men's steps. There aren't any men available. Well, none that I know, unless you count the reverend at the Methodist Church!"

"Ooo-er! Imagine that. Doing the foxtrot with a man of the cloth. Did you ask him?"

"Of course not."

"Sounds like you will be even busier than ever! Four kids and a job and evening classes. Ooo-er! I couldn't do that."

"No one could. So I'm giving up the refuge-for-troubled-children. After that experience with Ngozi, I just couldn't take the risk with another problem child coming from a warring tribe. I've done my bit. God knows I've done my bit for troubled children."

"True. But what about little Akanni? He's grown so much hasn't he? How old is he now?"

"He's three and a half."

"Doesn't someone need to be here to look after him?"

"Oh, he can't stay. He will have to go back to his real mother."

"Ooo-er! And he calls you mummy, and he seems so happy here."

"Yes, but I'm not his real mother. He needs to call me Auntie Emily now. And his real mother is coming over on Saturday to take him back."

"Ooo-er! Well, I'll be sure to come round and say good-bye."

The hinges on his box bed have rusted so badly that I don't know if the doors will close when we fold up his bed on Saturday.

73

There are two plastic Co-op bags by the door. We put his clothes and the Lego and the teddy bear in them. The teddy bear is called Little Bear. We put the sippy cup in one of the bags too but he can drink from a big boy's cup now. He has to call her Auntie Emily but he keeps calling her mummy the way any little boy would. She said he is going away for a while, just for a while, so he's holding onto her dress.

We looked at the thin, piss-filled mattress and decided to let it air out before we fold up the bed and close the doors. The door has a lock but we've never had a key so we can't lock the bed away. We'll use the bed for guests who come to stay in the summer or at Christmas.

And he wouldn't eat his Farley's Rusks and warm milk for breakfast. He pushed the dish away until it fell on the kitchen floor, and Mum never said anything. He drinks weak tea with milk, but he isn't thirsty today. He knows what's happening—the same as we all know. We all know what's happening today.

It didn't seem so long ago that we had his birthday party and his sister came and we put "Puff the Magic Dragon" on the record player and danced with our hands in the air like boys from far away would dance. It was soon after that he asked about being white and why and when and why again.

He thinks I am his real brother and he said he wants to be white like me now or when he grows up and I told him that's not possible and he asked me how I got so white and was I white when I was little like him or was I black? We're all white around here. So it's not surprising that he doesn't understand why he's black. Then he goes back to asking why. Always why.

They're here now. They came in a Ford Anglia. It's pale blue and has silver chrome down the side like a rocket ship and hubcaps like flying saucers. Rockets and flying saucers.

"This is a handwoven *asho oke* cloth from my tribe. It's for very special occasions and ceremonies."

"I know. You wore it for the tea party. Don't you remember?" Mum replied.

"Oh. Yes."

"What happened to you?" Mum asked Akanni's father.

"I was walking home from night school. There were six white men across the road, and they shouted, 'Get the nigger!' I tried to run but they were too quick for me."

"But your face..."

"They grabbed me and beat me with their fists. And one kicked me in the groin, and I went down."

"That's disgusting!"

"Yes. And I curled into a ball as they kicked me. But one of them held my arms back so that they could get their boots into my face. They rubbed the soles of their big boots into my mouth and kicked my head. And another one took my hand and bent the fingers back until they snapped like twigs."

"Oh my God."

"They told me to get back to the jungle where I belonged."

"We're not all like that."

"I don't belong in a jungle. I didn't come down from a tree. Lagos is a city. They wiped the blood off their boots on my jacket. It was my blood. I heard them laughing while they walked away."

"What happened?"

"I thought I would die, and I became unconscious. I woke up in hospital."

"This is terrible."

"They broke three of my fingers. And four ribs. And fractured my jaw."

"Did they catch them?"

"No. The police don't have time for that. It happens all the time in Stockwell."

Akanni can sing the alphabet and he can count to ten. He does wet the bed occasionally but he's dry during the day and he likes to play with his Lego. He has his bear in bed with him at night and he calls him Little Bear but sometimes he creeps into bed with his big brother and takes Little Bear with him. Everything is in the bags; he doesn't have much, God Bless him.

He's a brave little boy. He will stop crying soon, stop begging soon through his desperate tears for his mummy, soon down the road and into the distance in the blue Ford Anglia with the silver rockets and the flying saucers, he will stop crying. Soon, when he forgets all about his mummy and his big brother, he will stop the crying and the begging to be back home. Yes, he will stop soon enough when he forgets.

He's got a bear. He calls him Little Bear.

They peeled his fingers away from Mum and pulled his arms to his side as they ran down the garden path to the car, all in tears, with the Co-op bags and Little Bear. They never finished their tea. And I never heard his screams after they slammed the car door.

I only heard the screams from my mum in the evening and in the dark, dark night.

And the blanket smelled musty from the wet of my tears.

74

No one knows why Margueretta was on our porch roof, screaming. It doesn't really matter. Everyone screams in our house, and you don't even need a reason. But if anyone needed a reason, we had tinned sardines on toast for tea. And everyone hates tinned sardines because you have to eat the whole slimy fish with its scales and head and eyes and tail and bones. And then it's Sunday and anyone would scream on a Sunday because we always have to watch *Songs of Praise* on the old telly. Mum sings along to most of the hymns, especially "What A Friend We Have In Jesus." But I think it was the sardines.

Margueretta climbed out of her bedroom window onto the porch roof, which anyone could do. And it was Joan Housecoat, coming back from the fish and chip shop with Fred's supper, who saw her there and heard her screaming in the dark. Joan couldn't stay because Fred's supper would get cold, but she thought it would be a good idea to call the police or the fire brigade or the doctor.

She wouldn't die if she fell off the roof. It's not high enough and there are bramble bushes on one side but there's a hydrangea bush on the other side and it would be upsetting if she fell on that bush because Mum planted it in the summer and put an old pan in the roots to make the flowers grow blue. She said it was from Japan and was a symbol of calm and tranquility. It will bring peace to the refuge-for-troubled-children, like a guardian angel.

"A guardian angel is sent from God to protect you and to listen to your prayers and whisper them back to the ear of God. It's really good if you've got a guardian angel because God is very busy," she said.

And when Margueretta wouldn't come down off the roof and wouldn't stop screaming, Mum went up to her bedroom to drag her back in through the window before one of our neighbors called the police. I ran after her, of course, because I wanted to see inside Margueretta's bedroom again. But the only thing that was different in there was the empty bottles lying on the floor. Bulmer's Strongbow apple cider. And Cliff Richard was gone from the wall.

Mum managed to get hold of her by the arm and the hair and dragged her back into the room and Margueretta made sounds like she was a dog growling at someone trying to steal its bone, which made Emily gasp a little bit standing there in the bedroom door.

"Let go of me, you fucking witch!"

"Get in here and stop this nonsense!"

"You're one of them! You witch! You sent them here! You fucking sent them here!"

"Get off the floor. Stand up!"

"You know what they're doing. You fucking know! Witch! Witch!"

"You filthy-mouthed little trollop. Stand up!"

"You're a fucking witch!"

She spat in Mum's face. Mum slapped her for that and I'm surprised she didn't slap her sooner but she still didn't stand up. She started growling like a dog again and rolling around the bedroom floor, scattering the cider bottles. And Mum told Emily and me to get out of the room but I stayed in the doorway and watched and Emily looked over my shoulder and gasped again like girls do.

I stared at Margueretta's face as she writhed around on the floor. If I stare at the mirror for long enough, my face changes into someone else's face. It's a much older face and it looks back at me like it is not me. So I don't stare at the mirror any more. That's what happened when I stared at Margueretta's face tonight, writhing around on the floor, groaning like a dog. Her face was old and angry and it wasn't her—it didn't look like her face at all. I think it was the Devil. Yes, I'm sure it was the Devil's face, staring back at me.

Now I know. Now I know what the Devil looks like. He's inside her.

And Mum got down on the floor to sit on her because it looked like she was going to hit her head on something or smash the glass cider bottles as she rolled around. And the growling sound changed into a gurgling, choking sound like a dog that's got a bone stuck in its throat.

Then she was sick and the vomit spewed out of her mouth in a small orange fountain and fell back onto her face and hair and eyes. It smelled sweet and sickly, not like the sick when Gary Gibly puked up his Weetabix at school. And Margueretta's sick didn't have any bits in it. But that's probably because she didn't eat her sardines on toast for tea or else I suppose it would have been full of bones and scales and bread and smelled more like fish than something sweet.

You shouldn't mix Valium and alcohol, even cider. That's what Dr. Wilmot said when he came round later. And it could cause liver failure and violence or a coma or something worse. Mum said she doesn't know where the cider came from. We never have alcohol in the house except for a bottle of Crabbie's Green Ginger Wine that Mum won at the Methodist Church Summer Fête. It's right at the back of the larder, unopened. She won first prize in the fancy dress competition by pinning Heinz baby food labels all over Akanni when he was nine months old. She entered him as a Heinz Chocolate Pudding.

Margueretta's sleeping now. I think they gave her another sleeping pill. Mum had to clean up the sick with the old mop and bucket but Margueretta had to clean off the sick on her face and hair herself. Serves her right.

We need to get the reverend round to say some prayers with us. That's what Mum says. But it won't be an exorcism because we aren't being haunted by an evil spirit.

So we just need to say some prayers.

75

She came to tell us she was dead. We were the first people she told. Mum asked her how she knew, and she said she knew because she asked her to put her teeth in earlier in the day. No one wants to die without their teeth. That's how she knew her mother was dead. That's how we all knew that Joan's mother was dead.

I'm not going to tell them again about her coming into the backyard in her nightshirt and scaring me half to death. Joan said her mother could never leave her bedroom because she always locks the door, so there is no way she could have been in the backyard. But I know what I saw.

"Are you sure she's not sleeping? Sometimes people are just sleeping. I should know," Mum asked.

"Ooo-er, no. She's not sleeping. She's as cold as ice, and she's not moving or breathing. I'm sure she's dead. And her face is different."

"Peaceful?"

"Yes, that's right! Peaceful."

"Do you know what to do?"

"I said the Lord's Prayer. That's the only one I know."

"Well, that's right enough. But, after that."

"I was going to call the doctor. Or the Co-op. I've never done this before. It's all too much."

"You should call the doctor. But you only have a short time. Have you folded her arms across her chest?"

"Across her chest?"

"Yes. Like this. And make sure her legs are straight. And put two pennies on her eyes."

"Ooo-er! I'd better go. I haven't done anything like that."

"Well, go now. And make sure her legs are straight before the rigor mortis sets in. That's a terrible thing. Or they'll be breaking your mother's legs to get her out the door. You don't have much time. Believe me, you don't want someone from the Co-op breaking your mother's legs."

"Ooo-er! No! I…I…"

"What?"

"I haven't cried yet."

"Cried? You will. It's the shock. You will."

"I'll go now. Yes, I'll go now."

"I've got to go myself. It's Local History classes tonight. Yes, I really need to leave."

I don't like this feeling. A dead person is just the other side of our wall. A dead person who came into our backyard even though Joan said she could never leave her bedroom. It would feel better if Mum was here but she's away learning about John of Gisors. He founded Portsmouth. But she prefers the foxtrot or a good waltz.

Margueretta's in her bedroom and I hope she stays there. We haven't seen much of her after she tried to jump off the porch. Well, she didn't actually try to jump but she wouldn't go back into her room because something was in there waiting to kill her. It will kill her one day, I hope. Doctor Wilmot said she should take up a hobby. It will help her to relax. So Mum bought her some oil paints and brushes and some canvases. We have more money, now that Mum has a job.

Margueretta says she is painting two pictures. One is a picture of good. And the other is a picture of evil. She wants to paint good and evil because it's all she knows. Mum says it's all nonsense and she should paint some flowers or a tree like anyone else would. But Margueretta says she's seen things that other people haven't seen and she knows things that we don't know and it all comes down to good and evil.

And even though everyone tells her that it's all in her mind, she says that's just the way some people see things and that terrible thing, that thing that talks to her, can even come into her mind and control her thoughts if it wants to. So saying it's all in her mind doesn't make it better because sometimes the thing is in her mind. And sometimes it's in her room.

I'm sure it's the thing from the cellar. Margueretta was the first one to tell me about it. Now it's here, like she said. It followed us here. It lives in the attic or the toilet and it goes into her room in the night. It will kill her first. But that won't be the end of it.

He hasn't been here yet but the reverend has agreed to come round to our house. He will say prayers but he won't do an exorcism, even though Mum didn't ask for one, because he says that's not something that he could do without permission even if we wanted one. And if Margueretta is possessed by an evil spirit then we should join hands and say prayers together and that should help but only if she joins in with us. But Margueretta still doesn't believe in God. She says God was invented to make us feel better and Jesus was just a man in sandals with long hair. I told her she's wrong but she says I'm just a stupid little boy who only believes what I'm told. And she said when we die we just rot in the grave and maggots will eat our eyes and swarms of flies will be all that's left and nothing more. I think that's why Mum wants to be cremated.

But if we all die and that's the end of it then I don't know where ghosts come from or that thing that comes into her room and can even get inside her mind or why the toilet handle swings on its own when there's no one around or who is screaming in the attic. Or the thing in the corner of the cellar in our old house, black and cold, and the drip, drip, drip. And the creatures that knocked inside the walls. Nana said they would stop once someone died. But they kept knocking even after Pop was dead. Nana said that means someone else is going to die.

Mum forgot to make us our tea tonight before she left. She always forgets things. She put the kettle in the oven last week and nearly went bonkers trying to find it to make some tea for her and Joan. Then she went to work in her slippers and didn't notice until she was on the Number 45 bus, the green one. And she talks to herself all the time. No one knows what she is saying.

So tonight after Joan left, we told Mum we were hungry and she told Margueretta to come down from her room and make some chips. But Margueretta waited until Mum was gone to evening classes and told me I was a pathetic little boy who could go hungry and when I complained she slapped me round the face and went back to her room. All I said was I'm hungry. God knows I want to get bigger. Just big enough so my arms can reach her and I can slap her back across her fucking face. Or punch her in the mouth. God knows.

Anyway, my arms are long enough to get the chip pan down from the cabinet. It's full of hardened fat and bits of old chips and things that probably shouldn't be in the pan but it doesn't matter. Mum heats up the fat until it boils and makes the chips and then she leaves the pan to cool and the fat goes hard. I've watched her do it so I know what to do, even though I've never made chips before.

I've cut the potatoes up into chips with the bread knife and you have to be really careful not to cut a finger off because the potatoes are wet and the breadknife slips everywhere and you have to saw it to cut through the potatoes. I put the pan on the gas stove first, of course, so that the fat would be really hot by the time I cut the chips. It's really hot now and the little bits of old chips are popping and jumping about in the boiling fat.

Emily thinks we should wait until Mum comes home but sometimes Mum goes out afterwards with her friends from evening classes and doesn't come home until we are in bed and we're not allowed to stay up after nine o'clock. So Emily spread some margarine on the bread so that we can have some chip butties.

I've put the cut chips into a cereal bowl so I can pour them into the hot fat. We will use the fish slice to get them out once they are nice and golden. You have to wait for them to cool down but we will put them on the bread

THE ATTIC

first and they will make the margarine melt with the fat and that's the best part. And it will be delicious. I'm so hungry.

The gas flame is blue and yellow and it's the only thing lighting up the kitchen now that the shilling has run out in the meter and the electricity has gone off. It's very dark in here. Emily says it's a good thing we don't have an electric stove or we wouldn't be able to finish cooking our chips for tea. But we've lit a candle from the gas flame and stood it on the side by the stove to help us see.

And now I'm pouring the chips into the fat and my face is just about at the right height to see into the pan and the boiling fat glistening and popping by the light of the candle.

76

t stabs like someone is sticking a knife into my face. It was the water that drained from the chips into the bottom of the cereal bowl that made the fat explode over my face the way it did. You're not supposed to pour water into boiling fat. Dr. Wilmot says I'm lucky I didn't lose my eye but he thinks it will be some time before we will know if my face will be scarred for life. We never ate the chips.

Mum shouted at Margueretta when she came home but it didn't do any good. She told Mum to look after her own bloody little brats and she shouldn't be out every night doing the Gay Gordons and learning about the history of fucking Portsmouth.

Danny thinks our house is possessed.

"How can I be expected to look at your fucking face? It's fucking horrible. My dad always says he's not just a pretty face but he's fucking ugly if you ask me. Did it hurt?"

"Of course, it fucking hurt! Anyway, the doctor said he hopes the scars will go away."

"If they don't, they'll call you 'Scarface' all your fucking life. Fucking Scarface!"

"Thanks."

"Sorry."

"It's alright. I hate my sister. It's her fault."

"Let's fucking kill her!"

"She's going to kill herself. Sooner or later. Or that thing will kill her that comes into her room."

"That's a fucking poltergeist! My dad's got a fucking book about poltergeists. I fucking told you all about that! It threw boiling fat in your fucking face. Have you fucking seen it? The poltergeist?"

"No. But I've heard it. It screams up in the attic."

"Let's fucking go up there!"

"I've told you. I've been up there. There's nothing. Just a water tank."

"And a fucking vent where we can spy on your naked sister!"

"It's still got cardboard over it."

"Fuck it. Anyway, I wouldn't want to be you. No fucking way. You need to get the fuck out of that house. Soon. I'm tellin' you. It's fucking haunted. Haunted by an evil poltergeist."

"I know."

The Darkness

The Haunted House, England
March 1969

77

She was crying in the front room when we came home this afternoon. We knew that wasn't right because she should be at work and we should be coming home to an empty house after school. And she wouldn't stop crying even when Emily asked Mum what was wrong. She just said it was our sister.

I have a nightmare some nights. It's always the same. A giant black cloak smothers my face and slowly suffocates me. I can't scream of course. People who scream have mouths but I just have skin beneath my nose where my mouth should be and then it pulls apart and bursts open and out comes the scream like a massive swarm of black flies. But it doesn't make a sound.

Sometimes I get that feeling during the day. It comes into my head for a tiny moment like a glimpse of someone who's behind my back and I know what it is and I wait for the feeling of the big black cloak. I got that feeling today when Mum was crying in the front room and she kept saying it was our sister who was upstairs where the music was coming from.

I hate that song—Mary Hopkin singing, "Those Were the Days." She was on *Opportunity Knocks*. Mum doesn't like Hughie Green because he has a fake smile and a fake accent. Margueretta thinks she's Mary Hopkin. She sings that bloody song all the time like she's famous.

But it isn't her singing the song—it's the radio.

It was Emily who said we should go up the stairs and I followed her even though I thought Mum should tell us why she was crying and what was going on. And it was Emily who pushed Margueretta's bedroom door open because it was only ajar and we could hear that song from inside. But Margueretta wasn't in the room. I looked around and there was a picture of a man propped up on the dressing table. It was an oil painting.

So we turned around and walked back towards the stairs and that's when I noticed that the toilet door was closed. That's where she was. We could hear the toilet chain being pulled and it had to be her inside.

The toilet door handle started to turn.

We stepped back even though the door opens inward and there was no reason to step back. But we stepped back. And the toilet door opened slowly inwards and her hand came around the frame. And then her shoulder.

Mum should have warned us.

Emily gasped and stepped back again and that made me step back even further and my foot hovered over that space at the top of the stairs, looking for solid ground, but I grabbed the banister and stopped myself from toppling down. And I could feel the air being sucked from all around us as the door swung back to show us her face and I forgot about my face and the boiling fat and the stabbing pains that wouldn't stop.

Emily's gasp became a scream.

We could hear the water flushing in the toilet and see the green rubber handle swinging and twitching on the end of the long rusty chain. Swinging and twitching. And I could smell the vomit, sweet like before.

Red and brown lacerations ran down her face and neck, torn in finger-width lines, one eye slightly closed and black. Congealed blood sat in broken dried-up streams. What was left of the skin on her face was yellow and blue and wrinkled like the crêpe paper we use at school. Her hair was matted and glued into the crusty blood. And a slimy trail of vomit curled down from the edge of her lips to her neck.

"What are you looking at?" Margueretta shouted.

And the curl of vomit dripped from her chin.

Drip, drip, drip.

78

A policeman came round to our house last night. There's nothing unusual about that. There are two of us in this house with scarred faces. My scabs are starting to peel off in long strands and it's leaving thick brown stains on my skin and Danny was right because people are calling me Scarface. I think Emily will be next, which is a shame because she is very pretty.

The policeman said there would be no charges. Not now. It was a fight, he said. A terrible fight.

Everyone hopes that our scars will heal: the scars on my face from the boiling fat that Danny says was thrown into my face by a poltergeist; and the scars on Margueretta's face from the thing that tried to kill her. Yes, everyone hopes the scars will heal.

I think it was that thing that comes into her room. That's why there are no charges. You can't arrest a poltergeist.

Mum is smoking a lot more Kensitas now and her hands shake all the time. She always says it's the black floors and she told us she has to get out of this house to save her sanity. I hate this house too. But there's nowhere to go. There's never anywhere to go.

Margueretta told us that she has a surprise. Something we all should see. I'd like to surprise her. I would creep up behind her and swing from her hair as I pull her down to the ground and beat her face until she begs me to stop but I won't stop and then I'll twist her ears and spit in her mouth. A great big glob of slimy spit. And would I laugh—I would laugh so much she would think I was laughing at one of Auntie Dot's really good farts. But

I'd be laughing at her, the fucking bitch, retching on the floor from where I punched her full force in the stomach.

I think the best surprise would be if she packed a bag and bloody-well moved out. She is fifteen now and she says she's a woman so she should just fuck off and never come back. Or she could buy a real knife and cut her own head off. That would also be a very nice surprise. Then maggots can eat her eyes out because she doesn't believe in God.

And now she thinks she's an artist and we need to see her paintings. They're the paintings of good and evil that she's been working on in her room all this time. But she doesn't want to show us the picture of good because she says that is private between her and her lover, whoever he is. And no, her lover is not Cliff Richard because he is not someone a woman like her could love. So she just wants us to see the picture of evil.

That's why we are all in the kitchen waiting. And Margueretta is there with the picture behind her back ready to surprise us because God knows it's all about what Margueretta wants.

"Before I show you this, have you thought about something?" Margueretta begins.

"What?" Mum replies, dragging on her Kensitas.

"With all of your children being born on the same day?"

"So what?"

"All born on the sixth of January. Three children born on the same day. The sixth. It's a sign."

"A sign of what?"

"The Devil. We're the Devil's children."

"I won't have you saying that in this house. The sixth is the Epiphany. It's the Twelfth Night. That's when the Wise Men came to..."

"I don't know why you believe in all that childish nonsense. And if they were so wise, why did they arrive twelve days late?"

"You'll be sorry you said that, one day! One day—when you need God."

"Never mind. He'll need me first. 666. Devil's children. You gave birth to the Devil's children. Weren't you born on the sixth too? The sixth of June. Two more sixes. That proves it."

"What does that prove, exactly?"

"There was Mary and Jesus. She was a commoner. A human. God impregnated her. The immaculate conception. 'Without any stain.' The virgin birth. Ha, bloody ha!"

"You blasphemous little minx!"

"So there was Mary and Jesus. And there was you and the Devil. Making Satan's spawn."

"You're not too big to get the back of my hand across your face…"

"Oh, don't be so Neanderthal. Anyway, I've painted a picture of the thing that wants to kill me. It's a manifestation of evil. And all of you need to see it."

"I've no interest in your picture of evil."

"Well, you are evil!"

"What? What? Honor thy father and mother! I'm your bloody mother for the love of God! Apologize for saying I am evil!"

"But you are evil. I can't change that. I would be lying."

"You will go to hell for that."

"Oh, no. I'm not *going* to hell. I'm already *in* hell. You fucking created it! Now look at this bloody picture!"

Mum was the first to scream. She dropped her teacup on the kitchen floor and it rolled around in the turds. Then Emily ran from the room.

It's better not to describe that picture. Better not to have painted it in the first place. Better one day to burn it before it comes to life and kills us in our beds while we dream of giant black cloaks over our heads, smothering us, and screams like swarms of flies flying out of our silent mouths and blood bursting from our maggot-filled eyes.

That's why the other people left. The gypsies. They left in the night without a word; they left behind a cat that starved to death in the scullery— and a girl who screams in the attic.

But something much, much worse followed us from the old cellar. And now we have a picture of it.

79

What do you expect to happen if you lock your teacher in a cupboard all afternoon? That's a long time for a spinster to be locked up who's claustrophobic and needs to pee. So Margueretta has been expelled. Now she can be a real woman with a job and everything.

But something incredible happened. Something incredible happened last night.

Mum was out doing the foxtrot when Margueretta came into the front room with her transistor radio and switched the telly off when Emily and me were trying to watch *Steptoe and Son*. She knows that's still our favorite program on the telly. And she sat there listening to "Windmills of Your Mind" on her radio and singing along with that stupid smirk on her face.

Like a circle in a spiral. . .like a wheel within a wheel. . .

I told her to stop and she came over and swung her arm out wide, and there was that bony hand swinging in a huge arc—about to slap my face. I could feel the sting before it struck, and then there it was, sharp and intense and as normal as ever. Normal, because that is how it is every day. Every fucking day. Always the same stinging slap and the hideous laugh.

And she went for another strike, nothing unusual there. But I caught hold of her wrist.

I could see that look, ready to beat me again, ready as she always has been to beat the little boy every godforsaken day of his pathetic life until he ran and hid under the blankets in his room—or anywhere to get away from her. Ready to lock him in the cellar where he counted to one thousand and said the Lord's Prayer in the utter blackness with the drip, drip, drip. "Our Father, which art in Heaven, hello be thy name," eyes shut tight. Ready to twist his hair out by the roots and spit in his face and make him eat cat food when all he said was, "I think we are having risotto for tea."

Ready—and no one to stop her. No one, ever, to stop her.

But I held on tight to her wrist and twisted it, and I realized something. Something incredible. Something I had never known in my life before. I was stronger than her. So I stood up and pushed her backwards, and she looked angrier than I'd ever seen. She clenched her fingers to dig her nails into my neck. But she didn't look angry when I clenched my hand into a fist, pulled back my arm, and slammed my fist into her evil mouth with the strength of ten thousand beatings. And it wasn't enough, I wanted more, even though blood burst from her lips. So I swung my arm again and punched her in the face a second time.

Now, she didn't look angry. She looked terrified. A final punch to the side of the head knocked her flying, and she ran out of the room and left her transistor radio playing on the sofa.

Like a circle in a spiral,
Like a wheel within a wheel,
Never ending or beginning,
On an ever spinning reel...

So I turned it off, and we watched *Steptoe and Son*. And I could feel all the blood in my body boiling with rage and racing and pumping and making me feel alive. And it felt amazing. Really, really, totally fucking amazing.

I don't need anyone now. There never was anyone to stop her. No Nana, no Pop, no Dad, no Mum, no God. No one. But now I am eleven, and I have myself. I will never need anyone in this world again.

Never, never, never.

80

The police have a little flashing blue light on a big board with a map of our street. That blue light marks The Mitchell House, and every time someone calls the police to come to our house, which they do every night because someone is obviously being murdered again, they know instantly where to dispatch the squad car with the dogs and guns. And the helicopter. I can picture it in my head.

The police are here most nights now. Well, generally it's Constable Ferguson, and he has a cup of tea and a cigarette with Mum and asks people to please stop calling him out just because there is a lot of screaming and shouting and banging and smashing and more screaming. If this wasn't a violent council estate, then he would understand. But there are burglaries and muggings and more important things to deal with, and he doesn't have an hour every night to come to The Mitchell House.

Except when something really serious happens.

"So she was fucking running down the middle of the fucking road fucking naked?" Danny asked.

"No. I told you. She was in her underwear," I replied.

"No fucking way! With her fucking little titties out, fucking bouncing around?"

"No. She was wearing her bra and knickers."

"And her fucking panties fell down round her fucking ankles, right?"

"No."

"She's a fucking loony if you ask me. What the fuck was she doing?"

"Trying to get run over by a bus."

"Fuck. That would be amazing to see! Imagine the fucking blood and guts!"

"Well, she didn't get run over. The bus driver stopped the bus."

"Pity."

She's seeing a psychiatrist now. Dr Wilmot said it's gone beyond the scope of a family doctor, and she's already taking the maximum prescription of Valium, and it's obviously not working any more. Mum's taking the Valium too, but I don't think she's told Dr. Wilmot.

The psychiatrist is called Dr. Browning, and he asked to see Emily and me too. He asked me what I thought about all of this palaver with my older sister, and I said nothing really because now I can beat the shit out of her if she so much as looks at me the wrong way. I never told him that. I just said I was fine, and that's all. He said it's nothing for me to worry about, and everything will be all right once they find out what is wrong with Margueretta.

She's got a job at the Tampax factory. It's just up the road. I asked Mum what they make, and she said it's for women when they get their monthly period and bleed. Danny said that women stuff a Tampax up their fucking quim, and it gives them an orgasm. An orgasm is a feeling you get like when you climb a rope and it rubs on your cock and you get all the way to the top of the rope and nearly fall off because it feels so good. That's what Danny says. Women don't have a cock, of course, they have a quim; but it's the same feeling. Anyway, she's working on the tampon production line, and Mum says that's a good thing because the Devil makes work for idle hands, and you can't be too idle making tampons on the production line at the Tampax factory.

They're going to do some tests on Margueretta, but Mum said it can't hurt to have the reverend round so that's why he came over.

"An exorcism is not my decision alone," he explained.

"Oh, I don't think we need an exorcism."

He was sitting with Mum in the front room, holding her hand.

"We should always look first to the love of Jesus Christ, our Lord. We should take the Holy Sacraments together. The blood of Christ. The body of Christ. I have always found that works best. We will bring the love of Jesus, our savior, into this home."

"Thank you," Mum replied.

"The Holy Trinity is no match for the Devil! Father, Son, and the Holy Spirit will be here with you. Where is Margueretta?"

"She's upstairs in her room. She doesn't..."

"Doesn't what?"

"She doesn't believe in God. I'm sorry."

"We all lose our way at some point in our lives. My own faith has wavered. Yes, it is true. But it passes. We all find our way home to our Lord eventually."

"What should we do?"

"Well, if she isn't coming down, we should pray together. The Holy Spirit will enter her body and her mind."

We all knelt on the black floor.

> *Our Father, which art in Heaven,*
> *Hallowed be thy name.*
> *Thy Kingdom come,*
> *Thy will be done,*

> *On earth as it is in Heaven.*

I could have done that. And I could have told him he's wasting his time with that prayer. You need a Guardian Angel to whisper your prayers into the ear of God. God's busy with famine, pestilence, war, hatred, destruction, and death. And the Devil. But if God is All Powerful, why doesn't He just take away our desire to make war and kill people? For that matter, why doesn't He take away evil thoughts altogether? And send rain when there's a drought. And kill the locusts. And kill the Devil. But then people wouldn't pray to Him. And then we wouldn't need God or Guardian Angels.

And since He is the Great Creator and He made everything, did He make the Devil? And if He didn't make the Devil, who did? Is there another Creator? And that whole episode in the Garden of Eden does not make any sense at all. Everything was going really well in the Garden because God created it. Then Eve offers Adam an apple, which is really a serpent, and he eats it. And that's the origin of all sin. So a woman tempted a man, and he couldn't resist. The apple is a symbol of sin, even though it's really a serpent. But God made us *and* the apple that's really a serpent. So it's all His fault. And all this does is prove that we are pathetic weak mortals, which is how He made us. Because He is God.

Give us this day our daily bread,
And forgive us our trespasses,
As we forgive them that trespass against us,
And lead us not into temptation,
But deliver us from evil.

Deliver us from evil. That's when Margueretta burst into the front room.

"You have to save me!" she screamed.

"What from?" asked the reverend.

"Up there! In my room! You have to save me!"

"She talks nonsense like this all the time," Mum responded.

"Come and sit here," the reverend suggested.

"Can you help me?" Margueretta pleaded.

"God can help you, Margueretta. Will you take God into your heart?"

"You have to help me!"

"I will, child, I will. Hold my hand. We will pray together..."

The Lord is my shepherd; I shall not want.
He maketh me to lie down in green pastures,
He leadeth me beside still waters...

The reverend never finished the Twenty-third Psalm. He was just at the part about *"Yea, though I walk through the valley of the shadow of death"* when she jumped up and screamed.

"What is it, my child?"

She never answered. She ran out of the house, slamming the front door.

"She thinks there's something in this house that wants to kill her," Mum said.

"This is the Devil's work."

"She painted it," said Mum.

"What?"

"She painted a picture of the thing that comes into her room. The thing that wants to kill her."

"Really? Do you have the picture? It is important that I see it. I must see it now."

81

The reverend said we should burn that picture immediately.

"Take the Devil from this house and burn it. Burn it! I smell the brimstone. Forty days in the wilderness could not tempt our Savior. Destroy the Devil! Out, I say! Out with this evil incarnation of Lucifer! Get behind me, vile being! God deliver us from this power of darkness!"

Out! Out! Out!

I knew he should have done an exorcism.

And the other picture, the picture of good, is in fact a portrait of Margueretta's headmaster with whom she is now in love. He is fifty, and she is fifteen; that is disgusting, immoral, and illegal, even if she does look very grown up for her age. And she wants to run away with him even though he is married with four kids. She is sure that he is also in love with her because he stared at her legs when he was telling her she was expelled. And she was staring at his crotch because he is a real man. She has written a poem about him, but we are not allowed to read it.

Lots of men stare at my sister because she is very pretty, wears really high heels, and extremely short miniskirts so that you can see her knickers—especially when you are walking up the stairs behind her as she swings her bum from side to side. I have not told Danny about this.

She's been fired from her job on the Tampax production line. You cannot drink cider and make tampons. Unfortunately, this means that she is at home all day long, with one eye on the Valium bottle and the other on Mum's bottle of Crabbie's Green Ginger Wine. I knew Mum should have taken the fruit basket for a prize at the summer fête.

Margueretta doesn't care about getting fired for being intoxicated, and she spends all the money she made at Tampax on cider. She even gives me a glass to drink. She doesn't care about mixing Valium and alcohol because it's the only way she can sleep and stop the voices in her head that are telling her to kill herself. It's a shame that up to this point she has ignored them.

Dr. Browning is very concerned about the voices in her head. He asked us all to come and see him again, which is very annoying because we have to take a forty-five minute bus ride to St. James's Hospital, which is the local loony bin where Great-Auntie Maisie died. And it stinks of carbolic soap and boiled cabbage. Even though they try to keep the place quiet, there are lots of people hollering and screaming, which is enough to give you bloody nightmares.

"It's good that you are here," he said, looking at Emily and me.

Emily smiled. I tried to look intense.

"I told the twins that this was important," Mum replied.

"How are you coping with all of this, John?"

"He's fine," Mum interrupted. "It's me who's losing my mind! Ha! Ha! I mean, how could anyone cope with all of this, for the love of God? How am I going to cope? That's what I want to know. How? How?"

"Well. Let's see. Why don't we let John answer for himself? Eh, John?"

"I'm fine," I replied.

He knew I was lying.

"Your sister is not well. She has been having a difficult time with bad thoughts in her head. Do you ever have bad thoughts in your head, John?"

"No."

Lying again. I have thoughts about killing my sister by pouring paraffin over her bed and setting light to it while she is in it.

"Well, we all have bad thoughts. We call them *intrusive thoughts*. They come from somewhere within us, but they are not really *our* thoughts. Not conscious thoughts. Sometimes they're violent or sexual or inappropriate in other ways. But they're just thoughts. Your sister thinks the thoughts are coming from someone else, someone or something that exists outside of her. And sometimes she talks to that person or thing. Does that make sense?"

It makes sense. But they're not just thoughts. The thing is getting into her head.

"Your sister is also suffering from depression. We doctors call it *manic-depressive disorder*. But don't worry about that! Just take it that she's sad a lot. Do you get sad, John?"

"Not really."

More lies.

"Well, we all get sad. And sometimes Margueretta will seem perfectly normal. Then she might get some more bad thoughts, which make her sad. And she's having difficulty in knowing the truth about where the thoughts come from. OK?"

"That's all well and good," Mum added, "but how do mothers cope with this? It's been going on for years now. And it's driving me up the wall! Dr. Wilmot said it was her periods."

"I think we can safely say it is not her periods, Mrs. Mitchell."

Which is a pity because Margueretta was getting free supplies of tampons before she got fired. There's a whole box of them in the scullery.

We went home after that and Mum had a good cry and said she was going mad with it all, and the house makes her depressed, and she needs help as much as Margueretta, perhaps more. I think it is the black floors. Yes, it's the black floors.

But the good news is the scars have mostly healed up on my face, and I am going to grammar school and will not be called Scarface when I get there. According to Mr. Hudson, I am not nearly as stupid as I look and through some bloody miracle managed to come top of my year in our final exams. What is more, twins should not be separated, so Emily is going too.

The other 142 kids in my year will go to an open prison, according to Mr. Hudson.

We will need school uniforms, but we don't have any money for those sorts of luxuries. So Mum has got out her needles to knit me a uniform. She is a dab hand at knitting, but we don't have any money for wool either so she has retrieved a faux chainmail tunic she picked up from the Methodist Church jumble sale. It was used for the part of a knight in an amateur dramatics performance of King Arthur and the Knights of the Round Table. Mum has ripped the wool back down to balls ready for re-knitting. It is very shiny wool.

Things are worse for Emily. In the summer, girls have the option of wearing dresses to school. The School Bursar runs a second-hand uniform store from her office, and that's where Mum found Emily a dress that she could grow into. It is a very large dress. Emily has to wrap it around herself three times and pray that it won't be a windy day. A couple of good gusts, and she will be blown halfway to Portsmouth. And in the thirty years that it will take for her to grow into it, assuming she gets very fat, Emily will be able to throw small tea parties using the dress as a marquis tent.

Mum is knitting along to Gustav Holst's "The Planets Suite." We are up to the track "Mars, the Bringer of War." I can feel the tension, and I expect her cable stitches will be a lot tighter than usual. She has knitted a sleeve already. It is very metallic.

I will look like a Brillo pad.

82

Woolworth's has a sale on. Dunlop Superior Self-adhesive Floor Tiles are half price. Those bastards may have confiscated the Sweet Shop and my Fry's Turkish Delight bars, but they never confiscated the profits. I have also saved my pocket money for months. The tiles come in red, white, green, and blue. I like the blue best. It will remind Mum of the ocean.

Unfortunately, there were only three packets of blue tiles in the sale, which is very misleading if you ask me. I have, therefore, had to compromise on the color scheme, and it will now be blue and green. This is not ideal, but it is better than black. I shall start with the kitchen and create a contrasting pattern of blue and green to create an effect that is durable and yet decorative. But for now, I am keeping the tiles under my bed because Nana is coming to stay for a few days, and she's bringing a surprise guest.

"Och, ma wee Johnny, ma wee Johnny, ma Scottish soldier! How I've missed you so. God knows I've missed my wee boy. My, but you've grown. And bonnie like your grandfather!"

I love my Nana. But it makes me sad that she's starting to smell like other old ladies—of onions and perfume and pee. And always the same sweet smell on her breath from the wee dram to keep out the cold, morning, noon and night.

Mum thought the surprise guest might be my dad but it turned out to be a man called George who happens to be married, and Nana is having an affair with him. But she is sixty-nine, and he is only sixty, which Mum says is not right at any age. They met in The Hope on Acre Lane when he was telling a wee joke at the bar.

"A Scotsman is leaving a pub with a bottle of whisky in his back trouser pocket. He's trying to board a bus but he falls backwards and lands on the bottle. Feeling a wet patch he shouts: My God—I hope that's blood!"

"Och, that's a good one, isn't it just? He takes a meat pie with his pint, don't you, Georgie?"

Squeeelch!

"Och, it's the pickled egg, excuse me.

Georgie Porgie, pudding and pie,
Kissed the girls and made them cry.
When the boys came out to play,
Georgie Porgie ran away!

"Och, here's a couple of bottles of something to keep out the cold."

Nana pulled two bottles of Harvey's Bristol Cream from her bag.

"Don't mind if I do," Margueretta said and poured herself a glass of sherry.

"You shouldn't be drinking with the Valium!" Mum insisted.

"Och, leave the lassie alone. It's just a wee drop. Takes after her old Nana, don't you lassie?"

"Thank you, Nana, I do."

"Anyway, where was I? Oh, yes. I went to see ma sister Wilma last week. It's nae good. She'll be the next one to go—you mark ma words. She's carrying all her valuables around with her in her handbag. That's what I've always said would happen. Possessions imprison you. They'll be ripping that bag from her cold dead fingers, don't you know? Eh, Georgie?"

"Right enough, Scottie. Right enough."

"She has a man in to do the dahlias. He stands in her back yard. That house in Peckham is far too big for her. She's covered all the furniture with newspapers. She thinks she's got the decorators in. She's no more got the decorators in than I'm the Flying Scotsman. Have another drink, Margueretta."

"Thanks."

"She shouldn't be doing that. She's hearing voices in her head," Mum protested.

"Och, I've been hearing voices in ma head all ma life. Bonny Prince Charlie, mostly. Will you not credit it! Those voices run in the family. If they can put a man on the moon, and who'd believe that I ask you, then I'm sure we will all be hearing voices in our heads. A man on the moon, is it? And I'm Mary, Queen of Scots! Here, have a top up, Margueretta."

"Thank you, Nana. They did put a man on the moon. But Mum wouldn't let us watch it in case the old Ferguson blew a valve. She really thinks that!"

"You know we can't take chances with that old telly," said Mum.

"Try to concentrate, woman. I'm tellin' you about ma poor sister. So this is it. There was a terrible smell," said Nana.

"Smell?" asked Margueretta.

"Aye. A terrible smell. It was the lodger, poor wee beggar."

"The lodger?"

"Aye. Wilma was wondering why she hadn't seen him in a good few days. She went into his bedroom, and there he was. In his bed. Dead."

"Dead?"

"Dead. And do you know what else?"

"What?"

"When she pulled back the sheets his belly came away with them, for the love of God. Squelch! Had his guts out, stuck to those sheets like sausages. And maggots filling up the man's stomach like a barrel of rice. She thought the curtains were closed. But no. It was the flies buzzing at the window. It was the lodger trying to fly away!"

"That's not true!" Margueretta laughed.

"Mark ma words, lassie. It's as true as those voices in yer head. And that's why she thinks she's got the decorators in. To get rid of that terrible smell. Och, imagine that! A lodger rotting away in his bed, and you downstairs watching *Coronation Street* and having a nice cup o' tea."

"That's gruesome!"

"Albert. That was the lodger's name when he was alive. Smelled like dead chickens, apparently. Have another drink, lassie. You never know when it's your turn to go."

"Don't mind if I do."

"You could be hit by a flying piano! 'There was a young man from Peru. Who bent down to buckle his shoe. He found half a crown, lying there on the ground...' Ha, ha! I never could remember the last line. Have you thought about something?"

"What? Margueretta asked.

"There's nothing left when it's all gone, lassie. And what you had, you never will keep. Bagpipes. Now they'll make me cry. I'd like that song at ma funeral."

Oh, Danny Boy, the pipes the pipes are calling,
From glen to glen and down the mountainside...

"She's off!"

"Voices in yer head, is it? Just don't start an argument with them...you could end up giving yerself a good thumping..."

"It's not a laughing matter, Mother!" Mum interrupted.

"Och, no. Of course not. It's nae a laughing matter. Voices in yer head, is it? At least you'll never be lonely!"

83

I found out that I should not be going to grammar school. People who go to grammar school have wall-to-wall carpet and vinyl wallpaper. They do not have front rooms— it's called a lounge. And it's not tea—it's dinner. And they eat Black Forest gateaux if they are having tea, which would be in the middle of the afternoon. They also have a clean pair of underpants for almost every day and do not wear shiny metallic jumpers knitted by their mums from a faux, chainmail tunic she picked up from the Methodist Church jumble sale.

Mrs. Middleton, who teaches science, said we could do an experiment with some iron filings to see if my jumper is magnetic. She also said that with a diode and some copper wire, I could receive Radio Caroline. Or detect low-flying Russian spy planes. The whole class laughed at that.

She told me to tell my father to buy me a regulation school uniform jumper. I told her I do not have a father, and she said that's no surprise coming from a council estate, and even though it could help with some science experiments, she does not want to be offended by the sight of my jumper again.

Not having a jumper wouldn't be a problem if it wasn't for the accident I had in metalwork class. I was cleaning up some steel swath from a lathe, and when I swiveled round, I caught my bum on the sharp point of a turning tool. This put a precise three-inch cut straight through my trousers and under-pants and left my bum slightly exposed but luckily did not break the skin. I only have one pair of trousers, which Mum bought from the Littlewoods Catalog on a twenty-four month installment plan.

I showed my trousers to Mum, and she said a repair was the only answer, being that they are almost new. Somehow she managed to turn a precise three-inch cut into a massive square patch using a piece of offcut quilting material. I would understand if she was making an actual quilt because then it could tell the history, in patchwork embroidery, of our ancestors from the early seventeenth century to the current day. No doubt other relatives would offer to add their own quilted patches over time, and the whole thing could be handed down for generations. But these are trousers. She is better at knitting. Anyway, I have been stretching my metallic jumper down to cover the patch. Now everyone will see the green rayon quilting. They will think I am a homo.

Things are bad enough, so I have decided not to tell anyone at the grammar school about how Mum started a refuge-for-troubled-children and the mix up with the warring tribes. I am also not going to tell them that the police come to our house every night because my sister is expecting to be murdered in her bed by the incarnation of Satan and there's a dead child screaming in our attic. It is one thing for someone to have to sit next to some riff-raff from a council estate who only has two pairs of underpants and gets free school lunches because he lives below the poverty line and would otherwise starve to death. But knowing that I live with Lucifer in a haunted lunatic asylum could push them over the edge and want to expel me.

It is therefore extremely important that I stay out of trouble. This is very difficult because a couple of boys have already tried to start a fight with me after catching a glimpse of the quilting and blanket stitches on my bum, and I had to give them a good thumping.

I have also had one visit to the headmaster's office for throwing a plastic cocoa pod during the study of equatorial South America. It was our geography lesson, and we were told by Miss Sanders, who is a student teacher and wears distractingly short dresses and white knickers, to pass the pod from person to person. But I was at the end of the row, and it looked like a rugby ball to me, so I threw it at Peter Turner, and he is a rotten catch and it went through the window. Well, the window was closed at the time so it broke the window.

Now not only do I have to find the money for a regulation school jumper, but I have to pay for a new window, which is on the second floor and may also involve some scaffolding. This will therefore put a severe dent in my budget for Dunlop Superior Self-adhesive Floor Tiles.

Mum said there is no stipulation in the school's uniform regulations about shininess, and she would therefore complain to my form teacher about the obvious injustice. It was a short discussion, and the ruling stands. I cannot wear a metallic jumper to school. Unfortunately, Mum told my teacher that we are very poor, and there's no money for a Sunday roast let alone a regulation school jumper. This has confirmed that I should not be in a grammar school, and I am now very concerned that Mrs. Middleton will be offended by the rayon quilting and blanket stitches on my arse, even though she has made no mention of it up to this point. Either way, I need money.

And there is an answer.

We get tickets for our school lunches, and mine are free because of my state of extreme poverty and malnutrition. All the other kids have to pay for theirs because they are from middle-class homes. They bring money to school every Monday morning and get in a queue at the bursar's office. It's obvious really. I sell them my free lunch tickets for half the price that they would have to pay for their own. That way, they have money to spend on sweets, and I have money to spend on a regulation school jumper, a new window with some scaffolding, and Dunlop Superior Self-adhesive Floor Tiles.

Unfortunately, this means that I will have no lunch and will have to survive on a bowl of cornflakes all day, assuming that Margueretta has not used up all the milk for a cup of Camp coffee.

Another way to save money is by walking to school and back. Mum gives us the bus fare every morning, and I have been saving the money—but I will not add it to the jumper, window, and tile budget because that would be mean to my mum. She needs new knickers because hers are all worn out, and she is now wearing my dad's old underpants, which I had completely forgotten we had kept. And since we have not seen my dad for more than four years, it is possible that he now has no need for them, and I am glad my mum had the forethought to keep them. So I have given her all the money I have been saving on bus fares, and she now has the money to buy new knickers. For some reason, this made her cry.

Unfortunately, walking to school and back in what is left of my school uniform, marks me out as a target for the kids who go to the secondary modern school and think I am an upper-class snob for going to a grammar school. It would be completely pointless trying to explain that I am not really welcome at the grammar school because I am council estate riff-raff. I get free school lunches, and we do not have wall-to-wall carpet in our lounge. In fact, we have bare, black floors with a scattering of dried-up cat turds. We do not have a washing machine, fridge, bedroom heaters, enough milk, Sunday dinner, or a shilling for the electric meter. And my mum is wearing my dad's underpants. So I am not an upper-class snob. But they still want to thump me.

I found that walking down by the stream next to the woods usually throws them off the scent. But earlier this week, they were waiting for me in the bushes, and they jumped me and took my school tie for a trophy and threw my homework books into the stream. They also held my arms behind my back so that the smallest boy could punch me in the face a few times, and he landed a really good punch on my mouth that split my lip.

Now I also have to find a way to immediately pay for a new school tie and copies of Huckleberry Finn, Basic Algebra, and French Verb Conjugation (Regular and Irregular). But that is not why I am so worried and why Mum has not stopped crying.

Today, there was a terrible, terrible accident.

84

Our front door was open. There's nothing particularly strange about that because Margueretta still doesn't have a job, and she sits around all day listening to Radio One on her transistor. But Emily knew the same as I did that something was wrong because Joan Housecoat was there, blocking our way in.

"Ooo-er! You kids just home from school?"

I nodded.

"Best stay out here. I know it's chilly. Stay out here and play. . ."

It is chilly. The winter is creeping in now, and the big oak trees in front of our house look tired and dark—like they don't want to keep going. So I didn't want to stay outside and play in the cold, and I pushed past her housecoat and wondered why she gasped and reached for my collar. But I was too quick for her.

The front room was empty, so I dashed down the passageway to the kitchen. And there was Old Man Dumby with a mop and bucket. He glanced at me and mouthed words, the way deaf people do, and held up a hand to say stop at the door. Don't come in this place.

Never come in here.

For the love of God, never come in here.

There isn't much color in our house. Just the orange fiberglass curtains in the front room. They're fireproof but don't go trying to prove it. And I haven't started on the floor tiles yet, so the floors are still black. But today the kitchen floor wasn't just black. It was red and black. And Old Man Dumby was pushing the red around with two cat turds and some potato peelings.

Swirling, swirling, swirling.

"Don't look in there!"

It was Joan with Emily. She was too late, of course.

By the leg of the kitchen table, I could see a bottle. I focused my eyes on the label. Crabbie's Green Ginger Wine. It was empty—lying there on its side. Mum will be angry after all that effort for the summer fête with Akanni as the Heinz Chocolate Pudding. Now it's empty on the kitchen floor when she could have had a fruit basket.

Old Man Dumby started mopping faster. It didn't matter. I could see the blood on the kitchen table and the wallpaper and the ceiling and the sideboard and the floor and the sink and the cooker and the cat's bowl. There was blood on the mop, and red water in the bucket. Blood on the pile of rotting food scraps by the sink.

Purple-red like the halo around the dead man's head. Purple-red everywhere on the black floor.

If it was milk, it would just look like a bit of a mess. But even a tiny spot of blood looks like more than it is. And a huge amount of blood makes your stomach shrink and heave like it's trying to come out through your mouth. And your mouth is hanging open waiting for it to escape.

There was a pool of blood under the kitchen table, but it didn't look like a halo around a dead man's head. It looked like a clown's face. Yes, a clown's face, grinning up at me in purple-red and brown. And over by the sink there was a woman's high-heeled shoe. But the heel was broken off and lying close by.

Blood turns brown when it dries. Brown, like the red roses on the wallpaper after the man sprayed for the lice.

"You shouldn't be in here. No one should. Your mum will be home soon. I'll put the kettle on and make you some nice hot tea. Do you know where Mum keeps the milk?"

"It's in a bucket under the sink. Mum won't be home soon. She's going to Local History classes tonight. She goes straight from work," I replied.

"Not today. She'll be home soon, and everything will be alright. These are nice dishes."

"They're unbreakable. Look."

I dropped a cup on the floor to prove it. It landed by the purple-red clown's face so we left it there.

"Ooo-er! Whatever will they think of next! Let's go into the front room now. Do you know where your mum keeps her shillings for the meter? It's getting dark."

"We don't have any."

"Ooo-er! That's not right. You come next door with me, and I'll fry you up some delicious bacon and eggs and a slice of fried bread for each of you."

"No, thank you."

I hadn't eaten all day, but I wasn't hungry. Besides, I didn't want to shame my mum by going next door with Joan and eating her delicious bacon and eggs and a slice in her cozy, warm kitchen with the steam on the windows and the cobwebs that Fred painted over. And maybe a chocolate biscuit afterwards. I didn't want to shame anyone with my disgusting gluttony.

So we just waited for Mum. And I stared at the purple-red colors on the walls and ceiling, turning slowly into brown.

85

recognized Dr. Browning in the hospital ward. He thought I couldn't hear when he was talking to my mum. But I heard everything. Emily didn't hear because she was by the bed, sitting in the visitor's chair. I never sit beside the hospital bed. So I stood by the end of the bed even though the other chair was empty.

"Can I have a quiet word?" asked Dr. Browning.

Mum and the doctor stood away from the bed and talked softly.

"This is really very serious. She's a very sick young lady. We're going to have to try a different approach."

"Why would she do this?" Mum replied.

"If she hadn't been found..."

"Oh, she wanted to be found. This is how she gets attention. If it's not one thing, it's another," Mum interrupted.

"Look. We have a lot to talk about. I know this has been a terrible shock. But once she gets over this, we need to do something more."

"What?" Mum asked.

"Something different."

"What?"

"I'm thinking about ECT."

"ECT?"

"Electroconvulsive therapy. It works with depression. It may help Margueretta. We should consider it. I'm going to give you some information about it, and I want you to think it over."

THE BOY WHO LIVED WITH GHOSTS

"I've heard about it. Isn't that a bit drastic?"

"It's more common than you think. It's a simple procedure. We anesthetize her, and then we put an electrode on each temple. It's called bilateral electrode placement. Then we pass an electric current, and that induces a seizure."

"A seizure? That sounds awfully serious."

"She may get some frontal lobe issues later in life. Here," he said and pointed to his head, "but for most people their cognitive functions and memory loss return. Perhaps as quickly as an hour after treatment. You can get some memory loss that's permanent. But that's very rare."

"I don't know," Mum said.

"It's explained in this leaflet. We'll talk about it some more. It's not a decision for now. I just wanted you to start to think about it. There have been too many incidents, and this was the worst. Very serious. She's lucky someone found her. Another twenty minutes—and she would have died from the loss of blood."

"And how am I going to cope?"

"Cope...with what?"

"Her. Margueretta! Will I be able to cope with her after the treatment? Because I can't cope with her now. I don't want her back home. Not after this."

"She's your daughter. You have no choice. She can't stay in hospital forever. I'm moving her to St. James's after this for a while. But then she will have to go back home. You'll just have to cope. She nearly died."

"But she's an adult now. She knows what she's doing."

"Fifteen is *not* an adult. And she does *not* know what she is doing. She has no control over this."

"You'll have to leave now!" the nurse announced.

"I'm sorry. I'm so sorry," Margueretta whispered.

Her eyes were full of tears, and her face was as white as the pillow. White like the dead man's face on the black tarmac road.

"What happened?" Emily asked her.

Margueretta pulled her hands from under the blankets and held out her arms. There were thick white bandages around both her wrists.

"So she fell on her high-heeled shoes and cut her wrists?" I asked Mum for the fifth time when we got home.

The cat was sitting by its bowl, which was empty and clean. And all the food scraps and cat turds were gone from the floor. It was the cleanest the kitchen had ever been but no one spoke about the brown stains up the wallpaper and on the ceiling. Blood always turns brown when it dries, no matter where it is.

"Did she fall?" I asked again.

Mum sighed.

"No. You will have to know sooner or later," she replied.

"What was it?" Emily asked.

"She just cut her wrists," Mum replied and dragged deeply on her Kensitas.

"So how did her shoe get broken?" I asked.

"I don't know anything about a shoe."

"But how did she cut her wrists?" Emily asked.

"With a razor blade. Several times on each wrist."

"I don't understand. But why did she cut her own wrists?" Emily asked.

"To kill herself. To kill herself. She wanted to bloody kill herself. Your sister tried to kill herself. And she nearly damn well succeeded!"

A neighbor found Margueretta at the back door, bleeding from both wrists. And she went to get Joan Housecoat, who went for Old Man Dumby, as he knows about these things because he was in the war. He applied tourniquets and stopped the blood and that saved her life. Margueretta drank the Crabbie's Green Ginger Wine to numb the pain of slashing her wrists. It must really hurt to slice a razor blade across your wrists again and again. I wouldn't want to do that, even if I had someone inside my head telling me to do it.

"Why were the doctors and nurses so rude to us? Is it because we live in a council house?" I asked.

"A council house? No. Of course not. They were rude because Margueretta was wasting their time. They're busy with tonsils and broken legs, and they don't need some lunatic slashing her wrists and trying to kill herself. It wastes everybody's time."

"Will she be alright?" Emily asked.

"Oh, yes. Don't worry about her. It's me you should worry about. I'm the one who's losing my mind in this madhouse. Yes, I'm the one who's losing my mind and no mistake."

I don't have much time. I need to cover the black floors before it's too late. I will start tomorrow.

86

Two vehicles pulled up outside our house today. One was a British Leyland ambulance, and the other was a pale blue Ford Anglia 105E—the same one with the rockets and flying saucers. We are going to have a family reunion.

Mum thought it might save her sanity if she fostered Akanni again in the refuge-for-troubled-children. The Methodist Church has started a day nursery and he can stay there during the day. I will pick him up on my way home from school. The Social Services said it was a very unlikely case because there should be a responsible adult at home at all times when there is a child in the house. So they did an audit and asked me if I was a happy child, and I told them about magnetism and the solar system with a particular emphasis on Saturn. I think that impressed them. They said we had a very calm and happy home, and Mum was clearly very devoted to saving troubled children.

Luckily, they did the audit while Margueretta was away in the lunatic asylum recovering from electroconvulsive therapy and trying to kill herself by slashing her wrists with a razor blade.

And Mum's Japanese hydrangea bush has died because no one watered it, so our house will not be visited by calm and tranquility. However, I have begun the laying of the tiles over the black floors and started with a creative, though not quite geometric, pattern of blue and green in the kitchen. Unfortunately, when I ran out of tiles and went back to Woolworth's for more, they only had white tiles remaining in the sale. So it will be a decorative and yet durable design in blue, green, *and white*.

Mollie Midget came over with Robert and Folami for the reunion. Joan Housecoat was here too, but she wouldn't stay if there was any screaming because her nerves are shot to pieces, don't you know, and she is now on the maximum dose of Valium. Dr. Wilmot said it was no surprise, living next door to a total, blooming madhouse.

He should try living *in* the madhouse.

Mum said it would be nice if we could celebrate this family reunion with a musical soirée. I have therefore been practicing Mozart's "Rondo Alla Turca." I can also play "Für Elise" and the slow movement of Beethoven's "Moonlight Sonata," although I am not note perfect at this piece. We will, however, start with some background music from Rodgers and Hammerstein before the recital. *South Pacific* has been chosen yet again after Florie Atkins told Mum that the musical won the Pulitzer Prize for Drama in 1950. Jim Reeves's "Distant Drums" was discounted because it may bring back bad memories of the warring tribes tea party. And the "The Planets" suite is too dark for a soirée. So it will be "Bali Ha'i."

Two ambulance orderlies brought Margueretta up the path, each holding onto an arm. Her wrists were still bandaged, and they moved very slowly with her—like she might break. She was in the hospital and the lunatic asylum for four weeks.

"Have you hidden the knives?" Joan whispered to Mum.

We don't need to hide the knives because you would still have to use the bread knife and you would have to saw it across your wrists, and I don't even think a bottle of Crabbie's Green Ginger Wine would numb that feeling. And the only person I know who shaves is Auntie Dot, and she's not here so there are no razor blades that we know of.

Mollie stared into Robert's eyes when "Bali Ha'i" came on.

"Eech! 'Here I am, your special island. Come to me. Come to me. Bali Ha'i. Bali Ha'i.' Eech!"

"She had ECT," Mum whispered to Joan Housecoat.

"Who? Mollie?"

"No! Margueretta, of course."

"Ooo-er! The doctor said I should have some of that," Joan replied.

"ECT? You? Really?" Mum replied.

"Yes. For my depression. He said it could end the black days once and for all. Then I wouldn't have to take Valium three times a day. Either that or I'm going to have a nervous breakdown."

"We'll all be having a nervous breakdown sooner or later. That or a frontal lobotomy! Ha! Ha! Ha!" Mum replied.

"Ooo-er!"

"Eech! 'I'm gonna wash that man right outa my hair!' Eech!"

"Time for the piano recital! He's been practicing for weeks," Mum announced and stopped the record, which was just as well as Mollie had asked Robert to dance and God knows no one wanted to see that.

It was when I was on the ascending A minor arpeggio of "Für Elise" that Margueretta let out a piercing howl like a dog that's been stepped on. I knew I should have practiced more. And Joan said that's it, she warned us that she wouldn't stay if there was any screaming. She left to get another Valium and would not be coming back under any circumstances.

And even though she was in the giant tribal headdress again, I'm sure Akanni's mother could still run. She should have grabbed Akanni in an instant and taken her husband's hand, and they would have been out of this madhouse in a flash. Run down the path and into the Ford Anglia 105E with rockets and flying saucers, speeding seventy miles an hour all the way to London. Never look back. Change their address and their names. Have face-altering surgery.

But they stayed and drank tea and said goodbye like old friends when they left, and Akanni didn't even want to kiss them. And everything will be fine because we've passed the Social Services audit.

"I've got something to show you!" Robert announced and left our front room.

"Eech! He brought it with us! He's never done that before! Eech!"

"What is it?" Emily asked.

Robert pulled the cover off to reveal a tiny cage.

"It's my Madeira Chaffinch. Isn't she beautiful? She's my prize bird."

She was beautiful. She was green and white, but the cage was too small for her to spread her wings—even though she was tiny.

So she sat on her perch and shivered.

And Margueretta sat on the sofa and stared at nothing, her face a perfect, pure white— except for two red circles on her temples. But she was still beautiful.

87

They've had to bring forward our sex education lessons owing to an incident with Malcolm Beresford. Ten of us threw him out of the changing rooms because he has pubic hair already even though he's only twelve, which everyone agreed is ridiculous. He was wagging his huge cock at us and that was more than any of us could stand, so we threw him out. Serves him right.

He was completely naked, and we left him with only a football sock to cover his pubes. We locked the door to stop him getting back in and it was not our fault that the girls came along for their netball practice. Well, it was our fault for locking the door but not for the girls seeing him naked. And according to rumors, he didn't even try to hide his cock with the sock. Some said he wagged it at them.

Anyway, it was Leslie Flowers who complained to Miss Copeland because Leslie Flowers likes girls, and everyone knows she stares at the other girls in the showers. Miss Copeland wanted us all caned, but Mr. Curry, our Religious Education teacher, said we should not be punished because we are obviously confused about our sexuality and it is more of an adolescent issue where punishment could lead to bigger problems with our sexual orientation. Apparently, we have a lot of hormones buzzing around our bodies that could result in any one of us becoming a mad axe killer. Also, Malcolm Beresford did not complain because he is now getting a lot of girlfriends. So we are having sex education lessons to help with our adolescent issues with puberty.

"You know when you are reaching puberty," Mr. Curry told us, "because you will get hair around your penis. Your penis will also get a lot larger than it is now, and you will experience something called an erection. Do any of you have any questions?"

We had questions. Oh, yes, we had lots of questions. Boy, did we have questions. Questions? Oh, yes. Questions. You bet.

No one said a word.

"How about if you all write your questions down, then we will put them all into a hat, and I will read them out and answer them? Would that help?"

Would that help? Good God, yes! We could ask any questions about wanking and tits and tampons and anything like that without anyone knowing who asked. We scribbled furiously.

"How do you know when you can produce sperm?" Mr. Curry read out the first question.

We all leaned forward. We needed answers.

"Well. Have you ever gone into a newsagents and looked at the pictures in the girlie magazines?"

There is no way I could reach those magazines. They're on the top shelf. So I imagined Danny's Parade Magazine pictures hidden in his dad's sock drawer.

"And when you are looking at the pictures, do you get a warm feeling down there?" he asked, pointing to his crotch.

We were transfixed.

"Well, that means you can produce sperm."

I definitely get a warm feeling down there when I look at my Parade Magazine picture. Therefore I can produce sperm. I will investigate this later in detail. But right now we needed more facts.

"Why do men have breasts and nipples?"

No answer on that one. He will check with Mr. Randal in the biology department.

"Will I go blind if I masturbate?"

No. But it could become dangerous if you are obsessed with masturbating or if you do it in inappropriate places.

This is just not enough detail. For instance, what exactly does it mean to be obsessed with wanking? Malcolm Beresford says he wanked six times in one day. So is that dangerous? And Danny's brother was wanking three times a day on his bed. Is that dangerous and inappropriate? And what is an inappropriate place? The cloakroom? Bicycle sheds? I doubt Mr. Curry's real ability to answer these questions. He appears very flustered.

And he's sweating.

"Is it possible to get a girl pregnant who is your sister?"

That's a whole different issue. Even though the answer is technically yes, we should not ever think about such a thing because it is called incest, and it is illegal and against the will of God, and if there is anyone who wants to discuss this question in private, he should see Mr. Curry afterwards. It is most important, whoever it was who asked that question, that he sees Mr. Curry afterwards.

"What are homos? Exactly?"

They are men who like other men and do it to each other the same as a man does it to a woman even though neither of them has got a quim. The correct word is homosexual. We are living in a more enlightened society now, and sex between consenting adult males was made legal four years ago in England. So we should not worry anymore about fancying another boy.

We're having none of that! Timothy Newland spends all his time with the girls at playtime, and he even walks and runs like a girl. There's a story going around that he's got a Barbie Doll. And his mum brings him to school every day and comes to collect him. He is obviously a homo. So we lock him in the equipment cupboard when we get changed for football so that he will not see our cocks. And if you ask me, Mr. Curry knows way too much about this subject, and I am beginning to think he is also a homo.

And apparently that is quite enough question time for one day because we are all pent up like animals, and we should not be thinking about sexual matters too intently for too long. We will therefore return to the subject of Christ's crucifixion and resurrection without which there would be no life after death and we would be no different from the common beast.

We will press Mr. Curry for more answers next week.

88

There were lots of drinks I've never seen before or even heard of. The bottles were all different shapes and beautiful colors. Tia Maria, Crème de Menthe, Bols Advocat, Crème de Curaçao, and Angostura Bitters. And Napoleon Brandy, Taylor's Port, Captain Morgan's Rum, Smirnoff Vodka, and two bottles of Harvey's Bristol Cream Sherry. And a bottle of Gordon's Gin, lying empty on its side.

Beside the bottles was a small book called *101 Cocktails to Mix at Home*. Uncle Jack said we could help ourselves to anything we want but not his Johnny Walker whisky, which he was holding onto for safekeeping.

Margueretta was deciding where to start. She poured an Advocat and Corona American Cream Soda. She said it's called a Snowball.

It was Christmas Eve, but we were not at home. Mum said we should spend Christmas with Nana because she is getting old and lonely. But we were not in Nana's flat. We were in Uncle Jack's flat with Auntie Ethel.

They've got a Christmas tree, but it looked like it had fallen over because it was propped up with a dirty pillow and a cardboard box. The lights were switched on, but there weren't many lights actually on the tree. They were mostly trailed across the floor, lighting up the gray-black sticky carpet. Beside the tree were two tiny children, my little cousins.

"Johnny, my little cock 'sparra! Remember me? Do you want a drink? You're the bloody drinker, you are! You drank that whole glass of sherry straight down...just like yer dad, you are! Where is yer dad? Do you want a drink? 'Ave a drink for Chrishmas!"

"He does not want a drink," Mum replied.

I did want a drink. I wanted something from one of those colored bottles, maybe the green one.

"Can I have a drink?" asked the tiny boy.

"Sit down, you! I don't want to hear from you! I'm sick of your fucking whining!"

I looked at Auntie Ethel, but she never said a word. She was sitting on the sofa, head drooped down on her chest. She never said hello when we came in. I don't think she could even see us because her eyes were half closed—even though you could tell she wasn't sleeping.

"Merry Chrishmas! And help yourshelf to a drinksh! A drink? Don't mind if I do. Thanksh very mush..."

Uncle Jack took a swig from his Johnny Walker bottle and then held it back close to his chest in case anyone should steal it.

"Give yer Uncle Jack a little Chrishmish kisssh! Thatsh my girl. You were always the pretty one."

And he pulled Margueretta's face towards him with his free hand and kissed her hard on the lips.

"Urgh! He put his bloody tongue in my mouth! Disgusting animal!" Margueretta screamed.

"It wash jusht a Chrishtmish kisssh!"

"Jesus wept! Stay away from her! She's your bloody niece!" Mum shouted.

"Shut yer mouth, Scottie! If you know what's good for yer!"

Jingle Bell, Jingle Bells,
Jingle all the way.
Oh, what fun it is to ride,
On a one-horse open sleigh!

Miracle on 34th Street was just starting on their telly.

"Thatsh a good old film, that one. Load of bloody nonshense about Father Chrishmas being real! Ha! There ish no Father Chrishmas! But it makesh a good film though."

"Father Christmas is coming tonight! Tonight! Tonight!" the tiny boy shouted, jumping up and down.

"Shut up! Shut yer mouth or you'll get whatsh coming to you! We get all that booze from the Littlewoods Catalog. Get it on the weekly plan. We're still paying for last Chrishmas. And the one before that...and..."

He rubbed his belly. It looked like the same dirty string vest he was wearing all those years ago on the beach. Floppy brown nipples surrounded by black hairs, and the hairs poking through the holes. And there was his belt, wrapped high around his waist, just under his ribs. As usual, it wasn't pushed through the belt loops.

"Have a drink, why don't yoush!"

Margueretta stepped up and poured herself a brandy and gulped it down. The bandages are gone now, but you can still see the red scars on the insides of her wrists. The doctor said if she had cut any deeper, she would have sliced through her tendons, and then she would have lost the use of her hands because it's very hard to sew a tendon back together again.

"Look at her drink! She's a Mitchell, right enough!" yelled Uncle Jack.

"Steady on, young lady!" Mum shouted. "Have you taken your pills today?"

"Where'sh that husband of yoursh?" Uncle Jack asked.

"No bloody idea," Mum replied.

"I'd bloody punch his face if he wash here. Leaving you like that. And these kidzz of yoursh! I would never abandon my kidzz!"

That's when Auntie Ethel lifted her bum off the sofa and started crying like a little girl who's wet herself. I could see a big patch on the sofa, and she was standing that way you do when you've wet yourself or taken a shit in your pants.

"What is it, Alice?" asked Mum.

"Ignore her. Stupid ole' cow. She's pisshed herself. Bloody embarrassh-ment. You've pisshed yourself! Do you hear me? She can't hear a thing."

"Is that you, daddy? My daddy? I love you, daddy. I've missed you so much..." Auntie Ethel whined.

"God Almighty! She thinksh I'm her dead bloody father. You've had too much fucking gin! I told you! It always turns her maudling. Drank the whole bloody bottle. I am not your bloody father! He's dead, you stupid cow!"

"What's wrong with mummy?" the tiny boy asked.

"Shut up! I said, shut up! Jingle Bellsh, Jingle Bellsh, Jingle all the way... Have a drink, Emily. You can't 'ave Chrishmas without a drink. What would Chrishmas be without a good drink? We've got everysing. Just you name it! No expensh spared for my family. I am the man whosh got everysing. And the bill to prove it! Ha! Ha! Ha!"

"Father Christmas is coming tonight!" the tiny boy shouted.

"Aieeee! Aieeee!" Auntie Ethel howled.

Margueretta poured herself a brandy and lemonade.

"He's coming! He's coming! Father Christmas!" the boy squealed.

"Shutsh yer mouth!"

Uncle Jack had his hands in the pockets of our coats that were piled on a chair.

"What in God's name are you doing?" Mum shouted.

"Jusht stopping them from falling on the floor," Uncle Jack replied.

"No you weren't! You were going through our bloody pockets! You bloody pickpocket! Thief!"

"Oh, don't be like that. I always had a shweet shpot for you," he replied and grabbed Mum round the waist and pressed his groin into her hips, grind-ing slightly.

"Get off me! You animal!"

"Aieeee! Aieeee! Daddy, daddy!" Auntie Ethel howled.

"Shut up! Bloody old cow!"

"Father Christmas! Father Christmas! Father Christmas!" the tiny boy squealed.

"Keep your hands to yourself!" Mum shouted at Uncle Jack.

"Father Christmas! Father Christmas! Father Christmas!"

"Shush! You bloody well shush!" shouted Uncle Jack.

"Father Christmas! Father Christmas! Father Christmas!"

And in one single practiced motion, Uncle Jack had the little boy by the arm, up off the chair and feet off the floor, and the belt undone and in his other hand, as he dragged him from the room.

Thwack, thwack, thwack.

We could hear the beating. And the screams. And *Miracle on 34th Street*.

His pants were still round his trembling knees when Uncle Jack dragged him back into the room.

"That'll teach him to shut hish bloody mouth!"

But Uncle Jack wasn't done. One by one, he threw their presents onto the tiny fire.

The doll's blonde hair flared into a bright orange then purple, and the yellow skin turned liquid until her blue glass eyes were floating without a face, staring in different directions. Then the eyes fell into the grate. The paint on the bright red metal fire engine blistered until it was black. It lay on its side in the coals and the black rubber tires smoked like four little molten chimneys.

The tiny boy just stared at the filthy carpet—dried up tears on his cheeks, pants still half down.

There is no Father Christmas.

89

Mum has given up trying to learn Yoruba because she will not have any use for it unless she goes to Lagos. This is unlikely because you have to take a boat and she gets seasick. There is also a civil war going on there, and people are being butchered—that's according to the BBC. So to expand her mind, she is now reading another book that had to be specially ordered: *A History of Mental Illness.*

"Listen to this," Mum began. "Apparently, in less informed times, they used to submerge lunatics in baths of ice water until they passed out! They also gave them lobotomies."

"What's a lobotomy?" Emily asked.

"Well, first they gave you two electric shocks to the head. Then they stuck a metal rod the size of a pencil up behind your eyelid and moved it around to separate the frontal lobes from the rest of your brain. A bit like stirring a vanilla blancmange."

"What?"

"But this was quite a slow procedure so it says here that a man called Walter J. Freeman developed the 'Transorbital Lobotomy' to speed things up. It says here that a third of the patients died, and another third ended up as cabbages."

"That's terrible, Mum!"

Unfortunately, Dr. Browning had not considered giving Margueretta an ice water bath or a transorbital lobotomy. He has instead sent her to group therapy sessions. He said it's good for treating depression but not for patients with personality disorders. In other words, fine if you get dark moods but not if you are a raving lunatic who hears voices. He thinks the voices could be just an adolescent phase.

"Group psychotherapy treatment was first used in England to treat troops with combat fatigue returning from World War II. It explores the group psychodynamic on multiple levels and not only gains access to the unconscious processes of group members but also to the unconscious group dynamic," Mum said, reading another passage from her book.

What this means is that Margueretta can get together with other lunatics, and they can talk about their madness with each other in a group. I think it makes them feel better that someone is listening, even if that person is also bonkers. At least it keeps her out of the house because she still doesn't have another job even though she's sixteen now. She did have an interview to be a chambermaid at the Queens Hotel in Southsea, and she's waiting to hear from them.

But she was home today, and she said she would tell Emily and me how to kill ourselves if we wanted to know. We didn't, but she told us anyway.

"First you run a nice hot bath. Then take off all your clothes. Doesn't matter if they find you naked. You're dead, so you won't be embarrassed! Climb in the bath and lie back. Then relax with a bottle of sherry. Make sure your wrists are nice and hot from the water. It numbs them. So does the sherry. Then get a nice new razor blade. Look here!"

She pointed to the scars on her wrist.

"You slit the vein, right here. You can cut across it. Or slice down the length. Like this. Down the length is more effective than across. That's given me an idea. Maybe I will kill myself in someone's room at the Queens Hotel. Imagine that! And they will come back from their stupid night out at the Guildhall, and I'll be waiting for them in their bathroom. Dead in a bath of blood."

"Stop!" Emily yelled.

Margueretta smiled.

"Slash both wrists. Then keep them under the water. The blood pumps out really fast. But you don't really feel it because your wrists are under the water. And as you lose blood, you get light-headed and sleepy. Have one more swig of sherry while you can still lift your arms..."

"I'm not listening!" Emily shouted.

"Then it's, 'Good night, cruel world!' Would you like to try that, John? Would you? Would you? Would you like to try it? I can help."

"No!"

"Oh, don't worry, little boy. I'm not going to hurt you right now. You'll find out what madness means soon enough. Then you will join me in this living fucking hell we call life. This world is just one, fucking long cauchemar. Do you know what that means, little boy? No, of course you don't. It means nightmare. Cauchemar! And do you know what I am?"

"What?"

"I am Hecate. The Great Hecate! Do you know who that is, little boy? Do you? No, you don't. Of course you don't. Why would you? You only know about silly magic tricks and those ridiculous floor tiles. Ha! Ha! The Great Hecate! It's the Goddess of Hellfire!"

"What?"

"I'm the Goddess of fucking Hellfire! And I'm just two doors away from your bedroom at night. Remember that! You're just two doors away from a living, fucking nightmare! And clenching your hand into a fist won't help. If you ever hit me again, I will be sure that you die. I have ways. Lots of ways. You will die a painful death."

It would have been appropriate if she had screamed at that moment. But she didn't. She smiled at me.

Because she knew what was going to happen next.

90

M um has decided to make a fresh start so she is cleaning out the larder
and boiling up a pig's head. I'm helping her with the larder, but I'm
staying well away from that pig's head. It's grinning from the edge of
the pot with its tongue hanging out over its yellow teeth, panting like a dog
that's been for a run. Someone's going to have to eat that later. I've locked the
cat in the scullery.

Mum is very pleased with the floor tiles on the kitchen floor, but she did
comment on the unusual choice of colors. I don't think she knows how hard it is
to find the money to buy Dunlop Superior Self-adhesive Floor Tiles or the unacceptable way that Woolworth's put out a different color each time there is a sale.

She is also interested to know why the tiles currently form a large cross
in the center of the kitchen. The cross will not form part of the completed
pattern. You have to start in the middle or you will not have a true line to
work from. That's what the instructions said. So, first it is important to
accurately measure the distance from each wall and form a cross with chalk
in the middle of the floor as a starting point. Because I do not have enough
tiles to complete the room, we will have to live with the blue, green and white
cross for now. She also has no idea how hard it is to get those self-adhesive
floor tiles to stick unless you clean off all the hardened dirt and shit from
the floor. I have wasted several tiles finding that out—especially under the
kitchen table where the cat takes a shit every day.

Mum is very focused on cleaning out the larder. Most of the things in
our larder used to belong to Nana. I think they have been passed down for

generations. Mum knows the entire history of our larder. We have a bottle of red food dye that is made from the blood of the crushed bodies of cochineal insects that are farmed in South America. You use it to color things blood-red. There's that pre-war tin of Coleman's Mustard Powder that Mum remembers from when she was a girl and some silver balls that Nana bought to decorate a cake for the queen's coronation in 1953. Then there's the tin of Tate and Lyle's treacle that we've never been able to get the lid off and a packet of dried peas for keeping salt from getting damp. You use one pea per year in the salt pot. There are twenty-three peas left, so we will have to replace the packet when I am thirty-five.

Mum's done with the larder. The contents are spread across the kitchen table where they will stay until another time.

This is a fresh start. Soon we will start with the burning.

I hope the first thing on the fire will be that picture. Yes, I hope it will be that picture. We should have burned it a long time ago. But Mum wants to start with the love letter to her headmaster. The flames are growing now with the paraffin Mum put on the fire in the back garden.

"Burn this filth!" Mum shouted.

I threw the love letter on the fire. Then we went back for more things. Shoes, clothes, more love letters, poems, trinkets. And the painting of her headmaster. And a new painting, one we hadn't seen before. It was a painting of Dr. Browning that was hidden under her bed.

The last thing we took out into the garden was that other painting. It seemed like Mum was afraid to touch it.

Take the Devil from this house and burn it. Burn it! I smell the brimstone. Forty days in the wilderness could not tempt our Savior. Destroy the Devil! Out, I say! Out with this evil incarnation of Lucifer! Get behind me, vile being! God deliver us from this power of darkness!

Out! Out! Out!

Mum kept the paintings to one side. She piled the clothes and shoes and papers and oil paints into a neat heap and poured paraffin on. Esso Blue. It burns without smell.

Everything roasted in vermillion flames. The picture of Dr. Browning was first to burn. His face shriveled and warped, and he was grinning in the fire. It was an insane grin that stretched his mouth and teeth, and they molded around the broken shoe beneath, the shoe from the kitchen. His cheeks burst and popped, and he disappeared in the powerful heat.

And then the headmaster's turn. And his balding head was burning, his facial features were melting, and strange, silent expressions spread across his eyes. His lips and nose were blistering until the oils bubbled and whistled and melted back into their original form before turning into black tar.

The thick pile of letters and poems released scraps of charred paper that were caught by the breeze and floated into the dark night and were lost to the black, silent sky.

Then at last—that thing. We should have burned it long ago. Back when Margueretta first showed it to us. Then, perhaps the terrible madness would not have come.

Now it is rightfully condemned to the vilest death for all it has done. Mum laid it face up on the pyre so that we could see it suffer. It stared up at me. I knew it had to die in the fire, but it looked right back, defiantly. Looking back through the flames with live eyes, following me.

But the fire curled around the edges of the canvas. It held on for the longest time before it gasped a molten breath and committed its evil fuel to the flaming inferno. And the fire burst through its eyeballs, and for a moment, made it even more sinister than when we started.

And now it is gone, roasted in the fiery lake of Hell.

An immolation to exorcise the evil demon.

And we are saved.

91

I t was Mum who found her. She heard a scream and a bang or a thump or something in the night. She could have ignored it. God knows, there are enough screams and bangs and thumps in this house that we all try to ignore. But she didn't ignore it. And then Mum cried out for me because I am the man of the house, and that's the way it is I suppose. It's up to Mum and me to try to save her.

Mum found Margueretta lying on the floor in her room. She wasn't moving. Mum shook her and shook her and shook her. And she screamed in her ear. But she wouldn't wake up. There were empty bottles lying beside her, maybe two or three. And a small brown bottle.

I ran as fast as I could—out the front door and down the street in the rain. I never had time to put on my shoes, and the grit dug into the soles of my bare feet. I slipped over three times on the wet pavement and skinned my knees, but I didn't feel anything. And the giant oak trees leaned in and pressed against my eyes like the walls of the dark, dark cellar. But I kept my eyes open until I saw the light.

No one would care that I was in my torn pajamas. It was the middle of the night, and only the bats were out, circling as they do and darting and swerving. They never make a sound.

I pushed the door at first, and it wouldn't open. Then I realized that you have to pull, and it opened easily. Everyone knows the number. They told us in Cub Scouts what to say when the person answers. But my fingers were wet from the rain and the little holes on the dial were made from metal and my fingers slipped again and again. And even though I'm twelve, I'm small for my age, and I had to stand on tiptoes to see the numbers clearly.

But I did it. I dialed 999. And told them we need an ambulance. Yes. My sister. That's right.

I think my sister is dead.

The ambulance was there only minutes after I got back home. The ambulance men were anxious and sweating as they worked, mostly silently. They looked at the empty bottles. Then they put a tube down her throat, as she lay limp on the floor. And they pumped saline solution into her, and it all came out of another tube into a bowl. There were no pieces of carrot or little chewed up lumps of beef. No bread or cheese. No sardines. Just white pills bobbing around like little sailboats adrift in a choppy sea of foam.

And there was the smell. The sweet, sickly smell. Akanni never said anything; he just hopped from leg to leg, his huge brown eyes staring at everything. And I looked at the soles of my feet. They were bleeding and black. Purple-red and black.

They carried her down on the stretcher and stopped at the front door.

And one of the men turned to my mum.

"How did you let this happen?" he said.

And that made Mum scream.

Mum went with them in the ambulance but she wouldn't talk when she came back home.

It was four days later that she took us to the hospital.

"Are you aware how destructive aspirin is?" the doctor asked.

"No," Mum replied, "we don't keep aspirin in the house."

"Well, if you want to kill yourself, aspirin is a pretty effective way to do it," the doctor continued, "and if you hadn't acted in time she would be dead now. You have to get the aspirin out of the gut within an hour. There is no antidote for salicylate poisoning. And there are lots of possible severe side effects that can also kill you or debilitate you. The toxins shut down your organs. She's lucky to be alive. If you had left her until the morning, you would have found her dead. Quite dead."

"I heard a loud bang. Something fell on the floor."

"She will have to stay here for observation for at least a week. We have to monitor the toxin level and get fluids and salts in her body. Dr. Browning wants to see you before you leave. He's in the office at the end of the ward."

"Will she be able to see again?" Mum asked.

"See again? I don't know. She's only just come out of intensive care. She was in a coma. There may be permanent damage. We just don't know what has been damaged."

We were in the Queen Alexandra Hospital. Margueretta was connected to four separate monitors. When she regained consciousness in intensive care, she said she was blind. Apparently an aspirin overdose can blind you.

"Mrs. Mitchell. Come and sit here," said Dr. Browning.

"You two wait there with Akanni," Mum said.

So I waited with Emily and Akanni at the door of the matron's office. But the door was open.

"You need to hear this," Dr. Browning began.

"What? What is it?"

"Look. I think she will survive. Survive this overdose. And I hope she will get her sight back. It happens. The aspirin overdose can cause a temporary blindness."

"Thank God."

"Yes, thank God. Mrs. Mitchell, she very nearly died. You saved her life. Without you, she would be dead."

Mum began to cry.

"But it can't continue like this."

"No, it can't. Or I'll be joining her in here," Mum replied.

"She should be getting better. The ECT...the group therapy. Her group therapist said she's very intelligent, and she's a lively contributor to the sessions. She's very popular, you know."

"Oh, I'm sure she is. She can put on that 'little girl lost' look, right enough. But I know the truth. It's a living hell."

"I thought she was improving. We all did. And then this."

"Why is she doing this to us?"

"I have something to tell you. This is very serious."

"I'm sure it is serious."

"She's going to have to be locked up."

"Locked up?"

"Yes."

"Locked up?"

"I need you to agree to putting her in the lock-down ward of St. James's hospital. She came as close to death as you can come. It's for her own good. But you can still visit her. In fact, I would encourage it. But, perhaps not the children. It's not an easy place to see."

He looked through the open door at Emily and me.

"And one other thing—before you go."

He handed Mum a folded piece of paper.

"This is a letter."

"A letter? For me?"

"No. Not for you. This is a letter that Margueretta wrote to me. It's a common problem. We can deal with it another time. But it's my professional duty to bring this to your attention."

Mum read the letter on the bus ride home. It is a love letter. Margueretta is in love with Dr. Browning.

92

I was down on the kitchen floor trying to make an effective pattern with the tiles, which is not easy with the unexpected addition of red. I am extremely distressed that I have had to buy red tiles. Once these floor tiles are down, no amount of prying will get them back up. So the only answer is to go with a random red tile in amongst a geometric pattern of blue, green, and white.

"What's he doing?" asked Joan Housecoat.

"Covering the black floor," Mum replied. "Would you like some tea?"

"I would. But why is he using those red tiles? It looks like a blooming flag!"

"They sold out of blue. And green. And white."

"Ooo-er. I've got something to tell you. Something quite important."

"That's nice."

"Well, I'm having a nervous breakdown," Joan said.

"What? Here?"

"Well, not right here at the moment, but yes. I'm having a nervous breakdown."

"A nervous breakdown? How do you know?"

"Dr. Wilmot told me."

"What happened?"

"Ooo-er. It was Wednesday. And Fred always has steak and kidney pudding for his tea on Wednesday. But I forgot the kidneys."

"Go on."

"I started crying."

"That doesn't sound good."

"I couldn't stop."

"Oh, dear."

"I went up to the surgery, and they managed to get me in to see the doctor. And Dr. Wilmot said I was having a nervous breakdown."

"Just like that?"

"He said I had two choices. Either take the maximum dose of Valium for the rest of my days…or go in for ECT. So I'm thinking about doing the ECT. You're in and out in a couple of days."

"What caused it? Did he say what caused your nervous breakdown?" Mum asked.

"I shouldn't say really."

"Why? What did he say?"

"Well. Ooo-er. He said it was all the screaming and the shouting and all that."

"Screaming and shouting? Where?"

Joan pushed out her bosom and ran her finger round the neck of her housecoat and pulled her chin in.

"In here," Joan circled her head and pursed her lips. "All the goings on in here. It's given me a nervous breakdown."

"In here?"

"That's what Dr. Wilmot said. It's really difficult to live next door to it."

"Next door to what, exactly?"

"Next door to a bloomin' madhouse!"

"Well, I hope you told him that was a load of nonsense!"

"Why would I? He knows what's going on in here. Half the bloody street knows, excuse me! What with the psychiatrist and the police and the screaming and cutting her wrists and the obscenities and the doors slamming and…"

"Oh, I see you've got it all worked out, haven't you?"

"These walls are paper-thin, you know! No one should have to live next door to this! Fred's been to the council. We're on a transfer list. We're going to a better place where we all can get some peace and quiet. I'm not having ECT for nothing, you know!"

"Well, you can put that cup of tea down, Joan!"

"Ooo-er."

"You can put that cup down and get out of my house. You are not welcome here anymore!"

"Well! That's fine by me. I'll remember this when that daughter of yours cuts her wrists again. Don't come running to me! I saved her bloody life. And washed your dirty dishes. This place was filthy. Cat shit everywhere..."

"Get out!"

Margueretta's sight came back. She saw colors at first and then blurry images. But she should permanently give up alcohol because her liver is damaged, and it may not ever recover. Dr. Browning said she was very lucky. But she had to stay in hospital much longer than anyone thought. And then they sent her to the lock-down ward of St. James's.

That's where the real lunatics are.

93

need money. It's all well and good selling my lunch tickets, but it takes a whole month to make enough money to buy just one pack of floor tiles, and I've only done half the kitchen and haven't even started on the front room. And Miss Sanders said I am looking very pale, and she's worried about me. I was trying to see up her knickers at the time because she likes to sit on top of her desk in front of the classroom. The middle of the front row is the best viewing point, and I'm sure she knows I'm trying to see her knickers because she crosses her legs again and again and she watches my eyes and smiles at me, which makes it very difficult to study the terrace farming techniques of the rice paddies in Southeast Asia.

When she asked to see me after our geography lesson I thought it was because she saw me looking up her dress. She also does not wear a bra, and she has small breasts, which you can see when she bends down to look at your written work. I need a lot of help with my written work. I'm sure I've seen a nipple. But she didn't mention her knickers or nipples. She wanted to see me to ask if I was feeling all right and if there are any problems at home.

She told me to sit down and tell her anything I wanted her to know. There were several things I wanted her to know. She said our conversation was private.

"Is there anything going on at home that you want to tell me about?"

"No."

I wanted to tell her she was the most beautiful woman I had ever seen, and I desperately want to see her naked.

"Are you sure? I feel as if you are hiding something. Something that's not right."

"Not really."

She bent forward when she said that, and her dress moved up her silky thighs.

"Are you sure you're feeling all right?"

"Yes. I feel fine."

"Well. If there's anything wrong, at home, or anything at all—you can tell me. OK?"

"OK."

"I'm not an old fuddy-duddy teacher, you know."

She rubbed my hair when she said that. I nearly fainted.

"I know."

I would like to slowly undress her.

"Is it about a girl?"

"No."

"You're a very sensitive boy, aren't you?"

If only I could tell her that she makes me shiver when she's near me. And I still want to see her naked.

"Look. I know you haven't got a dad. But you've got a mum, right?"

"Yes."

"Well, can you talk to her about things? You know, about anything that's troubling you?"

It would be pointless to explain to Miss Sanders that my mum is going mad. Or that the reason I'm looking so pale is because I'm half-starved owing to the fact that I am selling my free lunch tickets so that I can buy floor tiles to cover the black floors that are the inexplicable reason why my mum is going mad in the first place.

So I said nothing about the asylum and the wrist-slashing and the filth and the leprosy and everything. She just shrugged her shoulders and looked sorry for me when I stared down at the floor.

I went to the park after school to think about Miss Sanders. I needed to be alone. When she was talking to me I got goose bumps on the back of my neck, and I felt this glow all over my head, like someone was pouring warm water on my brain. She's not married. And I think she likes me. I wish I was older or maybe just taller. I would put my tongue in her mouth. I would clean my teeth first.

And I wish I was in the park again right now. We call it a park, but it's really just waste ground with some swings and dog shit. There's brown, black, red, and even orange dog shit. Orange stinks the worst. If you ever get that shit on your shoe, you will need more than a dock leaf to get it off. Best to wait until it is hard and then chip it off with a stick.

There are packs of dogs running wild all around our estate. People buy dogs and then throw them out when they can't afford to feed them. The male dogs try to hump each other and that usually starts a fight that is great to watch. Then they go back to trying to hump each other. There's a small red-haired dog that the big dogs pick on. He gets humped a lot.

That girl in the park was amazing.

She came over to say hello, and even though I wanted to be alone, we sat on the swings together. Then I said we should play a game. So we played fizz-buzz. I don't know who she is, but she can't count. You have to say fizz if a number has a five in it or is divisible by five, or buzz if it's a seven, and fizz-buzz if it's both. It's pretty simple really if you concentrate and know your five and seven times tables. But I had to let her win a few times to make her think she was good at it. Then I said we should play for money. I let her win some money, and then I made my move. She started to panic when she owed me five shillings—and she didn't have any money at all.

She had blue knickers. And my legs started to shake like I was really scared. But I wasn't scared, I was excited, and then my whole body started shaking, and I couldn't believe that she agreed to my suggestion to take her knickers down in payment for the five shillings.

"A quick look! That's all you're getting! A quick look! And no touching!"

We were hiding in the bushes. I could hardly hear her because my ears were ringing with the excitement, and I was finding it hard to breathe as I had that same glow over my head again.

She held her dress up and then she slid her fingers into the top of her knickers and pulled them down slightly. But she stopped.

"That's all!"

"Do it! You have to show me!" I shouted. "Or pay me the five bob!"

She dropped her shoulders and sighed, and she flicked her long black hair with the back of her hand. And then she pulled a little further at her knickers until I could see a line of dark hair. It had to be pubic hair. It had to be. I held onto a branch.

"That's all!" she shouted.

"No way! Five shillings! You owe me! All the way!"

"God! You fucker!"

She slid them down further until I could see a triangle of hair. And then she pulled them right down to her knees.

"Go on then. Have a good look! You wanker!"

And there it was. Right in front of me. The thing Danny and I had talked about for years. We had seen the pictures. We had discussed it in every detail. That glimpse when we were getting undressed for PE. I had done everything I could to see a real one. And now here it was. Only a yard in front of me, in the fading light. And so near, I could reach out and touch it.

The quim.

An actual quim.

And it was the most beautiful thing I had ever seen.

94

J oan Housecoat has come home from her electroconvulsive therapy, which is free on the National Health. She could have come home in an ambulance but Fred has bought a car. He traded in his Vespa for a secondhand Bond 875 fiberglass three-wheeler. Some drunks turned it upside down in the road in the middle of the night, but he got Old Man Dumby to help him turn it back up the right way, and he used it to collect Joan from the nut house, after he refilled all the oil and petrol and wiped the grit off the roof.

Margueretta, however, will not be coming home as planned.

"Something terrible happened," Mum explained to Emily and me.

"Is she alright?" Emily asked.

"Who knows? If it's not this, it will be something else. But it's me who suffers through it all, for the love of God."

"What happened?"

"She stole some pills from the drug cart."

But that wasn't the worst thing.

They take away your shoelaces and anything else you could use to hang yourself or kill yourself within the lock-up ward. So Margueretta took the cord from a lamp and hanged herself in the toilet.

Diddle, diddle dumpling, my son John.

She isn't dead because another patient found her, but it's only a matter of time. She's thrown herself in front of a bus, slashed her wrists, taken an overdose of aspirin, and hanged herself. And I'm not counting the time when she tried to cut her throat with Nana's bread knife or when she threatened to throw herself off the front porch. There's no way that those were serious ways to kill yourself.

She has to stay locked up, of course, and they even had to put her in a straitjacket because she said she would find a way to kill herself or kill someone else. According to Mum's *A History of Mental Illness*, the straitjacket was invented by a French upholsterer as an alternative to tying down the lunatics and maniacs with metal chains. This was before the enlightened age of psychoanalysis and modern psychiatric medicines. These days the doctors know a lot more about madness, but they still use straitjackets. And they have padded cells to stop the nutters from braining themselves by bashing their heads against a wall. So they put Margueretta in a straitjacket and then in a padded cell.

She cried and begged and Dr. Browning said she could come out if she could prove that she was not going to kill herself or anyone else. And she must have proved it because they let her out of the padded cell, and that's why we have to visit her.

Akanni couldn't come because he might find the scene too disturbing, and he's too young to understand why my sister has a thing in her head that's telling her to kill herself. Or why she screams at the sight of a running tap and the colors purple or red make her want to bleed. So he's staying with Mollie Midget for the afternoon. But since Emily and I will soon be thirteen, we are old enough to visit a lunatic asylum lock-up ward. Dr. Browning thinks it might help if Margueretta can see the people around her who love her and want her back.

It is possible that Emily loves Margueretta and wants her back. I will ask her later. I, on the other hand, do not.

There's an old lady clucking like a chicken. Her dressing gown is loose because she doesn't have a cord, of course. And I don't want to see her wrinkled old breast, even though it's hanging there for anyone to see. And another woman is making a low-pitched groaning sound like a fire engine whose siren is winding down. Then there is a woman hiding under her bed with black eyes, and she's looking at me like I am the one who is mad, not her.

It smells of vomit and diarrhea and boiled meat and cabbages with a bigger smell of disinfectant. The nurse said Margueretta likes to listen to Anne Murray singing "Snow Bird."

Spread your tiny wings and fly away,
And take the snow back with you where it came from on that day...
And if I could you know that I would,
Fly away with you..."

She listens to it over and over again all day. So we should buy the record when she gets out, that's what the nurse said.

Margueretta wants to fly away. But she can't. She's in this cage.

And this other woman keeps tugging at my arm and asking when her mummy is going to be here. She says she's waiting for her mummy to come in a taxi to take her home. She's as old as Nana. I would think her mummy is dead. Now she's crying for her mummy.

"Please find my mummy. Please find her. She's coming for me today. She's coming to take me home to see my papa. I want my mummy. Please tell her I'm in here. She's coming today in a taxi to take me home. Please find my mummy..."

And I am sure that each one is waiting for her mummy to come and take her home at the end of school and whisper, "I love you," in her ear. And tuck her up in bed at night with an orange nightlight reflecting little moons and stars on the ceiling and give her a cup of hot chocolate to drink while mummy softly reads *The Tale of Jemima Puddle-Duck*.

And her daddy would sing to her.

Here we go loopy loo,
Here we go loopy light,
Here we go droopy-doo,
All on a Saturday night!

And twirl her around so that her little skirt would fly out. And he would call her "droopy drawers" because her skirt sat so low underneath her plump little tummy.

But no mummy or daddy is coming to take any of them home. They will always be here, staring out of the windows through the iron bars. And the others will be on the outside, staring back.

No sign of Margueretta, though. But there is another girl about the same age as Margueretta. Wrists are bandaged. She looks like a ghost. It's not nice to look like a ghost, but I don't think she knows.

Keep walking down the corridor. Take no notice of the people who are screaming. Ignore the arms that are reaching into the air. I think that woman just peed herself. Keep walking to the bed on the end.

There are only two chairs by the bed, so I will stand. And I don't know why we have to wait by this bed with that woman lying there under the blankets, staring at the ceiling.

"Kiss your sister. Give Margueretta a kiss. Go on."

I'm not kissing her. She doesn't look like Margueretta. She's yellow and gray and old with black circles round her red, red eyes. She has a wide purple-black ring around the skin on her neck.

And her hands are shaking, as she reaches her pale thin arms out to touch me. Reaching out like a dead person wanting to touch something that's still alive.

95

Mum bought that "Snowbird" record and, since we were in the music shop, she suggested we splash out on a new LP to listen to on Sundays. This could mean the end of "Bali Ha'i." It was a hard choice, but she came down in favor of the soundtrack to the *Sound of Music*. It was either that or Merle Haggard. His girlfriend does not love him anymore, and there is a hole in his shoe. His wine is all gone, and he needs some more. But for us it will be the Mother Abbess who is climbing every bloody mountain.

They're in it together. I know that it could not have been a coincidence that Florie Atkins gave me the piano score for the *Sound of Music* as an early Christmas present. So now I am learning to play "Edelweiss" while she stamps her foot and bangs her hand on the side of the piano. And since it is a musical, she is also singing along. Mum keeps asking me to play "Edelweiss" because a small white flower on a mountainside is just one way that we can see the face of God. She can't wait for me to learn "The Lonely Goatherd."

According to Miss Peabody, you should not listen to lively music on a Sunday, or it will distract you from your thoughts of God. Certainly not pop music, jazz, or rock 'n' roll. Permissible genres are classical, gospel, country and western, and anything by Rodgers and Hammerstein. This is why you cannot listen to *Paint Your Wagon*. Also, there is a lot of wooing in that movie, and the Fandango girls are women of ill repute. If not for this, Lee Marvin's "Wandr'in' Star" could be listened to because it has the Sabbath cachet of being sung in a tuneless and morose style, creating a musical sense of depression and grief.

We can also listen to hymns.

"Stand Up, Stand Up for Jesus" remains Miss Peabody's all-time favorite.

Stand up, stand up for Jesus, Ye soldiers of the Cross,
Hold high his royal banner,
It must not suffer loss.
From victory unto victory, his armies he shall lead,
'Til every foe is vanquished and Christ is Lord indeed.

Don't even think about asking or Miss Peabody will tell you everything about this hymn. It was written in memory of the Reverend Dudley Tyng, who died as a result of his silk tunic getting caught in a corn thrasher, ripping his arm from its socket. He lost a lot of blood, the wound got infected, and he died. Apparently, his last words were, "Let us all stand up for Jesus."

I am sure that Valium use increases on Sundays.

The television is no better. Tonight we watched David Kossoff on *Storytime* telling the tale of Cain and Abel. Cain was jealous of Abel because God did not praise him. This was after Cain only gave God a few grains of corn as an offering whereas Abel killed an actual lamb or two. It was God's test to see if Cain would let the evil take him over. So Cain takes his brother for a walk and murders him, and then God curses the ground so that it will never produce again. Miss Peabody says that the murder of Abel was the creation of evil after the original sin when man discovered woman. And Cain was the evil one, the origin of the Devil.

I think this answers the question about whether God created the Devil. He did.

It is permissible to laugh on Sundays but only at a religious joke. This is why the chief usher tells the same joke at the end of the sermon every week when he reads the Parish notices.

"The Young Wives Club will meet at five o'clock on Thursday. All those wishing to become Young Wives, please see the reverend in his study."

And the Sunday roast dinner was definitely invented to help people get through the day. The comfort of roast beef, Yorkshire puddings, roast potatoes, and lashings of gravy probably helps to prevent several attempted suicides per week. We, however, had something purple and hairy for dinner that the butcher thought was for our dog. Part heart, part udder. And without a decent meal from Monday to Friday, I am in real danger of starving to death. Any advert on the old telly involving food or sweets is becoming highly hypnotic to me—even the advert for Maltesers, the chocolate with the less-fattening center that should only be eaten by girls who are watching their waistlines.

I have told Mum that this cannot continue. Obviously, I did not tell her about my risk of starvation and the lunch ticket scam, even though the purple, hairy heart-udder we were supposed to eat for dinner needed some discussion. But I did tell her that from now on I will not be going to either Sunday School or Church because there is nothing further that I can be taught about God, Jesus, the Holy Spirit, the archangel Gabriel, the Bible in general, or specifically the concept of Original Sin.

This did not go well.

Mum has seen my demand to stay at home on Sundays as a clear sign that I have reached "that" age, and it is time that she told me a thing or two about the desperate plight of man and the need for procreation, and how, *exactly*, we all came into this world.

"There are things you need to know, Johnny. It's time that you knew. Some of this may come as quite a shock. I will spare you some of the detail. But the world is full of shocks. Sit yourself down."

Firstly, I should consider myself a servant of God, and since I have not yet reached the age of adulthood, I could not have served any worthy purpose, and therefore I owe God a great debt. Mum was right. This has come as quite a shock. I thought that my childhood double-duty of Sunday School with Miss Peabody and nightly prayers on my knees had been a clear sign of my belief and devotion. I had no idea I was racking up a debt to God.

Secondly, she said I must continue to attend church, as I will be tested later in life by all manner of temptations, betrayal, grief, death, and possibly by a general lack of purpose. It will be during these times that I will need to turn to God and will regret having selfishly abandoned Him before I have even reached my teenage years or repaid my debt. I will especially need Him if I do not know why I am here.

And finally, there are sins that I will encounter specifically involving the serpent and the apple but am still too young to know what these are in any detail. Adam and Eve are also involved.

"All men are the same. Mark my word. You'll get the taste for it, and that will be that. You're just a boy now, but, in a couple of years you'll be a man, and you'll be out there with Eve and the serpent. Do you understand?"

"Not really."

"And to think that you want to abandon God at this stage in your life. I've never heard the like of it. The serpent hides in the branches and in the leaves. Right, laddie?"

"Not sure what you mean."

"Once you've dipped your wick, you will not be able to resist it, no matter what."

"Dipped my wick?"

"The flesh is weak! We'll leave it at that for now."

This is the original sin. The technical term, I think, is "wooing," and this clearly demonstrates why I should not be listening to the soundtrack to *Paint Your Wagon*. Especially on a Sunday.

And there was absolutely no mention of the quim.

96

She howls like a desperate wolf in the smothering black air of the night. Then she screams the way anyone would scream who is convicted to the sentence of blind torture by faceless demons. Alone in a darkness that is too big for this world, swirling around inside her head.

And those things talk to her with their independent voices. Not pretty, adolescent conversations about boys and lipstick and babies. Just whispers of death and dying and the constant taunting to kill herself. Even sleep is no escape. They come to her in her dreams. They live inside her and outside at the same time.

But there is no dead child in the attic. No necrotic, entombed girl waiting to be released from her eternal purgatory. No half-life screeching in the emptiness for her freedom. To be released by those who cruelly abandoned her to her immurement.

After all this time, there is no child in the attic. It's Margueretta. Mum knew it was her all along—her voice coming through the vents in the ceiling like a child in the attic. Mum knew it but she didn't want to admit that Margueretta was screaming in the night. Mum wouldn't admit it for fear it would frighten Emily and me—for fear that it would terrify us almost to death.

Margueretta has been screaming for years.

But I'm more frightened now. It was easier to think of a ghost in the attic, or a dead child abandoned by the gypsies who fled in the night. A ghost that might find its way home—a terrible ghoulish nightmare in the godforsaken darkness. A nightmare that I might wake up from.

Now I know it's Margueretta, and I can hear the fear of death in those screams. She takes her pills before she goes to bed, but they never last the night. And then that thing comes to her that's rarely seen. It whispers first, and then it cries in her ears and inside her head like a prisoner trapped in a cell when all the other inmates have been released. A friend at first—and then the vile hands of a killer reaching down inside her throat to throttle her or wrap it's palms around her nose and mouth. Locked in the cell together.

She tells her story now. I have to listen.

Soon it will be me. Not the imagined skull smeared across the bedroom window glass like the slow motion of a hideous, haunting sludge. Or that person who always stands behind me but is never there when I turn around. Those are easy things to forget, easy to ignore.

No, she says there are embodiments of evil inside me, feeding on tiny random thoughts that don't mean a thing. Just a thought of savage death, slicing through the purple hairy beast with the mass of blackened veins. Eating the cow's rejected body of cancerous flesh that grew beside its udder. Or the suffocating darkness that's too big for the space and comes down through gaps in the trapdoor to join the ancient darkness that was there before anyone or anything. And still it's too big and wants the space that is inside me—the darkness that I stole from the cellar and keep inside my head.

I can't forget those things when the sun shines. Not the voices she says are inside me. Not the same voices from the water streaming from the tap like a vile, immovable glass rod. Those things don't only belong to the night.

So I am knocking on her door tonight. Some nights are worse than others, and it seems like an inevitable death will end it all. Most times I bury my head under the blanket, pull it around my ears, around my head, and pray for the screams to stop. But tonight I knock on her door, a gentle tap.

The screaming stops. Nothing.

And then the door opens with such a force that I fall back and down, away from her door. And I scuttle like a human crab, moving backwards on all-fours, headfirst, away from it all—away from the fear-wet face and the suddenness of my sister's violent grief. Away from the thing that comes inside her head and could so easily come inside my own.

"Help me...help me. For God's sake, help me. I'm going to die!" she screams.

She wants God now. She would renounce the Devil and let God back. She would say her passionate prayers like any sinner wanting redemption. Wanting to be released from the fiery lakes of Hell. Declaring with her mouth, "Jesus is Lord," and believing in her heart that God raised him from the dead. She will be saved.

For my sister has not sinned, save the offense towards God of trying to take her own life.

She is afraid for her life.

And when the silence returns, as it always does, I hear the rattle of the piss running through Akanni's thin mattress and bouncing on the floorboards below. Then he groans the groan of the first boy, turns over in his restless, box-bed sleep, and returns to his boyish dreams of heroic adventures.

97

Something wonderful has happened that means I can eat again. Emily and I have found jobs at the local greengrocers. Strictly speaking, it is illegal for us to be working at age thirteen. But Mrs. McWilliams, the proprietor, sees us as her "widow's mites," and she has taken pity on us. She will pay us in cash, no paperwork.

When she asked what our father does, I replied that we do not have a father, and for some reason she jumped to the conclusion he was killed in a terrible accident. I did not tell her that he went out to see a man about a dog just after Winston Churchill's funeral and has not been seen since, except for an episode in a pub involving a broken bottle, which we do not talk about. I did not correct her, and I may have encouraged her by looking like a sad and distressed little boy whose father was tragically killed in a terrible accident.

"A sudden accident?"

I just stared down at the floor.

Mrs. McWilliams knows all about death, having survived the Allied blitz of Hamburg in 1943. And that's where she met her husband, who is Scottish, when he was serving in the British Second Army after the war. So she speaks English with a German-Scottish accent. Unless she is angry, and then she just speaks German.

I am therefore learning some important phrases such as, "Vas ist zat, Scotch Mist?" or, "Bringen sie pastinak," which means, "fetch the parsnips."

I carry sacks of potatoes and crates of cabbages up two flights of stairs and restock all the shelves of fruit and vegetables, and I make enough money to buy three whole packets of Dunlop floor tiles per week. I have therefore picked out a mock-oak plastic design for the hall, which I shall lay in a parquet style, alternating the grain. I have decided to leave the front room for last just to see if Woolworth's pulls the same sale trick with the mock-oak. I do not want to introduce a color to go with the oak parquet.

I am also able to afford a packet of Camel unfiltered cigarettes to smoke with Carl. Carl is the permanent lad who works in the shop all week. He is almost sixteen and knows all about quims. His girlfriend is a slut, which means that she drops her knickers at a moment's notice for just about anyone, and if I want to do it with a real-life quim, he will bring her round one afternoon. I suggested next Saturday.

And Carl is much stronger than me because he lifts those crates and sacks all week. He says he is going to make something of himself one day but in the meantime he is trying to throw a potato over the next row of shops.

"If you throw it hard enough, you can get it over the building there!"

I cannot throw a potato further than the parking bays at the back of our shop. But Carl has a huge swing, and he can launch a potato with such a force that it flies over the opposite three-story building. We can't see beyond the building, but we know there is another street of shops over there.

He does practice throws with brussels sprouts, and when he's got a good aim, he throws a Maris Piper. It feels really good to drag on an unfiltered Camel and watch that Maris Piper potato rocket over the rooftops into the next street. It's a shame we can't see it explode when it lands. Maris Pipers are really good for baking because they are quite large.

We don't just sell fruit and vegetables. We sell Coca-Cola, flowers, fresh farm eggs, pickled onions, and Lucozade. But we've had to discount the fresh farm eggs by 80 percent because they have been on the shelf for over three months, and Mrs. McWilliams doesn't know exactly when they were laid. Actually, they were not even fresh farm eggs. She got them from the wholesaler. We are therefore selling them on a no-return basis and have had to put a limit of only one dozen per customer.

"Zis floor is nicht clean! Vash it again!"

We were washing the floor this afternoon for a second time, Carl and me, when a short fat lady in a faux-fur coat came into the shop.

"Vee are closed! Kannst du nicht read?

"Who the fucking hell did this!"

And that's when things went badly downhill. I can keep my job, but I will not be getting next Saturday's introduction to the full details of the quim. Carl was fired. And I was forced to agree that in no way did that woman's husband deserve to get hit on the head by a flying Maris Piper. It also broke his glasses.

"And before he was so cruelly struck, it was raining brussels sprouts like the fucking Plagues of Egypt!"

Mrs. McWilliams handled the situation very well, I thought. She gave the fat lady two-dozen, fresh farm eggs and a small bunch of freesias.

"Here," said Mrs. McWilliams, handing her the eggs. "You get zwei-dozen. Datz gut. Zehr gut, eh? Everyone else only got one! Ein!"

"Not fucking good enough! I'm getting the police!"

The fat lady wouldn't leave until she had claimed two pounds of Granny Smith apples, a pound of first-class Jersey tomatoes, half a pound of button mushrooms, six cans of Coke, and a bag of unshelled peanuts.

"I'll make him a mushroom and tomato omelet for his dinner tonight," she said, leading her husband out of the store. "Come on, Cyril. Let's go. You've had a difficult evening."

"Look vat zat cost me, Carl! You blithering dum-kopf! You're fired!"

Still, it's Friday night, and maybe Mrs. McWilliams will forgive him tomorrow. He says she's fired him before for pissing in the corner of the storeroom even though she couldn't prove it was him. He said a dog must have got in there. But she always hires him back in the morning when the potatoes need to be brought up from the store. I hope she does hire him back because I was really looking forward to doing it with a real-life quim.

Hopefully, next Saturday.

98

The police brought her back tonight. She was at her group therapy session this afternoon, and then she didn't come home—but that's nothing new. They found her trying to jump out of the ninth floor window of a block of flats. She was sitting on the window ledge.

"Do you know what happened?" Constable Ferguson asked.

Constable Ferguson is here again with a policewoman called Theresa. Margueretta just screamed and ran up to her bedroom.

"Nothing would surprise me," Mum replied.

She went drinking with her group therapy friends and they suggested she drink Tia Maria because she said she likes coffee and wanted to try something different to Harvey's Bristol Cream Sherry. She's not under arrest because it's not illegal to dangle your legs out of a ninth-floor window and attempting suicide is no longer a crime.

"Did you know she was missing?" Constable Ferguson asked.

"She's not missing. It's only nine o'clock at night."

"Well, did you know where she was?"

"Yes, she went to her group therapy session."

"We found her trying to climb out of a window."

"Really? Huh."

"On the ninth floor. She said she was going to jump. We've spent most of the last hour talking her off the ledge of the window, Mrs. Mitchell."

"She won't jump," said Mum.

"Why? How do you know that?"

"Because if she was going to jump, she would just do it. She wouldn't wait for someone to call the police and then spend an hour talking to you, would she? She would just jump."

"I don't like the way this conversation is going, Mrs. Mitchell. Is Mr. Mitchell at home?" asked Theresa.

"Ha! If he was at home I would like a word with him first. He's been missing for six years! In fact, you should be out looking for him instead of messing around with her. He owes me six years back maintenance for these children. He hasn't paid a damned penny towards their upbringing!"

"This is serious."

"Oh, I'm deadly serious. How am I supposed to survive bringing up three kids on my own in this day and age?"

"We're not here for that. You need to have tighter control over your daughter. This isn't the first time. We've got a file an inch thick on her."

"Tighter control? And, tell me, do—how exactly do I do that? Ask Constable Ferguson. He knows."

"She should have a curfew," Theresa replied.

"A curfew? Oh, don't make me laugh, young lady. Try putting a curfew on a cat!"

"It may not be such a good outcome next time!"

"Well, why don't you give me those handcuffs?"

"What?"

"I will take them upstairs and handcuff her to her bed. Will that satisfy you?"

"But you're her mother!"

"Oh, I'm well aware of that. Well aware."

"She's just a girl," said Theresa.

"A girl? Are you kidding me? She's seventeen years old. It's her life now, and if this is what she wants to do with it, then so be it. I've tried everything I can to be a good mother after their father left them. And this is the result."

"Look. We don't want to have to enforce it. But you need to give her a curfew. And no more alcohol. She's been drinking, you know."

"Drinking? They shouldn't serve her. She's underage. Of course she looks old enough to drink with all that makeup on and those clothes of hers. How do I stop her? Eh? I'm sure they like a pretty girl in a short skirt in the pubs around here."

"Please try."

"Oh, I'll try, right enough."

Constable Ferguson and Theresa left, and Margueretta put her record player on in her room, but she doesn't play "Snowbird" anymore. Now she plays a song about a rose garden, over and over and over again. And she sings along.

So smile for a while and let's be jolly,
Love shouldn't be so melancholy,
Come along and share the good times while we can...

And Mum cried when the police left. Tears and the rose garden. Over and over. So I laid the last of the tiles in the kitchen and showed her. That seemed to make her happier.

But she didn't stop crying even though the black floor in the kitchen is gone forever.

99

We knew there was a problem as soon as we got there this morning. An angry mob was waiting outside the greengrocers, and the shop wasn't even open. Mrs. McWilliams was standing by the Radio Rentals shop, nervously watching the crowd.

"Go round zee back of the shop. I vill call ze politz if it gets violent!"

We all gathered in the dark at the back of the shop.

"You, Carl! You stand at zee front when I open zee door. You're the biggest. Hold them back if you have to! Vee vill let in only one at a time."

I think this means she's hired him back.

"Don't worry," Carl said, cracking his knuckles loudly, "I'll thump the first person who tries to push past."

"Zat iz zee spirit, Carl!"

"Dunkirk spirit."

"Vat?"

"Nothing."

"OK. To zee door!"

They all burst in at once when we opened the shop door. Carl ran behind the counter.

"Look at this!" a woman shouted. "It's a green egg!"

"And this one is just a lump of mold inside!"

"How old are these eggs?"

"Vat did you expect? I mean, it vas a vee bit o' a bargain."

"But there were no *good* eggs," a woman shouted. "It can't be a bargain if *all* the eggs are rotten."

And then there was a familiar face. A familiar face and a familiar faux-fur coat. And a man with glasses stuck together with sticking plaster.

"Look at this! That was supposed to be Cyril's dinner!"

She threw the dozen eggs on the counter. He was really looking forward to that mushroom and tomato omelet. She probably had a bit of sharp cheddar in the pantry to give it some extra zest.

"Och! Werden Sie zurück! Stand back! Everyone getzen compensation."

Despite several remarks from the angry mob involving Hitler's testicles, which I thought were totally uncalled for, Mrs. McWilliams negotiated a truce. Everyone gets a bag of slightly bruised fruit, a jar of pickled onions, and a savoy cabbage. It was quiet after that.

But the fat lady wasn't leaving. She said the eggs were a penalty for hitting Cyril on the head with a Maris Piper.

"Ha! Und zwei bottles of Lucozade. It aids recovery!"

So Mrs. McWilliams sent me and Carl to fetch a crate of Lucozade from the downstairs storeroom. We stood in the store and lit up a Camel and each took a long drag.

"Can you believe that?" I asked. "Two bottles of Lucozade!"

"That's what she thinks!" Carl replied.

"What do you mean?"

"You'll see."

Carl carefully pulled down the yellow cellophane wrapper from one of the bottles and unscrewed the cap. He guzzled down the warm fizzy juice, spraying it all around his mouth and onto his shirt.

"What are you doing?" I asked.

"Blurrrrrp! Blurrrrrp! I'll get them for blurrrrrp this fucking blurrrrrp mess. Fucking blurrrrrp fuckers! Glad he got that spud on the blurrrrrp fucking head! Now he blurrrrrp will get more than he fucking blurrrrrp is expecting! Blurrrrrp."

Carl whipped out his cock and pissed into the half-empty bottle, neatly filling it back to the top. It is helpful that Lucozade is the color of piss.

"That should do it!" Carl said, screwing the top back on the bottle and squeezing the cellophane back in place.

"You can't do that!"

"Ha! Watch me! 'Lucozade Aids Recovery!' Ha! Ha! Ha!"

It's not going to be a good day for Cyril. He will be sitting down to a fresh bowl of fruit tonight for desert. And he will wash it down with a tasty glass of Carl's piss.

But at least Carl is back. And Saturday is only a week away. Only one week until the quim.

100

arl is a liar. He is also a virgin and has not done it, as he claimed, with seventeen different girls, including the girl who serves behind the Pick 'n Mix counter in Woolworth's. And his girlfriend is not a slut because she is also virgin, and you can't be a slut if you are a virgin. He said he will make it up to me, but I have been anticipating the quim all week and thoughts of the serpent and Eve have been keeping me awake for days. So nothing will make up for this. Nothing.

I have also been thinking about suicide. I just realized that Margueretta has tried all the different ways I can think of to kill herself, and quite honestly, I can't think of another way except drowning. We do live near water, and I think if you want to be sure of killing yourself, you have to jump off a bridge so that you are dragged deep under the water by strong currents. Even if you fight it, you will still be drowned. You could also bind your hands and legs together or put really heavy rocks in your pockets.

According to *A History of Mental Illness*, drowning is a popular way to kill yourself because the body is not marked or disfigured in any way, and you can therefore look perfect and peaceful when displayed in your open coffin for your grieving relatives. This is, of course, dependent on being found quickly, or your body will become swollen and sallow, the skin will become soapy, and it will slowly detach from your bones in slimy strips. Also, your head becomes floppy when you are dead, and it bounces around in the water and runs the risk of hitting a rock or a post or something that could lead to some quite disturbing damage. Sea spiders or other carnivorous crustaceans could also eat you. It might therefore be better to drown yourself in a bath-tub or a swimming pool.

Ruling that out, she will have to try one of the other methods a second time. Or she could shoot herself. But I discounted that because we don't have a gun.

Mum says Margueretta needs to get a job or her mind will constantly dwell on dark, depressing thoughts of death and despair, and things will only get worse from there. She only lasted a week as a chambermaid at the Queens Hotel. She found a used tampon on a bathroom floor, and that was that. She also said that one of the male guests tried it on with her when she was trying to tuck in his eiderdown. But I think it was the tampon. No one would want to pick up a used tampon with their bare hands.

Mum has also said that without a wage coming in from Margueretta, I will have to make a weekly contribution to the household budget from my wages. This is completely unfair, as I don't think she realizes that I am using the money to buy floor tiles to cover the black floors to stop her from going completely bloody bonkers. Floors don't cover themselves. And if I am going to make a contribution to the household budget, I want an actual Sunday roast dinner and not a hairy purple heart-udder that has to be boiled all night. If not, I will starve to death, as I will have to go back to selling my lunch tickets to make more money.

Anyway, Carl has brought a bottle of VSOP sherry into the shop this afternoon as a peace offering. Once we get this new load of vegetables off the lorry and into the storeroom, we will open the sherry and have a nice drink with our Camel unfiltered cigs.

If things work out around here, Mrs. McWilliams says she will let me serve behind the counter, the same as Emily. But I prefer working down in the storeroom with Carl. We can smoke and talk about quims in private.

"I get completely pissed down the pub every Saturday night. Sixteen pints of mild, mate! Have you ever drunk VSOP?"

"No. My sister drinks Harvey's Bristol Cream. I've tasted that..."

"Tasted? Tasted? We're not going to *taste* it! We're going to have a serious drink here. I'll show you. Gulp it down like this. We're gonna get hammered."

"OK."

"Here. You take a good swig. We can stay down here the rest of the afternoon and get pissed out of our fucking skulls. So what's your experience with the quim?"

"I saw one in the park. It was a bet."

"What color was it?"

"Black."

"I like red ones best. Mind you, hic, there aren't too many red ones about. Hic."

"This tastes good. It's sweet."

"Yeh. It's not really a man's drink. Hic. We're gonna polish off the whole fucking bottle. Just you and me. We're mates. Drinking mates. They're the best kind. Let's have another cig."

"Yeh. Hic. Glug. Glug."

"Yeh. We need to get some quim. My girlfriend is gonna give it up. She says I have to get a jonnie. Hic."

"Jonnie?"

"Yeh. A Durex. Condom. Don't want her getting fucking up the spout. Bun in the oven? Fucking bitch."

"Carl! Carl! Vere zee bloomin heck are you? I turn my back und zis is vat happens! You disappear!"

It was simple really. Carl had already put a coin in the light bulb socket, and when she flicked the light switch—that was it. Zap. Kaboom. Sparks. Storeroom in darkness. Carl is a genius like that.

"Carl! Who turned out zee fucking lights? Carl! Are you in there? Carl! Carl!"

We're hiding behind the cabbages.

"Carl! Do you hear me? Sie sind gefeuert! You're fired!"

101

Firstly, the reason Mum is so upset this morning is not because I puked all over my bed in my sleep last night and then puked out of my bedroom window. Or because it was quite a windy night and the vomit blew back and landed on the outside of our kitchen window, where it still is.

I admit that this was very upsetting for my mum to find when she came downstairs for her morning cup of tea, with her initial thought being that a massive bird had been pulverized against the glass in some freak accident. And yes, I could have died by inhaling my own vomit, in which case, Mum would now be grieving over the cold, lifeless body of her thirteen-year-old son who is covered in dried up sick and stuck to the sheets and will never see the benefit of his good Christian upbringing and five years of piano lessons.

I can understand that this episode alone would be enough for any mother to consider abandoning her children forever to an orphanage, especially as she has worked her fingers to the bone scrimping and saving to bring them up without that lazy good-for-nothing father of mine.

But that is not why she is so upset and has spent the entire morning crying and smoking. She does not know that I smoke as well as drink, so I did not offer her one of my unfiltered Camels when her Kensitas ran out.

The reason Mum is really upset is because Margueretta was kidnapped. This explains why my older sister has been missing for two days.

I have only caught a few of the facts from the conversations this morning in between episodes of being voluntarily locked in the toilet. I am never drinking VSOP sherry again. Carl also lied about drinking sixteen pints of mild in the pub every Saturday night because if he really was that experienced with drinking, we would not be in this mess. And Mrs. McWilliams has really fired him this time because it's one thing to fuse all the lights by putting a coin in the socket, but he puked into the gypsophila vase and that is just unforgiveable even if there were no customers in the store at the time.

I still have a job because I was lead astray by an older boy. And I am now supporting a poor, widowed mother who has hungry mouths to feed.

I have to take all my bedclothes to the launderette later, but now I have to take the mop and bucket and clean that bloody mess off the kitchen window so that it will not continually remind my mum of what a thoughtless, ungrateful, and uncaring child she has for a son.

"This is not *Tom Brown's School Days* you know!"

I'm not sure, but I think Mum is referring to the book that has been serialized on the BBC on Sunday night. It's about schoolboy bullying and juvenile drinking in 1830s England. And I am not Tom Brown.

"You're your father's son, all right. Just like him. The apple does not fall far from the tree. Out drinking when you should be working. Irresponsible. I know how all of this will end, mark my words, young man! And how old are you?"

"Thirteen. I said I was sorry."

"Oh, yes. Sorry. I've heard it all before. All my life. Sorry. Until the next time. And then where will I be? Weeping at your grave, that's where. And you still haven't told me why you did it. Are you hiding something from me? Did you drink to prove something? Eh?"

Mum has decided not to call the police. Not for my underage drunkenness, and not for Margueretta's kidnapping.

Margueretta escaped through a tiny window, which she could do because she is so thin. They kidnapped her in the Black Dog pub after group therapy. The good-looking one said he was going to put her into films because she is so pretty and obviously talented. And they had a nice car, and they drove her around for a while, and then they took her to a house in a street she didn't know.

And they locked her in a back room and told her she was now to do it with men for money, and she should start by giving a free one to the good-looking one. So they stripped her, and he did it with her. And he slapped her when she complained. He had a knife, and he said he would not hesitate to slit her throat and leave her there to bleed to death.

She thought she was going to die. That's what Margueretta told us.

"How did you get back here?" Mum asked.

"On the bus," Margueretta replied.

"But you said you didn't have any money. They took all your money. That's what you said."

"They did. I didn't have any money. I looked out the bus window when the conductor came over, and he must have thought I already had a ticket. I always do that."

"You expect us to believe this kidnapping story?"

"It's true."

"So you were kidnapped by three men in a pub?"

"And raped."

"That's your story."

"It's true."

"You left with them in their car. You were drinking! What do you expect?"

"I knew this is what you would say. You never believe me. How could you say I am making this up?"

"I never said you were making all of it up. But it seems a bit of a wild tale to me!"

"I need to lie down."

The vomit was really crusty, and it took a lot of scrubbing with the mop to get it off. Then to the launderette with my bedclothes—and that woman who is always there. She's always there looking for me and the black children, wanting to know what I am washing. But the launderette was closed because it is Sunday. I will therefore have to sleep on the bare mattress.

If it was Thursday, I would watch the telly tonight. Thursday is the best night for the telly. Last Thursday, Raymond Baxter showed us an electronic calculator on *Tomorrow's World*. Mum thinks we should make do with multiplication tables. I think they should invent something really useful like x-ray spectacles.

Margueretta still watches *Top of the Pops* because she likes Tony Blackburn. And last week there was a man singing about killing a man who did something sinister to Maria. And a band called Middle of the Road is number one. A baby called Don has lost his mama and papa after falling asleep.

It goes chirpy, chirpy, cheep, cheep.

102

R ape is when a man steals a woman's chastity without her permission. And if a man lies with a woman without her agreement, and she is not betrothed to another man, he is supposed to marry her. It's more complicated than that, but Mum says that's as much as I should know until I am older and is also why I should not sing the words to "Foggy, Foggy Dew," even if I have heard Mum sing it many times. You never know who could be listening.

Margueretta will not be getting married, but she will be coming home soon after her latest treatment.

"'Psychopharmacological treatment is contraindicated.' I have written that in her notes because these drugs have what we call 'teratogenic potential.' What this means is they could cause deformities, Mrs. Mitchell. This latest news means we have to stop all drug treatments. But these voices are alarming. She is also experiencing powerful hallucinations. This is an extremely disturbing development. Right now we only have one alternative."

"Which is?"

"We should try another course of electroconvulsive therapy."

"It didn't work before."

"Yes, but it's the only treatment open to us. It's the only treatment we can be sure won't cause harm."

"Harm? To who?"

"It won't harm the fetus. And after she has had the treatment, we can decide if she has the mental stability to bring a child into the world. If we terminate the pregnancy, which is quite likely, we will put her on a course of lithium."

"Lithium?"

"Yes. It's very effective at preventing suicide."

"She isn't going to commit suicide."

"We don't know that. You don't know that. There have been many attempts."

"She's doing it for attention."

And if lithium doesn't work, then the doctor will have to try some new and even stronger pills, but then she will have to take them for the rest of her life—if she lives that long. I suppose no one believes her story about being kidnapped. But if she's pregnant, it must mean that she has done it with a man. Maybe it was that man who kidnapped her in his car, locked her up, stripped her, and had a knife. Mum should have called the police, and they should have asked people in the pub what happened. At least they should have asked someone.

If you ask me, things are getting a lot worse around here, and even though I have covered the black floors in the kitchen and have begun laying the mock-oak parquet floor tiles in the hall, Mum cries most days. She even cries when I bring her a bag of bruised fruit and a bunch of freesias from Mrs. McWilliams on Saturday after work. That's why she takes Valium every day. Not because of the freesias, but because Dr. Wilmot said she is depressed, and anyone would be depressed with what Mum has gone through with Margueretta.

Mum says she doesn't want Margueretta back—not now, not ever. I don't want her back either because it would be easier to do my homework without some lunatic screaming the house down, the neighbors banging on the walls, and Constable Ferguson coming around for a cup of tea to calm things down.

And then the letter came. It was postmarked London, and I took it to Mum in the kitchen as soon as the postman delivered it. But I don't think she wants that letter. No one would want that letter.

Three million people died—mostly starved to death. Lots of them were children. It should never have been this way. But it's over now. It ended eighteen months ago, so maybe now it's safe to return. It should be safe, even if the children will never know their grandparents who perished in the conflict. And the timing is good because the education they came here for is done, and that means a good job.

A good job back in Lagos.

A time to rejoice in the new Nigeria. A time to rebuild under the new government, and a time to reunite the family, what is left of it. God rest the souls of those who are no longer with us. God bless you all for what you have done. You will live on in our prayers and in our thoughts forever. God bless you.

"Eech! They're taking my baby away! They're taking my baby away!"

Mollie Midget has a letter too. That's why she's at our front door. They're sailing on the P&O Line from Southampton to Lagos with a few ports of call along the way.

"Eech! I can't do it. I just can't do it. Please stop them! My little Folami. My little girl. She's my little girl. They can't take her from me. I won't let them!"

"I know. I know. Akanni is my little boy, you know. My special little boy."

"Eech! I thought she would stay with me forever. Until she was grown up. We have to do something!"

"At least they will fit in. Everyone will be black. Not like here."

"I don't care. Eech! I don't care. This is the end of everything. Everything."

Mum said we should keep the "Puff the Magic Dragon" LP because she wasn't sure if they have record players in Africa, and it might not survive the journey. After all, it's three thousand miles away, maybe more.

Mum said she will watch him sail through the Netherworld to the Afterlife on his funerary boat. And for his sake, she will not cry.

But the two mothers are clinging to each other and weeping and screaming and wailing. Two mothers who have to plan for the premature deaths of their beautiful children. Something no mother should ever have to do. They packed a cuddly toy and some tiny clothes to sustain them in the afterlife.

And every time these dear, loving mothers look at the sky, they will remember their dead babies and know they have gone to a good life. Forever making the sun shine brighter.

But in the darkness when we cry alone, we will have nothing.

Nothing but the despicable, vilest absence of something we once loved.

103

Carl has done it with his girlfriend. He told me all the details, and it sounded very messy—especially the bit about the toilet paper. He didn't have a Durex so he wrapped some toilet paper round his cock first. There was no sign of the toilet paper when he was done. But there was blood everywhere. He didn't know where that came from and neither do I. So she is probably up the spout. He was so angry that he gobbed in four jars of Mrs. McWilliams' pickled onions and put the lids back.

Margueretta isn't pregnant anymore. They gave her an abortion, which is where they kill the baby before it is born. She wanted to have the baby and then have it adopted, but I think they thought she would kill herself before the baby was born, and then the baby would die too. Either way, the baby is dead. I don't know how they killed it.

Margueretta says she has been betrayed. She has been betrayed in a terrible conspiracy, and Mum is at the center of it. I don't think she means "betrayed" the same way as Jesus was betrayed by Judas in the Garden of Gethsemane for thirty pieces of silver.

My mum is not Judas.

"Do you know what happened, John?" Margueretta asked.

"No," I replied.

"She...I don't want her to hear. I'm going to whisper. Come closer...she wouldn't let me out. She...made me stay there. Don't say anything to her. She'll send me back. She can do it, you know. She's got those doctors exactly where she needs them. They're all in it together. She wants me locked up."

"Mum wants you to get better."

"You don't know anything. Why would you? I was fucking locked up in there by her. She wants me locked up. She...come closer and listen to me... she wants me...dead."

"No, she doesn't."

"I've got proof. She doesn't know, but I know. Do you know what it's like to be locked up with fucking maniacs with bars on the doors and windows? No, why would you? I pretended to be mad. It was the only way to survive. I stripped all my clothes off and dug my nails into my skin until I was bleeding everywhere. Those male orderlies took their time getting me dressed again, I can tell you. Fucking perverts. Anyway, I've got proof..."

"What proof?"

"It's all in the notes. I read my case notes."

"What does it say?"

"I can't tell you. But now I know. She's out to get me. Her and a lot of other people but mostly her. She's jealous you know."

"Of what?"

"Of me, of course! And why wouldn't she be? I'm everything she's not. And she smells because she never takes a bath until she's filthy. Can't you smell it? I bathe every day. Sometimes twice a day. That's why she wants me locked up. That's why she made them do that fucking ECT on me again. It's supposed to make you into a bloody zombie. Then you can't stop them doing whatever they want to you. Just like her next door. Joan whatsername. It worked on her. But she was always a bit simple. But it didn't work on me. Oh, no. I know what's going on now. I'm on the lookout for their next move. She'd give me a bloody lobotomy if she could! Well, I'm watching her. Don't say anything..."

"To who?"

"To her! Look. I'm never going to be locked up again. Get it? Never. They're all fucking mad in that place. I'm never going back. Never. And another thing..."

"What?"

"I *was* kidnapped. Some people think I imagined it. You can't imagine that sort of detail. I was kidnapped, and locked up, and raped. Just how do they think I got pregnant? Immaculate conception? I am not the fucking Madonna! I was raped."

"Why don't you tell them?"

"Tell them? They're all in it together! Haven't you been listening to a word I've said? Watch her. You're next. I know these things. Emily will be alright. She's compliant. Mum doesn't see her as a threat. Emily will be alright. Has Mum said anything strange to you lately?"

"No."

"Didn't she say you were just like Dad? You know, after you puked on that cheap sherry?"

"Yes."

"That's the start, John. She said the same to me. I'm just like Dad. Dad said she was mad. He always said she was the fucking mad one. That's why he ran off like that. He ran off to get away from her before she had him locked up…he's the lucky one, wherever he is…"

"It's not like that!"

"Really? And how do you know? Does she ever thank you for what you do? I've seen the way you did that kitchen floor for her. Has she ever thanked you? Or does she just wallow in that same self-pity, blaming others for everything. Blaming Dad, blaming me, blaming the floors. Blame anything except herself!"

"She likes the floor."

"She expects you to do it. She will never thank you. I loved my father. He was a good man. He loved me. But her? She only thinks about herself. And anyone who doesn't fit in with her plan gets the same treatment. Dad ran off just in time. She had the police onto him, you know?"

"I don't know."

"Sure you do. You were there when the police came for him. Looking for that biscuit tin with the money. She called them. It was Mum who called the police. No one else. She wanted him locked up. Now it's me. Then it will be you. Get out of here as soon as you can. I'm getting out. I'm getting a job, and I'm getting away from this fucking place. Same as Dad. And she'll never see me again. Never."

"OK."

"OK? That's all you can say? She's only interested in herself. She's a self-pitying woman! Why do you think she goes out every night to bloody evening classes? Eh? Because she has no sense of responsibility, that's why. But she brought us into this world. She was twenty-one when she had me. Then along came you twins. She always said she could have put us in a home. What kind of thing is that to say to your children? I'm getting out of here, I tell you."

104

Mum is slipping further away, even with so much of the black floors now red and white and blue and green and mock-oak. Maybe it's because those black floors are still there, still black beneath the colored tiles.

I'm ashamed of everything. Ashamed of the turds under the kitchen table. Ashamed of having only one pair of underpants to wear and one in the wash. Dirt and filth everywhere. Rice and an Oxo cube for tea. Purple, hairy heart-udder for Sunday roast. Blood on the wallpaper and the ceiling. Dead lice. Sister in the asylum, scars on her wrists, scars on her neck.

No father.

I'm ashamed.

Margueretta is out of prison now. She was only in Holloway for a week, but it's her own fault for throwing that brick through the chemist's shop window on Saturday night. She said she had run out of lithium so she went to get another prescription, and they were closed—so she just snapped.

Constable Ferguson said it was really wrong that the magistrate sent her to Holloway. For one thing, all Mum needed to do was take her back and enforce a curfew, and they would have let Margueretta off with a suspended sentence. And when Mum refused to do that because enforcing a curfew on a cat is nigh on impossible, they had no alternative but to stick her in Holloway because all the young offenders facilities were full. She had her own cell. But she could only take one bath a week, so she is lucky she didn't have to stay in there for a month.

They locked her up again in the asylum when she was released. There's no way Mum is letting her back home, not after the disgrace of prison.

Joan read about Margueretta's conviction in the *Evening News*, and that was it. They left in the middle of the night without saying goodbye. At least she's had her ECT to help her with her nervous breakdown.

Now Dr. Browning thinks he knows what is wrong with Margueretta. He said it's all now down to drug treatments. If you are just depressed, then Valium is really good because it makes the sun shine, and you feel good about life. And if you are suicidal or manic, then lithium is good because it stops you wanting to kill yourself. But none of this has worked on Margueretta because she still wants to kill herself. So in a way, the treatments have helped to reveal the diagnosis.

"We have come to a fundamental diagnostic conclusion," said Dr. Browning.

"Which is?" said Mum.

"All along we've thought she was suffering from depression, probably manic-depression. But we now believe that your daughter has a significant personality disorder."

"Disorder?"

"Look. Just listen. You need to listen carefully to this. We believe that she has something that is rare in a girl of her age. We believe that she is schizophrenic."

"Split personality?"

"No. That's a common but entirely incorrect view. It's quite clear now that Margueretta cannot distinguish between real and imagined events. She is having profound and detailed hallucinations. We have observed her in the ward, and she continues conversations with people who are not there."

"That's nothing new."

"It's a very rare condition. Childhood-onset schizophrenia is highly unusual."

"But she's not a child! She's almost eighteen!"

"It started when she was younger. We don't know what causes it. But it is probable that it is part genetic and part environmental."

"Genetic? There's no madness on my side of the family. I can't speak for her father, though."

"I don't think you should call it 'madness.' It's a mental illness. And it's probably only partly genetic. Her upbringing could have been a significant factor."

"Her upbringing? What do you mean?"

"Well, in girls, particularly sensitive girls..."

"Oh, she's sensitive alright!"

"As I was saying. In some girls a severe trauma could start things moving in the wrong direction."

"I'm the one who has had the severe trauma. You should try living with her."

"She lost her father, didn't she?"

"Lost her father? We didn't *lose* him. He abandoned us!"

"And how old was she when that happened?"

"What's that got to do with anything?"

"How old was she?"

"She was ten. Or maybe eleven. But that was years ago."

"Well, we can be sure that her father abandoned her. That must have been highly traumatic. She's been very sick for a long time. I am convinced this is childhood-onset schizophrenia. More specifically, she is almost certainly a paranoid schizophrenic."

"Paranoid?"

"The people and things she imagines, the things she hallucinates, are plotting to harm her. That's what she thinks. She thinks people are trying to harm her. Or kill her."

"Well, she has nearly been the death of me!"

"I've put her on a new drug. It has worked wonders with thousands of patients who have psychosis from profound personality disorders. It's called chlorpromazine. You should see a significant difference in her behavior. Trust me on this. Let her back home. One last time, Mrs. Mitchell."

"No. Never."

"Think about it."

"Never."

"And one more thing, Mrs. Mitchell. I would like you to organize something we call an 'intervention.' The chlorpromazine will help to eliminate the psychosis, but it won't help with the addiction."

"What addiction?"

"Margueretta is an alcoholic. And she shouldn't drink when she is taking chlorpromazine, or she will become very drowsy. But more importantly, she has liver damage from the aspirin overdose. She mustn't drink again. Ever. So I want you to organize a family event and invite all of her loved ones to come along. Don't tell her about it. It should be a surprise. I'll explain more later, but you should all prepare a statement for her. Say how much you love her, need her, and want her to change her behaviors. Write it down if you like. It can be very effective at stopping addictive behaviors."

"I don't want her back."

"Think about it. This may be her last chance. For the love of God, give her one last chance. Please."

105

am very excited about this party, once we get the serious bit over and done with. Mum is going to start with "The Planet Suite" because it is an astrological journey rather than an astronomical journey. We can therefore start with an exploration of the star signs that are imbued in all of us. Margueretta is a Capricorn. And through this astrological link, we will be able to talk about Capricorn's personality traits, and how we would like to change Margueretta's addictive behavior. And once we get past the addiction intervention part, we will move on to the *Sound of Music*.

Mum has agreed to let Margueretta back just one more time.

"Eech! I'm a Taurus! Do they have a song for a Taurus? I'm a bull. Eech!"

Mollie was the first to arrive because she only lives around the corner, of course, and she is very excited because never gets invited to parties. But she is also depressed and taking Valium to help with the trauma of losing her beloved Folami, which is like suffering the death of a child.

Mum wrote to Nana to invite her and Auntie Dot. I don't think it was a good idea to use the word "intervention" in the letter for two reasons. Firstly, it is not a very common word and most people would not know what the hell you are talking about. And secondly, Nana's eyesight is not what it used to be and together with Mum's shaky handwriting, it should not be a surprise if Nana misread the word.

Also, when Dr. Browning said that we should surprise Margueretta with the intervention, he did not say that we should surprise all of her friends and loved ones as well. We should have explained that we are trying to intervene in Margueretta's addictive behavior to stop her being a total alcoholic because it does not mix well with anti-psychotic drugs and liver damage. If we had explained things in detail about breaking the pattern of Margueretta's addiction, Nana and Dot would not have bought a box of Mackeson, Strongbow Cider, Johnnie Walker Whisky, and Harvey's Bristol Cream Sherry at the Off-License on the way here.

But I have to agree that the change in Margueretta has been profound now that she is taking the new wonder drug. She seems completely normal now, and she has had several interviews for a job—but she won't tell us what it is yet. If she gets the job, she will tell us, and we will be amazed.

Mum waited until everyone had a drink before she tapped a spoon on the glass she was holding.

"Och, we're going to have a wee speech!" Nana said.

"Mother, quiet please," Mum replied.

"Well, I need another drink if I'm going to have to listen to a speech! Come on, Margueretta, let's have a wee top up for that glass of yours," Nana added.

"Don't mind if I do," Margueretta replied.

"Mother! She should not be drinking. She's taking pills, you know," Mum insisted.

"Och, aren't we all? I've been taking pills for my lumbago for years," Nana replied.

Squeeelch! Nana farted.

"Oh, for the love of God, Mother! You do not have lumbago. I'm trying to be serious here! And please stop farting like that."

"Beg pardon."

"So. We are gathered here for a reason. I have a something here I want to read..."

"Och, no! It's nae a speech, it's a blooming sermon. This is why I gave up on the Presbyterian Church. I always said I would nae listen to another sermon. 'Dearly Beloved, we are gathered here...'"

"Mother, just drink your drink, and let me be. I have had a very stressful few weeks. You may know that I lost my little boy, Akanni..."

"Eech! And my little girl, Folami!"

"Yes. Well, that was the most terrible thing," Mum agreed, "and I don't want to live through that feeling again. A mother losing a child is a terrible thing. That's why we're here today...I miss my poor wee boy. He's on a boat out to sea..."

"'I must go down to the seas again, to the lonely sea and sky, and all I ask is a tall ship and a star to steer her by.' Och, you need a drink, lassie," Nana said, looking at Margueretta's glass. "Yer glass is empty. Johnny Walker, is it? Dot, get Margueretta a wee refill, lass. And while yer at it, give them wee twins a Mackeson each. Right enough, Emily and John? It'll put hair on yer chest."

"As I was saying," Mum continued.

Squeeelch!

"Beg your pardon! It's the gas, you know. What do you say, Dot?"

Thluuuump!

"Better out than in!" Dot added.

"Och, right enough, Dot. Can you not turn that mournful music off an' put something cheerful on? Some party this is with that dreadful sound. 'The Plant Suite,' you call it? More like the 'Painful Suite.' Fortunate that some of us thought to bring some wee refreshments to get the party going, though..."

"Mother! Be quiet. There's something Margueretta needs to know..."

"Och, there are things in this world that no one should know. Some people know far too much. Am I right, Dot? Are there some things no one should know, Dot?"

"Yes. The smell of a donkey's arse," Dot replied.

"Och, that's right enough. 'I've seen lots of bonnie lassies travelin' far and wide, but my heart is centered noo on bonnie Kate McBride.' Let's dance, wee Johnnie."

"You need to sit down now!" Mum protested. "You are not taking this seriously! We are here for a reason..."

Squeeelch!

"And for the love of God, stop farting! I have something to say..."

"It's just wind," said Auntie Dot.

"Just wind?" Nana began. "It was *just wind* that blew doon the Tay Bridge, you know! It was twenty-one years before I was born, the Tay Bridge collapsed in a violent storm. That bridge connected ma home town of Dundee to Fife, across the Firth of Tay."

Squeeelch!

"Och, and there was a train crossing the bridge at the time, traveling from Edinburgh to Dundee it was, sure enough. In the darkest, foulest night. Over seventy poor souls drowned. There were no survivors. Bodies were washed up on the shoreline for days. But some were never found. I have a piece of the communication cord from the train, you know!"

"Look! We are here for a reason. We are here to talk to someone. Everyone has something to say. I have something to say..."

"Och, I've something to say, right enough. 'The boy stood on the burning deck, his feet were full o' blisters. He thought he had on his mother's shoes, but no they were his sister's.' Now put a record on. And none of that last load of rubbish, mind. Dot, we need to refill all these glasses."

"For the love of God, will you be quiet, Mother! I'm trying to make a statement here, and you are not making this easy. It's something for Margueretta."

"Have you got her a wee gift? You know I was given a pretty doll when I was a wee lassie. It was from ma father for Christmas. It was the happiest Christmas. We had a beautiful hoos. There was a huge Christmas tree. And a roaring log fire in the hearth. I curled up beside the fire wi' ma wee dolly in my arms. She had on a red dress. A beautiful red dress. I fell asleep by the fireplace. And when I woke up the doll's face was all pushed in. It was a wax head. The heat of the fire had melted it. She wasn't pretty any more. Oh, I cried. I cried and cried for that wee, pretty dolly. Her face was all squished in. All squished in and ugly."

Nana started to cry for that doll on the sofa in our front room with the black floor.

"And when are we going to see the invention?" asked Auntie Dot.

"Invention? What invention?" replied Mum.

"The invention. You said we were to come here for an invention…"

106

I don't think she told them that she has a prison record. But it doesn't matter because she has had four interviews, and she's got the job. She's completely normal now that she's been taking the new pills for the past two months. Dr. Browning was right. It's a wonder drug.

It's a pity that Joan Housecoat moved away in the middle of the night without leaving a forwarding address because now she would be able to see that we are a normal family, and Margueretta is just a normal young woman. And everyone at school is going to be really jealous when I tell them that my sister is going to be a Bunny Girl at the Southsea Playboy Club.

"Listen to this: 'The Bunnies, in their brightly colored costumes, with rabbit ears and white cottontails, add beauty and glamour to these surroundings...you are with girls who, like yourself, possess excellent character, striking good looks, charm, intelligence, and friendly personalities...'"

Margueretta was reading from her Bunny brochure.

"Did you tell them about your problems?" Mum asked.

"What? You're always trying to spoil things for me. I took the Bunny Test, and I passed. I am going to learn the Bunny Poses. They said I was perfect Bunny Material."

"Perfect Bunny Material? Don't make me laugh. Let's see how long this lasts. How long was it at the Tampax factory? A month?"

"I didn't like working shifts. Anyway, I will meet famous people, like Tony Curtis. He's a 'devoted Keyholder' at the New York Playboy Club, you know."

"Tony Curtis? That's a good one. Southsea is not New York."

"You don't believe me. I will meet a movie star and get out of this bloody dump. Just you see! People like you belong here. In this filth and squalor. You were born to it."

"Oh, la-di-da! Aren't we Lady Muck? You're the Queen. And I'm nothing. That makes you the Queen of nothing. Ha! Ha! Ha!"

"You know I hate you, don't you?"

"My dear Margueretta. No one cares what you think anymore. Whatever time we might have cared about what you think has long passed."

"Really? No one cares what I think? We'll see. You'll be laughing on the other side of your face when a Bunny Scout finds me and takes me to the Playboy Mansion in America."

"You're right, Margueretta. I will be laughing."

"Don't spoil my dreams!"

"Spoil your dreams? Spoil your dreams? Are you damn well kidding me? God, if you could hear yourself! All of your dreams are bloody nightmares! And we are the ones who have to live in them!"

"They're going to teach me how to mix cocktails. I've got to learn the recipes from a little book they gave me. Manhattans, Harvey Wallbangers, Gimlets. You've probably never heard of those things."

"And how long will it be before you're drinking those cocktails, eh? Enjoy it while it lasts, Margueretta."

"Oh, I will. I will enjoy every minute of it. I've been fitted for my outfit and everything."

"Can we see it?" Emily asked.

"As soon as I get it, you will see it. This is the turning point in my life. You'll see. Some movie star will sweep me off my feet. They said they get all types of movie stars in the Playboy Club. This is my chance."

"How exciting!" Emily exclaimed.

107

She sleeps during the day because she doesn't get home until three or four o'clock in the morning. They bring her home in a taxi because there are no buses in the middle of the night, and she doesn't have a car to get home from the Playboy Club.

She puts on her Bunny outfit before she leaves in the evening, and it has a little cotton tail on the bottom, which she wiggles for her customers. But they are not allowed to touch it because that is against the rules. She said that some customers do touch it, and some of them even pat her bottom. She never says anything because that's just the way it is when you are on the lookout for a movie star to take you to America.

I hope she will take me with her.

Constable Ferguson still comes here because Margueretta is on probation, and he just wants to be sure that everything is going well, and she doesn't get into any more trouble. He thinks it's a miracle the way things are now with my sister being a Bunny Girl, and he says it's lucky they have to wear gloves because she can cover up the scars on her wrists.

She gets up in the afternoon and takes a bath every single day. She said all the Bunnies do that. I still take a bath once a week. She puts on her makeup, and she looks like a movie star herself—all glamorous and amazing like Twiggy.

She asked to speak to me yesterday afternoon in my room.

"Look John. I don't want you to go through what I've been through. It's over now, and I will be leaving soon. I've met a man at the Playboy Club. I don't want to talk about it in case *she* tries to stop it. She's jealous of me, you know. She will do anything to destroy my life."

"Who?"

"Mum, of course! I've told you already! You know who I mean. I watch the way she looks at me when I get dressed up in my Bunny outfit. If looks could kill…anyway, I'm almost out of here now. I've saved some money. And things are going very well with this man. We're in love. This is the real thing. I've been in love before, but now I am a woman. This is real love."

"Is he going to take you to America?"

"He says he will. But he's not American. That doesn't matter. You need to look out for yourself, John. That woman will have you in the asylum if she feels threatened by you. Locked up. No one is safe. No one. She's in a conspiracy with other people."

"Who?"

"That Mollie woman for one. They're in it together. There are others. They have ways of doing things to you. Terrible things. Do you have nightmares?"

"Sometimes. Why?"

"What are they about?"

"Different things."

"Well, watch out for the ones that are real. Watch out for the people who come into your room in the night looking for you. Watch out, John."

"I will."

"Has anyone been to the house looking for me?"

"Not really."

"Not really? What does that mean? Who's been here? Tell me!"

"Constable Ferguson comes round for a cup of tea…"

"Constable Ferguson! Why didn't you tell me? He's in it with her! Oh, for God's sake, there isn't much time. When was he last here?"

"Yesterday. He comes here a lot."

"I think I'm frightening you. Forget what I said. Just look out for yourself. She'll stop at nothing and remember she's done it before, and she'll do it again. You're never safe. Not while you're in this house. Do you understand?"

"I suppose."

"I'll be gone soon. This man is...well, let's just say he's handsome and wonderful and he's in love me. You're too young to understand what that means. He says I am the prettiest girl he has ever seen. The other Bunnies said to watch out because it's against the Bunny Code. But they're just jealous. He's really handsome, John. This is the one. I can't tell Emily, or she will tell Mum..."

"No, she won't!"

"Well, that's unproven. The hall floor looks nice."

"Thanks."

"What are you going to do when all the black floors are covered?"

"I'm going to start painting the walls."

"She'll never thank you. She expects it."

108

She thought they called her in for not declaring her prison record. But the ethics they were talking about were the ethics of fraternizing with customers. Especially with a middle-aged, married man who should know better, pretending he was going to take her to America with him. They're sure his wife would have something to say about her husband having an affair with an eighteen-year-old Bunny Girl. And the Bunny Code is very strict. They took away her outfit and her Bunny Manuals.

You can't keep those things when you have been fired.

She got up as usual to run her hot bath today.

"First, you run a nice, hot bath. Then take off all your clothes. Doesn't matter if they find you naked. You're dead so you won't be embarrassed! Climb in the bath and lie back. Then relax with a bottle of sherry. Make sure your wrists are nice and hot from the water. It numbs them. So does the sherry. Then get a nice new razor blade...you slit the vein, right here. You can cut across it. Or slice down the length. Like this. Down the length is more effective than across...."

It was the plan she already had in her head.

But she isn't dead.

The bathroom door wasn't locked when I heard the cries. And the ambulance got here really quickly after I ran to the call box. The blood looked like cumulonimbus clouds before the storm. We're learning about cloud patterns in geography.

Mum says I am very brave, and I am definitely the man of the house now, but my daddy already made me the man of the house when I was seven.

Trust you are looking after Mum, as you are the man of the house now. Are you doing a good job? Yes! I thought you would.

I say my prayers every night to God and to Jesus. I've never missed a night. I tuck my knees up to my chin and count to a thousand. And sometimes I say the Lord's Prayer.

Our Father, which art in heaven. Hallowed be thy name.

God help her. Please, Jesus, help her. For the love of God.

109

They've sectioned Margueretta under the Mental Health Act to be locked up for her own safety and for the safety of others. She's eighteen, and that's the only way you can lock up an adult against her will. She said she would change, and she would never stop taking her pills again. And everyone said they've heard it all before, but it's too late now.

So they've her locked up.

I don't think they will ever let her out again. And for now, she is in a straitjacket because she said she would kill herself or someone else if she was ever locked up again. Mum said it's too stressful to go to that lock-up ward so she's not going back anymore to visit Margueretta. So Margueretta will just have to stay in there on her own with all the mad people and the bars on the windows and doors. Yes, she can stay in there for the rest of her life. On the inside.

"Maybe some movie star will find her in there and take her away from all of this!"

Mum had to come home early from work last week. She said she was staring at some numbers at her desk when the lights went out, and she thought it was a power cut. But the lights were still on, and she was blind. So they helped her into a taxi.

Her sight has come back already. It was the mind's way of shutting down. Dr. Wilmot said she's had a complete nervous breakdown, and I need to look after her. I don't mind looking after my mum, but she doesn't seem like my mum anymore. She says things I don't understand about the mysteries of the world, and the other day she started crying and handed me a letter to read.

"Look at this, Johnny. I'm sorry for you to have to find out this way. He's dead. You need to know how he died. Your father is dead. He had lung cancer. They cut one lung out, and then he contracted pneumonia. I'm so sorry." I read that letter, of course.

St Mary's Hospital

My Dear Emily and John

Many thanks for all you have done for me, and tried to help me. Well, we are hoping my operation will be a success. But if it's the Lord's Will to call me home, don't grieve about me as I am an old man now and I have had my day. I would have liked to have been with you and the dear children a while longer, but it can't be helped. Just stick to each other and the children. Dear Wee Margueretta, Wee Emily, and Wee Johnny. They are nice Wee Bairns.

God Bless you all and keep you till we meet again. Remember me to every one.

All the Best

Your loving Father

The letter was dated 22 November 1959. I told Mum that this letter was from my dad's dad, and my father isn't dead at all as far as we know.

"Mum! This letter is dated 1959. It's not from my dad. It's from my grandpa, and it's addressed to you and my dad."

But she said she was sorry my father was dead. Dr. Wilmot said not to worry because she will get better, and all of this will pass.

110

gave Mum the choice, and she said she wants the kitchen repapered first because those roses have turned from red to brown. So I've picked out a vinyl wallpaper with green and white flowers from Le Bon Marché in Portsmouth. I will make a start on the walls on Sunday. And with the oak-effect parquet being finished, we've got a carpet for the front room. A bright, orange carpet from the Littlewoods Catalog. I cut it to fit with scissors because it is wall-to-wall carpet.

People who go to grammar school have wall-to-wall carpet and vinyl wallpaper. They do not have a front room—it's a lounge. And it's not tea—it's dinner. And they eat Black Forest gateaux if they are having tea, which would be in the middle of the afternoon.

I sleep without a nightlight, and the dark night sky has come down already tonight and it's rushing into every space between the stalks in the wilderness outside my window. It is dark at the beginning, and it is dark at the end. The dark joins with the giant blackness that is in the attic because it is too big for that space. And then to the darkness inside my head that I stole from the cellar.

We will always know what is inside Margueretta's head because we all lived there for a long, long time not only as voyeurs but also as participants, taking secret photos.

That's why I lie awake at night until some vile hallucination makes me think my arms and legs are suspended from the ceiling while my body is sliding down the stairs like limbless, black treacle. I'm a helpless, drowning amputee in a sea-anemone forest of arms.

They come into my room, but I never look at them. Angels of death knock inside the walls, always waiting for someone to die, until there is a death. And when they grow silent, the thing from the corner of the cellar comes down from the attic, eyes bulging out like my big, green marbles.

And then I sleep. And the nightmares begin.

Night, night Margueretta. Now you can sleep with an orange nightlight glowing in your bedroom after dark, reflecting little moons and stars on the ceiling. And dream the sweetest dreams of little girls and wear your pretty party dress for your daddy. He will dance with you, and you will swing on a star.

And when you reach up, we will hold your hand.

The ghosts are all gone now.

111

They took Mum away for a short break. It was obvious, really. The doctor said it won't be for long—just until she gets her mind back and stops thinking in that mixed up way where she believes people are dead when they are still alive.

Almost everyone is gone. Pop, Dad, Nana, and my little brother...and my mum.

And Margueretta. She's locked up forever.

The dangerously insane have to be locked up and shackled for all of our protection. She's still in a straitjacket. No one can get out of that device. She can't even scratch her nose or go to the toilet without asking politely for help.

They used to give them ice baths—that certainly silenced them for a time, and then they passed out. When they regained consciousness, the skin was peeling off their bodies like wet tissue paper.

I shouldn't think about these things anymore. Not now. Margueretta is never coming back.

The moon is shining through the window tonight, making shadows of tree branches on my bedroom walls. The shadows dance like ancient slaves wanting to be released. You can't see those shadows when you close your eyes. You can only see them when they are open.

Mine are open.

At first, it sounds like a dog, howling in the distance. Not every night. But tonight, she's there—and soon she will be screaming again in the attic. Just above my head.

Some people don't believe in ghosts. They didn't know the man who hanged himself in the toilet—a man whose eyes bulged out like giant, green marbles, swinging there by his neck from the water pipes.

And they didn't have a sister who locked them in the cellar where it was so black they wouldn't know if their eyes were open or closed. Nor did they count up to a thousand and say the Lord's Prayer, rocking back and forth in that silent, breathless prison.

And they didn't hear that girl who screams in the attic.

She painted a picture of the thing that came into her bedroom time and again and told her to kill herself. The reverend said we had to burn it. As though it were alive. But it never died.

I am glad for people who don't believe in ghosts. The rest of us have to live with them. They are inside our heads, and they are as real as we make them.

I'm staring at the attic door again. Staring, staring, right above my head. And now I know—because the door is slowly starting to move.

Epilogue

Even though it is told through my eyes, this is **Margueretta's** story. She wanted it told but she could never write her story herself, despite many attempts. I wish she was here to read it now, but sadly, Margueretta is no longer with us. There is another story to be told of her continuing fight against the incredible demons that invaded her sanity into adulthood. She fought valiantly with the disease of paranoid-schizophrenia and eventually it won. Now she is at peace and I forgive her with all my heart for everything.

Childhood-onset schizophrenia is thankfully very rare. It is an appalling and incurable disease, although it can be somewhat controlled with effective medication. It often manifests itself in the child hallucinating and hearing voices that seem to have an independent existence. I can only imagine the horror of living with a voice inside my head telling me to kill myself or it will kill me.

Mum has celebrated her eightieth birthday in amazing health. She is the true survivor and I will always love her dearly for the incredible way in which she managed to hold things together. God knows that it would have been hard enough to survive being abandoned by my father to bring up three children alone in an era when a single parent was very uncommon and even despised. But to deal with the additional horror of a child suffering from schizophrenia is frankly more than most people could cope with. But my mother did cope and she did survive and because of her, we all survived.

Dad drank himself to death. He died alone and penniless at the age of fifty-seven. I did not meet him again until I was eighteen. Bizarrely, he died on my birthday—the same birthday that I shared with my two sisters. I don't read anything into this and before he died, I forgave him for abandoning us, but I am not sure if he ever forgave himself. I still crave his recognition and keep his postcard with me at all times, for I am the man of the house now.

Emily, my beautiful and lovely twin sister, has an incredible outlook on life and always seems to be happy and optimistic. She has a wonderful family and I will forever look up to her, even though I am her big brother, having been born thirty minutes before her. And now that I am a grown-up, I don't mind holding her hand—even if she is a girl.

Nana died in her ninety-fifth year. When I die, I will run to meet her. She will hold me tight and whisper stories of the Highlands, of chasing the golden-tailed dragonfly in the dappled dusk. She will cook me bubble-and-squeak on the old stove and sit me on her lap by the fire. For you are never cold or hungry in Heaven. And you are always loved.

A man did hang himself in the toilet. It was before I was born and Nana and Margueretta enjoyed embellishing that tale. But even so, for all of my life, someone or something has lived right behind me, just visible in the corner of my eye. Fragments of the black cloak continue to smother me in dreadful, breathless moments. I am still anxious about everything, especially the darkness that comes down from the attic and joins with the darkness of the night. I have a dark place inside my head that I stole from the cellar but I fill my life with the bright light of my wonderful wife and children.

At times, the pain of writing this book has been unbearable. As the words found their way onto the page, I realized something: every emotional detail of my childhood was still alive. The fears and horrors were still living inside my head. The ghosts of my childhood were still haunting me.

But I realized something even more profound: twenty years of my adult life were missing. I had been sleepwalking through my adult years by numbing myself from those childhood horrors. The story of my life had a beginning but it had no middle. I had surrendered my life to the banality of a meaningless job, the drudgery of monthly bills and the anesthetizing effect of the daily cocktail hour.

Someone had stolen my life. And I was the thief.

EPILOGUE

That's when my life took on a new meaning. I could not waste another minute. For the first time, I wanted to do something that actually mattered, something I loved doing and something that might make a positive difference to other people's lives. I had to finish writing Margueretta's story.

There is a book inside every one of us. It is being written every day. Don't leave any pages blank.

Make it memorable until the end.

CPSIA information can be obtained at www.ICGtesting.com
Printed in the USA
LVOW12s1544180813

348461LV00016B/238/P